THE BOOK OF
ADDISCOMBE

VOLUME II

CANNING & CLYDE ROAD RESIDENTS

ASSOCIATION & FRIENDS

First published in Great Britain in 2002

THIS BOOK IS DEDICATED TO:

*Albert Jackson (shown left and see Chapters Eight and
Fifteen). He did much to improve the quality of life for
people in Addiscombe.*

*Our thanks to the Millennium Awards for All who made the
production of this book possible. They requested that we did
something enduring for the community and we hope that this
is a fitting project.*

British Library Cataloguing-in-Publication Data
A CIP record for this title is available from the British Library

ISBN 1 84114 176 3

HALSGROVE

Halsgrove House
Lower Moor Way
Tiverton, Devon EX16 6SS
Tel: 01884 243242
Fax: 01884 243325
email: sales@halsgrove.com
website: http://www.halsgrove.com

Frontispiece photograph: *Addiscombe at home, 1921. Mrs Annie Elsley and daughter Ivy (married name
Ivy Binstead) with Smut the cat. The photograph was taken by Ivy's father, Mr Harvey Elsley, in their back
garden in Leslie Grove. The doll was a gift from a French lady to Mr Elsley during the First World War
and was carefully brought back for his daughter in his backpack. Mr Elsley used to give recitals on his
gramophone.* (I.B.).

Printed and bound in Great Britain by Bookcraft Ltd., Midsomer Norton.

Preface

Someone once said that a historian is often only a journalist facing backwards. Well, just to confuse you, here is a journalist looking forwards about what has passed. It is, as you may have noticed, an old trick we often play, to find something from years ago to bring a relevance to a present-day event. But in this case it is thoroughly merited, because what I have found from years gone by is this book you have been clever enough to have. Sequels can frequently be disappointing. They lack the freshness of the impact of the original. But not, perhaps, in this case.

Volume II of the Addiscombe story unleashes more memories of the days before yesterday, in words and particularly in evocative illustrations. It is a result of the great success of the first book, and that success helps to show how much people enjoy local history. This is important, especially in this part of the world; so much of the borough of Croydon has changed so radically in the past 30 or 40 years that many struggle to remember what it used to be like. Newcomers have no idea at all, and it is through valuable publications such as this one that they can be told, and those memories preserved.

To many Addiscombe may seem, at the most casual of glances, undistinguished. It is an area stuck between the town centre and the districts beyond. But stop and stare for a moment, stop and read, and you will begin to sense more. Much more. It is like opening a big door and, as it creaks ajar, it reveals a wealth of unexpected sights. In this case forgotten stories and curious facts which to many were simply unknown until now. What helps to furnish an area with its character are the people who live and have lived in it. They deserve to be remembered, and not only the famous. The ordinary, average man and woman have parts to play here. Scan the photographs and see them going about their day-to-day tasks and routines.

If only we were able to stop them and talk with them, to find out what life was like then, how they lived. In a way, books such as this provide at least a glimpse of that. The hours of painstaking research, and the careful preparation of presentation, now pay dividends. The words and pictures can come to life with the lightest nudge of your imagination.

I began with a quotation. Let me end with another: 'The past always looks better than it was; it's only pleasant because it isn't here.' A trifle cynical, perhaps, but you get the meaning. Whether this past looks better to you, minus today's endless traffic, the crowds and the noise, or not, this way it comes alive again. Just for a moment. History can live, and the people responsible for this volume deserve fulsome praise for that. Read on... into the past.

ROGER BING, COLUMNIST, *CROYDON ADVERTISER*
2002

Addiscombe Road, c.1907. (J.G. & P.C.)

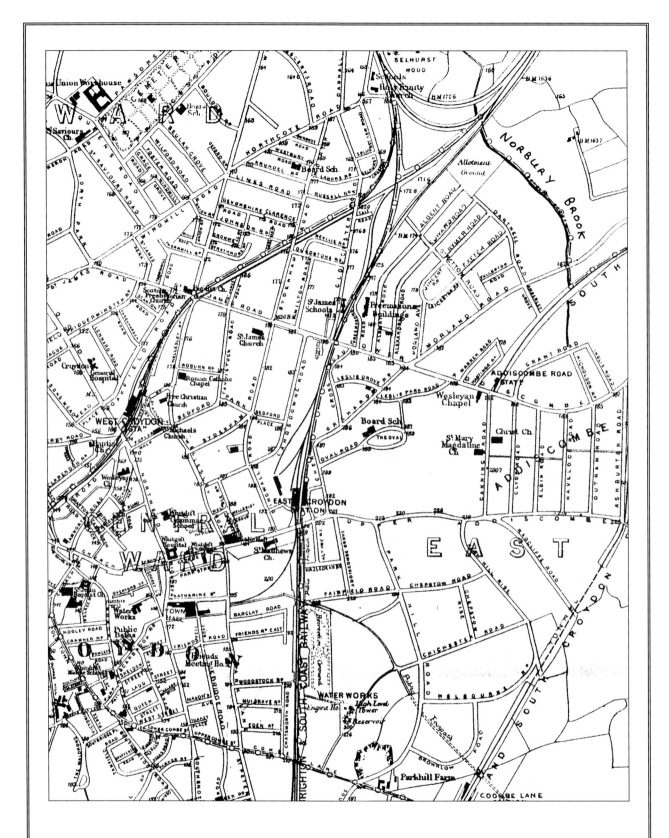

Street map of 1904. This comes from Edward A. Martin's Croydon New and Old, *3rd ed. (The Homeland Association).* (C.N.H.S.S.)

CONTENTS

Mary Chandler

Denis Driscoll

David Gilbert

Anne Bridge

John Haybittle

Paul Jordan

Vera King

Ivy Binstead

Cliff Marlow

Ray Misson

Bill Maile

Eric Burley

Steve Collins

Barbara Edwards

Ernie Maynard

Cecil Hadfield

David Blake

Bill and Joan Angell

Ivy Ayling

Oval School

Oval School

David Pleasance

Bill Wood

Steve Wickenden

Arlette Beelitz

Elsie Pamphilon

Margaret Robson

Brian Roote

Evelyn Adams

Shirley Roberts

Kath Spalding

Gordon Weaver

John Cartwright

Tony Stelling

Eileen Weaver

Steve Roud

Jonathan Moore

Chris Bennett

CONTRIBUTORS

Evelyn Adams
Addiscombe Rifle Club
Bill and Joan Angell
Dorothy Anglers
Ivy Ayling
Peter Barry
Arlette Beelitz
Chris Bennett
Ivy Binstead
David Blake
Lynda Blaker
John Blunsden
Dick Boetius
Anne Bridge
Barbara Broughton
Eric Burley
Arthur Burns
Jean Burrows
Ann Butler
John Cartwright
Mary Chandler
Robert Cogger
Steve Collins
Peter Crosier
Croydon Advertiser
Croydon Local Studies Library with special thanks to Steve Roud

and Chris Bennett
Croydon Natural History & Scientific Society
Jean Davis
Pamela Davis
G.M. Donaldson
Denis Driscoll
Jan Dyer
Barbara Edwards
Ron Elam
Jackie Fuell
John Gent
David Gilbert
Richard Gilbert
Marian Gilliam
Liz Goodall
David Gowers
Geoff Green
Chris Groom
Cecil Hadfield
Pat Haworth
John Haybittle
Veronica Hickox
John Hobbs
Hounsfield family
Stanley Howey
Ken Hughes
Gill Hulne

Gerald and Betty Huston
Les Ives
Joan (Jay) Jenkins
Paul Jordan
Vera King
Kobal Collection
Christine and Peter Lockley
Leslie Lockley
Isabel Macleod
Ken Maggs
Bill Maile
Cliff Marlow
Paul Mason
Jean Mayes
Ernie Maynard
Michael Mead
Ray Misson
Jonathan Moore
Chris Morgan
Paul Moynihan
Paul Nihill
Oval School Year 6 with special thanks to Chanelle Howland, Cleonie Austin-Khandelwal and Niashoni Clarke-

Fortune
Angela Palmer
Elsie Pamphilon
David Pleasance
Alan Pollet
Mike Roberts
Shirley Roberts
Margaret Robson
Brian Roote
Steve Roud
St Mary Magdalene Church; special thanks to Richard Williams and Julia Pentecost
Roy Saunders
John Scrace
Pat Smith
Paul Sowan
Kathleen Spalding
Ivor Steer
Tony Stelling
Jean Tucker
Gordon and Eileen Weaver
John Wellfare
Steve Wickenden
Don Williams
Bill Wood
John Wood

PICTURE CAPTION KEY

A.B.   Anne Bridge
A.Be.   Arlette Beelitz
A.B.K   Associated British (Courtesy Kobal)
A.P.   Angela Palmer
A.R.C. Addiscombe Rifle Club
B.B.   Barbara Broughton
B.E.   Barbara Edwards
B. & J.A. Bill and Joan Angell
B.R. & C.M. Brian Roote and Cliff Marlow
B.W.   Bill Wood
C.A.   *Croydon Advertiser*
C. & H. Chorley & Handford
C.H. & C.A-B. Chanelle Howland and Cleonie Austin-Berry
C.L.S.L. Croydon Local Studies Library
C.N.H.S.S. Croydon Natural History and Scientific Society

C.T.   *Croydon Times*
D.D.   Denis Driscoll
D.G.   David Gilbert
D.P.   David Pleasance
D.W.   David Webber
R.G.   Richard Gilbert
E.A.   Evelyn Adams
E.B.   Eric Burley
E.M.   Ernie Maynard
E.P.   Elsie Pamphilon
G. & B.H. Gerald and Betty Huston
G.M.D. G.M. Donaldson
G.W.   Gordon Weaver
I.B.   Ivy Binstead
I.S.   Ivor Steer
J.B.   John Blunsden
J.F.   Jackie Fuell
J.G.   John Gent
J.H.   John Hobbs
J.Ha.   John Haybittle
J.M.   Jean Mayes
J.Mo.   Jonathan Moore
J.M.B. J.M. Bates
J.S.   John Scrace

J.T.   Jean Tucker
J.W.   John Wood (junior)
J.We.   John Wellfare
K.H.   Ken Hughes
K.M.   Ken Maggs
K.S.   Kathleen Spalding
M.A.   Merton Atkins
M.C.   Mary Chandler
M.M.   Michael Mead
M.R.   Margaret Robson
M.Ro.   Mike Roberts
N.C-F. Niashoni Clarke-Fortune
N.S.   Noakes Studios
P.B.   Peter Barry
P.C.   Peter Crosier
P. &. C.L. Peter and Christine Lockley
P.D.   Pamela Davis
P.J.   Paul Jordan
P.M.   Paul Moynihan
P.N.   Paul Nihill
P.S.   Pat Smith
R.C.   Robert Cogger
R.E.   Ron Elam's Local

Yesterdays
R.G.V.O. R.G.V. Ottaway
R.K.K. The late R.K. Kirkland, reproduced from *Croydon to East Grinstead* (Middleton Press)
R.M.   Ray Misson
R.S.   Roy Saunders
S.C.   Steve Collins
S.H.   Stanley Howey
S.M.M. St Mary Magdalene Church.
S.R.   Shirley Roberts
S.Re.   Sporting Record
S.W.   Steve Wickenden
V.H.   Veronica Hickox
V.K.   Vera King
W.A.   Whitgift Archive

ALL ITEMS ATTRIBUTED TO *CROYDON ADVERTISER* AND *CROYDON TIMES* REPRODUCED BY KIND PERMISSION OF THE *CROYDON ADVERTISER* GROUP.

Introduction

The first *Book of Addiscombe* was published at the end of 2000 and was intended to be a composite history, designed to answer the who, what, when, where, why (and what happened next) questions about our area. Surprisingly, this had never been done before, so our trusty gang of volunteers boldly went and did it. After painstaking research, we thought that we had covered most of it. The subsequent feedback received from readers revealed that we seemed to have unlocked many memories, and they felt a bit miffed that we had not included them. The reason was simply because we did not have the information at the time. Now we do, and so you now have *Volume II.*

Extraordinarily we have some 108 contributors, the oldest of whom is 97 years of age, whilst the youngest is just 11! One of the most satisfying of our contributor links concerns the cousins who were reunited after 60 years and are included in the 'And Finally...' section of the book. Many of the excellent photos come from family albums that otherwise would not have been seen. Without you this second book would never have happened - nor without the invaluable computer skills of the infinitely patient Richard Ogden. Thanks to Anne Bridge, who not only wrote some major chapters, but typed the book, scanned, captioned and categorised all the images, undertook major research, provided her own computer equipment, room for meetings, and, despite a full-time job, has managed all of this. Well done! Read on and learn more. In the Jubilee Year, why not start with the Royal connections...

> **AUTHOR NOTE:** Before February 1971 there were 12 pennies (d.) in the shilling (s.), and 20s. = £1.
> For easy conversion: $2^1/_2$p = 6d.; 5p = 1s.; 10p = 2s.; $12^1/_2$p = 2s.6d. (half a crown); 50p = 10s.

Stretton Road, c.1920. (J.G.)

The Duke and Duchess of York, later King George VI and Queen Elizabeth (Queen Mother), at the Freemasons Home near Windmill Bridge, 1931. (C.T.)

Oval School pupils greeting the Queen along Lower Addiscombe Road on her Golden Jubilee visit, 4 July 2002. (C.A.)

One

❧❀❧

Addiscombe's Royal Connections

A Pictorial Overview

*I*n *Queen Elizabeth II's Golden Jubilee Year we thought it fitting to start with a brief pictorial look at Addiscombe's royal connections.*

Above: *This coronation party was intended to be a street party but owing to bad weather transferred to Oval School. Pictured are: Keith Capon, Lynda, Janice and Pat Angell.* (B.& J.A.)

Right: *Princess Margaret at the dedication of St Mildred's organ, 4 May 1959.* (B.B.)

∽ Relevant Geological Periods & Their Leftovers ∽

Solid Deposits:

Chalk, London Clay, Woolwich, Reading and Blackheath Beds and Thanet Sand.

When?

THE CRETACEOUS PERIOD started about 136m. (million) years ago and lasted for 71m. years. Land bordering the sea consisted of far-reaching swamps. Rivers flowed slowly and formed enormous deltas. There were widespread deposits of chalk – this was our earliest bed. The White Cliffs of Dover formed, and further afield, a great period of mountain building took place (with the formation of, among others, the Rocky Mountains, the Andes and the Panama Ridge, giving rise to the Gulf Stream). The local climate was mild and vegetation grew abundantly as far north as Greenland. Parts of Australia meanwhile were covered by glaciers.

TERTIARY means 'early recent' and refers to the early forms of evolving mammals following the extinction of the dinosaurs. The times that we are interested in start with the Palaeocene and Eocene periods about 65m. ago which lasted for around 27m. years. The Eocene was the second epoch of the Tertiary period. This saw the subsidence of much of Europe, and the seas advanced again. The Cretaceous mountain ranges continued to grow, and the weather in our area was the best part of tropical. Volcanoes erupted in the Atlantic and Indian Oceans and a great deal of lava flowed in Scotland and Ireland.

Some 7m. years back and lasting for around 5m. years we had the Pliocene period, the last epoch of the Tertiary period. Land subsidence led to the formation of the North Sea and local weather conditions were much as they are today. It was during this period that the earliest hominid – human-like ape – Australopithecines, evolved in Africa, and Suffolk and Norfolk had herds of happily grazing elephants.

A mere 10,000 years ago we had the end of the Pleistocene (not to be confused with Pliocene) era. Ice sheets and glaciers covered most of Europe. This included us – probably the most southerly point of the ice invasion in the UK. Through occasional melting the sea levels rose and the weather was extremely changeable. But against all the odds we seemed to have managed to make tools, had the enjoyment of hippopotamuses in the Thames, discovered the uses of horses and witnessed the appearance of the first oxen. It was during these periods that the other solid deposits arrived.

Drift Deposits

River Gravel, Plateau Gravel and Clay with Flints.

When?

PLEISTOCENE (QUATERNARY EPOCH) occurred far more recently (in the last 100,000 years). By way of glacial and melting water wash, we acquired our neighbours' leftovers as top-dressing for the solid deposits. Drift at this time was fluvial (originating from rivers), accumulated in the Thames flood plain and with river development and major changes in sea level basically got washed our way.

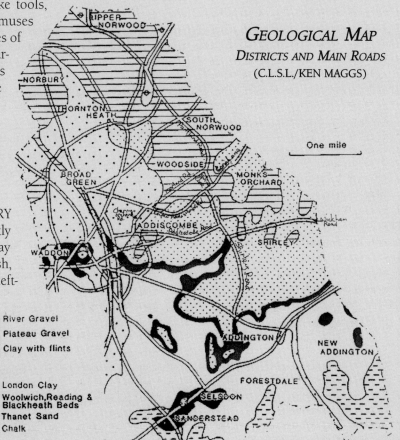

GEOLOGICAL MAP

DISTRICTS AND MAIN ROADS

(C.L.S.L./KEN MAGGS)

One mile

River Gravel
Plateau Gravel
Clay with flints

London Clay
Woolwich, Reading & Blackheath Beds
Thanet Sand
Chalk

Two

It's in the Soil

The Lay of the Land & The Chaffinch Brook

The Lay of the Land:
A Geological & Hydrological Underview

Paul Sowan & Steve Collins, with help from Ken Maggs

We thought that it would be appropriate to take a short subterranean exploration to help to better answer some oft-asked local questions:

Why are some of the properties in our area awash with water?

Why do some subside?

How come some plants flourish in one garden, but just a few hundred yards away (same aspect) perish in another?

What happened to our natural overground water?

According to Kenneth Williams in the iconic 1950s radio show 'Round the Horne', the answer lies in the soil, and this is precisely so for us. So hard hats on, Jurassic Park, Planet of the Apes and Flintstone fans tune in. We are nipping back in time to discover more about the geological beds over which we now sleep.

Beneath us is a mattress that separates into 'solid' and 'drift' components. The solid stuff happened first, and the drift, as we will learn, washed over it later - and in best part, this is what you see on the surface today.

Drift deposit types include: river (terrace) gravel deposits of uncemented gravels and sand thought to be derived from the Woolwich and Reading Beds; plateau gravel, a relatively weak mix of clayey gravels, about 1.2-2.5m thick; and clay with flints, a firm to stiff silty clay with numerous flints. Solid deposits include the following:

LONDON CLAY: A stiff dark grey to brown clay, in parts sandy. It contains limestone and is of low permeability. This basically means that water will run over the top. Near the surface it weathers to a brown or yellow-brown. It has a very high shrinkage rate - normally caused by drying out through tree-root action - and is the main cause of subsidence in the area. It also causes 'heave'. This is when the clay becomes wet again and expands upwards - so take advice before cutting down your adjacent tree! There are exposed strata of London clay at Brickfield Meadows.

WOOLWICH, READING AND BLACKHEATH CLAYS: These beds are typically laterally variable clays overlying a bottom bed of glauconitic (blue/green) sand, loam and pebbles. Blackheath is typically pebbly sand and characterised by the pebbles being well-rounded flint. Readers may be pleased to learn that the clay component does not shrink as much as London clay. Exposed strata can be seen at Shirley Hills.

THANET SAND: A fine-grain typical quartz sand, sometimes greyish green, which in places could contain small amounts of clay. Unfortunately, in the course (pun) of time this can be washed away by a concentration of water, and this too can lead to subsidence.

CHALK: Known as upper chalk in our parts, this is soft white limestone mixed with flints. Typically over 600 feet thick, it is present throughout the area. If water meets with chalk then it will percolate into the depths and not reappear until it hits a more impervious barrier. On the surface, chalk only appears south of a line from Waddon Ponds to Coombe Road. Because the area is heavily built up, the only chalk exposure to be seen is in Lloyd Park, at the children's playground. This is the big pit - with an excellent slide - which was an old quarry.

Knowing what we do now, take a look at the geological map opposite and it will explain quite a lot about what you find in your back garden.

How Do We Know?

Geological exposures have always been scarce in our area. Even when the subsoils have been temporarily

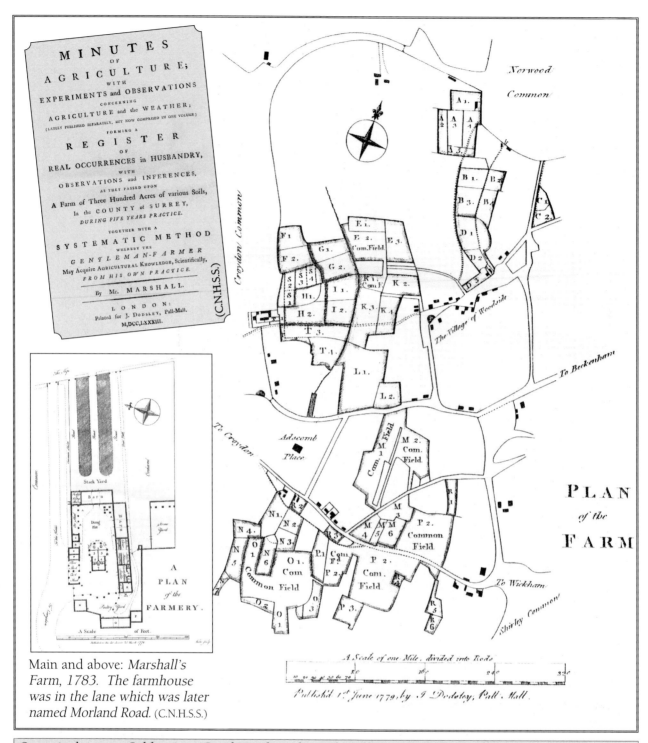

Main and above: *Marshall's Farm, 1783. The farmhouse was in the lane which was later named Morland Road.* (C.N.H.S.S.)

Opposite bottom: *Coldstream (Canal Mead) in the mid 1850s, showing the newly-built East India College Gymnasium. Note the bridge over the (now) Lower Addiscombe Road. W.C. Sayers, long-standing Croydon Chief Librarian, gave a lecture in 1921–22 to Addiscombe societies entitled 'Croydon a hundred years ago' (in which he imagined walking around Addiscombe in the 1820s):*

The Lower (Addiscombe) Road runs east, but is not a road in any sense in which we recognise it. It is a country lane with hedges and fields on either side. On the right, reached by a stile, is the hospital of Addiscombe College. On the left is the old red-tiled roof of a farmhouse (now in Hastings Road), which stands on the edge of its farm-lands. Some 100 yards east, we cross a little brick bridge spanning the Coldstream, which runs into the Coldwater. The Coldstream rises where Radcliffe Road is to be and, running under this bridge on the Lower Road, falls into the Coldwater (or Canal Mead) large pond. Noble trees rise on the margin of the pond and a stile from the Lower Road gives access. It was 462 feet in length and 54 in breadth and kept at a high level by springs in it, which can yield 60 tons of water in a day. It deserves its name, for an officer (of the East India College) swimming here was seized with cramp and drowned - which demonstrates that the water is deep. (C.L.S.L.)

exposed – through brick-clay and gravel pits, sewer trenches, railway cuttings, bomb craters and major building foundation making – there was little or no record made of the findings. They were buried again under whatever the new development happened to be. But all is not lost. Good records exist from three prime sources: well and borehole sections; the brick-making industry and gravel pits; and, wonderfully, a detailed soil condition report from Marshall.

In 1783 William Marshall worked a farm of some 300 acres, consisting of scattered fields throughout Addiscombe and Woodside, extending from south of the Addiscombe Road to the north of Woodside Green. He kept meticulous records of the varying soil conditions, field by field, and generously published his findings some five years later (see maps and tables). He classified the subsoils as absorbent, quicksands, retentive, or springy – all according to their drainage properties. His descriptions of the topsoils speak for themselves and will likely ring a bell with modern gardeners as a description of their own patch.

Referring to the plan of the farm, all the boggy fields lie either side of the Addiscombe Road (marked 'To Croydon/Wickham') which dovetails well with the geological map.

Note that on the Lower Addiscombe Road (marked 'To Beckenham'), the Canal Mead or Coldstream is clearly shown below field T4 and to the left of field L1. This is where the grounds of Havelock House now lie.

And if you are wondering about that distinctive thoroughfare abutting fields M2, M3, M4 and R1, it is Love Lane. See the Ashburton Estate (*page 51*).

Love Lane in 1908, which ran between the Addiscombe and Shirley Roads. (J.G.)

The stile at the entrance to Coldstream. Left to right: cadets Henry Doveton (1857-58), Thomas Walker (1857-58) and James Waterhouse (1857-59). This photograph and that below represent very early photography in England and demonstrate how technically advanced the East India Company College was, where cadets were trained largely as engineers. (C.L.S.L.)

TO THE EXPERIMENTS.

DESCRIPTION OF THE FIELDS.

Names	Size	Soil	Subſoil	Aſpect, &c.
A. 1.	5 Acres *	Clayey Loam	Retentive ‡	Very gently Eaſtern
2.	3 ——	Tenacious Clayey Loam †	— —	Gently Southern
3.	3½ ——	— — — —	— —	Bold to the South
4.	4 ——	— — — —	— —	— —
5.	1½ ——	— — — —	— —	Eaſtern ; but nearly level
B. 1.	3¾ ——	— — — —	— —	— —
2.	2½ ——	— — — —	— —	Gently Northern
3.	4½ ——	— — — —	— —	— —
4.	4⅛ ——	— — — —	— —	— —
C. 1.	2⅛ ——	— — — —	— —	— —
2.	3 ——	Clayey Loam	— —	Northern ; but nearly level
D. 1.	7¾ ——	— — — —	— —	Various ; principally Weſtern
2.	2 ——	— — — —	— —	Gently Northern
3.	1⅞ ——	— — — —	— —	Level
E. 1.	2⅞ ——	Adheſive Clayey Loam	— —	Very gently Weſtern
2.	2⅝ ——	— — — —	— —	— —
3.	4¾ ——	Clayey Loam	— —	Gently Weſtern
F. 1.	4⅛ ——	Black Moory Sandy Loam	Quick-ſand	Eaſtern ; but nearly level
2.	5⅛ ——	— — — —	— —	— —
G. 1.	4⅛ ——	Strong Sandy Loam	— —	— —
2.	5¾ ——	— — — —	— —	— —
H. 1.	3½ ——	Spongey Sandy Loam	— —	— —
2.	6½ ——	Sandy Loam	— —	— —
I. 1.	5½ ——	Strong Sandy Loam	— —	— —
2.	6½ ——	Loam	Retentive	Gently Eaſtern
K. 1.	1⅞ ——	Clayey Loam	— —	Level
2.	5⅛ ——	Mellow Clayey Loam	— —	Weſtern ; but nearly level
3.	11½ ——	Tenacious Clayey Loam	Retentive	Nearly level ; inclined to nor.
4.	6⅞ ——	— — — —	— —	Very gently Weſtern
L. 1.	20⅛ ——	Clayey Loam, Loam & Sandy Loam	— —	Very gently Northern
2.	4¾ ——	Tenacious Clayey Loam	— —	Very gently Weſtern
M. 1.	5⅝ ——	Loam and gravelly Loam	Various	Gently Northern
2.	3⅛ ——	Loam	Retentive	Very gently Weſtern
3.	4⅝ ——	{ Rich gravelly Loam with boggy	Various	Very gently Northern
4.	3½ ——	{ Patches	— —	Gently Northern
5.	1⅞ ——	Gravelly Loam	Abſorbent	— —
6.	4½ ——	Gravelly and boggy	Various	— —
N. 1.	5 ——	Gravelly Loam, &c.	Abſorbent	— —
2.	3 ——	Sandy gravelly Loam	— —	— —
3.	3 ——	Strong gravelly Loam	Various	Various
4.	3 ——	— — — —	— —	Various ; chiefly Southern
5.	4¾ ——	Gravelly Loam	Springy	Various ; chiefly Northern
6.	4 ——	Gravel and gravelly Loam	Various	Gently Northern
7.	1⅛ ——	Strong gravelly Loam	Retentive	Bold to the South
	196⅝			

* The fractional Roods and Perches are omitted, as well for conciſeneſs as perſpicuity.

‡ Every Subſoil is conſidered as *retentive*, which retains or checks the ſuperfluous rain-water which drains through the Soil or Vegetative Stratum ; whether the Retention proceeds from the tenacity of the Subſoil itſelf, or from the Retentiveneſs of ſome inferior Stratum, or from a partial Landſpring, &c.

† This is a peculiar ſpecies of Soil : it is uncommonly adheſive and difficult to plow. It is particularly mentioned in a MINUTE of the 6th of February, 1776.

Marshall's findings of the state of the fields, 1783 (Marshall's Farm 1778–83). (C.N.H.S.S.)

Brick Making & Gravel Pits

Clay is of course needed for making bricks, and gravel primarily for road building. These were in high demand during the explosive development of the area starting in the mid 1800s. There were large numbers of small gravel pits (from the surface drift), many of which escaped being recorded on maps. One can, however, gain clues from artificial differences in ground level and the fact that when gravel pits were worked out (like clay pits) they were liable to flood. It is clear that the Oval Road area was once a gravel pit.

The best records come from brick making. In 1858 W. Vaughan was based on the west side of the south end of Morland Road. This was on what is now Morland Avenue, near the corner with Morland Road, just beyond the 1930s semi-detached houses. When the clay pit became unviable (probably because it was too wet and difficult to work) it was abandoned and became Morland Pond.

The 1868 Ordnance Survey Map also identifies brickwork activity on what is now Hastings and Warren Roads and extensively in Dartnell and Jesmond Roads. In the same area we have brick workings in the Bredon, Kemerton, Laurier, Dominion and Brampton Roads, including what is now the Davidson School site. And we have Handley's Brickworks at Woodside – the largest and most enduring of the lot (see *Vol. I*). What remains is Brickfields Meadows – now a local community area. This comprises a large lake, the only extant local example of a flooded clay pit.

Throughout the area the flooded pits were subsequently incorporated as ornamental water in the gardens of newly-built houses, or, as was far more commonly the case, used as landfill sites and built over.

Main: *Morland Pond on the corner of Morland Road and what is now Morland Avenue, 1898. Mora Hobson is pictured by her father, Mr J.M. Hobson MD, the doctor at 1 Morland Road.*
Left: *Morland Pond, 1901/02.* (Both C.L.S.L.)
Bottom left and right: *Brickfields Meadow, 2001.* (A.B.)

Wells & Boreholes

If you want to abstract water by making a well or sinking a borehole to discover if you are on a firm footing, then it is a statutory requirement to report your findings to what is now the British Geological Survey. The records are precise. The following gives an idea of the local London clay strata:

Location	Thickness of London clay (metres)	Depth below made ground (metres)
Dartnell Road	16.45	2.43
East Croydon Station	0.60	6.09
Gloucester Road	15.23	5.79
Leslie Park Road	No Clay present	
Morland Road	10.36	2.74
St. James Road	26.51	4.47
Stroud Green	8.53	1.52
Woodside Brickworks	17.37	0.00

Deep well sections further north have proved a clay thickness of up to 112 metres.

The Leslie Park Road data (below) comes from a borehole sunk in September 1930 as a precursor to the building of the South Suburban Co-op Central Dairy. This was to abstract water from an artesian well, which was tapped at a depth of 390 feet (c.118 metres). This shows:

Co-op Dairy	Thickness (metres)	Depth (metres)
Drift (surface soil)	4.26	4.26
Blackheath Beds	12.49	16.76
Woolwich and Reading Beds	13.10	29.87
Thanet Sand	12.19	42.06
Chalk	76.80	118.87

The Morland Road data is from a borehole sunk in 1896 to provide water for the famous R. Whites lemonade factory. This shows:

R. Whites	Thickness (metres)	Depth (metres)
Made ground	2.74	2.74
London Clay	10.36	13.10
Blackheath Beds	11.43	24.53
Woolwich and Reading Beds	12.95	37.49
Thanet Sand	12.49	49.98
Chalk	56.69	106.67

This gives an idea of the lay of the land. If you want to find out more, then the excellent Croydon Local Studies Library will help.

Water

As the geology suggests, surface streams and waterlogged gravels were abundant in the area. Water would not be absorbed by the ground as it would with chalk or sandy terrain.

The many streams were typically short and ephemeral, taking a downhill course via the easiest route. Basically they would run or dry up according to rainfall. The Sandilands area, south of Addiscombe Road, also had springs, small ponds and more than its fair share of streams. But the two most substantial, permanent and existent streams are the Chaffinch and Norbury Brooks (brook means a small stream). Heading northwards, combining with many other streams and rivers on the way, they finally issue into the Thames at Greenwich. Chaffinch Brook runs from the Stroud Green area northwards. For a short stretch, it is now the only example of an overground stream in the area. See 'The Chaffinch Brook'.

Recent records describe Norbury Brook as running from somewhere near Grant Road and the end of Nicholson Road, before making its way to what would now be the south side of Northway Road.

Locally, the Brook is known as the Beverley Water or Spring, since its prominent point of presence is indeed the Beverley Cub and Scout Hall in Grant Road. From there it appears to meander through the old railway lines to Capri Road, then Dalmally Passage, and Northway Road before making its way under the huge triangle of railway lines at Selhurst on its way to Thornton Heath. From there it runs to Norbury, the River Graveney and the Wandle. The Brook is clearly shown on the map on page 4. By that time Canal Mead (or Coldstream) had been filled in for building development, but remains the underground spring head for the Brook.

This means that the Coldstream or Canal Mead (pictured on page 15) - now the grounds of Havelock House - is the natural spring headwater for the Norbury Brook. This is its source! And just to top it up, it was trickle-fed by streams from the Lloyd Park/Sandilands area.

So Canal Mead provided potable water for Addiscombe Place and was surely a good piece of ornamental water for the estate. But before the 1850s where did other people get their water from? Supplies of water for domestic use could (before mains water started to be laid from 1851 onwards - see *Vol. I*, p.131 for the Baldwin Latham story) be locally obtained from relatively shallow wells, typically tapping the water from drift gravels at a depth of less than 10 metres. Domestic wells were very unreliable, particularly in times of drought and through surface contamination.

We are pleased to report that we still have a couple of viable domestic wells at the Croydon end of Addiscombe Road. These are at Ashleigh House and 30-36 Addiscombe Road, both of which draw water at a depth of around 12 feet (4.4 metres). A map drawn by an East India cadet demonstrating water flow in the area confirms local knowledge that there is a spring line along the north side of the Addiscombe Road. Indeed, a disused well exists underneath the bungalow next to The Cricketers pub.

On a commercial scale, deeper water supplies were obtained by sinking wells through the London Clay to the more pervious Blackheath Beds, or the underlying Thanet Sand. A well sunk in 1863 at (what is now) East Croydon Station, to provide water for steam locomotives, abstracted from the Blackheath Beds at a depth of just 7.31 metres. This accords with the local domestic wells.

For Addiscombe Station (1864, rebuilt 1899), there is no evidence of a similar well (for similar steam reasons) - even though water lies just beneath. It appears that Baldwin Latham piped it in from his underground Park Hill reservoir as part of a reliable water supply for the emerging area.

Nowadays rainwater mostly falls on house roofs, pavements and roads and flows through modern drains and sewers, taking a shortcut to the River Wandle via the Beddington Sewage Works! And the ephemeral streams have been culverted and buried as building development required. This is all rather sad really, so we will nip back to the Chaffinch Brook for our last bit of natural running water.

The Chaffinch Brook: Addiscombe's Lost Waterway
Jonathan Moore

On the grounds of the Addiscombe, Woodside and Shirley Leisure Gardens lies hidden an untouched stretch of the Chaffinch Brook, almost a quarter of a mile in length and a rare example of a disappearing brookside environment. The Chaffinch Brook still meanders and circles old oak trees. Even to this day the namesake of this stream, the familiar chaffinch, sings in the nearby trees. The brook itself cuts through the London clay and the Blackheath pebble beds. The clay is on the uphill rising gradient to the east on which many allotments now occupy several acres of land, a green oasis surrounded by Addiscombe, the Ashburton estate and Shirley. The marine pebbles, sands and clays are on the other side of the brook to the west, known as the Woolwich, Reading and Blackheath beds. On the west side of the brook stands the imposing Stroud Green well-pumping station which dates to 1906 and was once owned by the Croydon Corporation waterworks. Thames Water now occupies this site and has a small depot there.

Chaffinch Brook, 2002, and Jonathan Moore, 1981. (Both J. Mo.)

unlucky adventurous fox cubs would be found drowned. Perhaps on a wet and cold night as many as five or six drowned fox cubs were found by myself and various plot-holders; one was discovered trapped under the iron grid - a devastating blow to a small pocket of the rural fox population.

The fauna on the banks of the Chaffinch Brook is quite varied. Butterflies include meadow browns, speckled woods, gatekeeper skippers, various blue butterflies, brown argus, orange-tips, small and large white butterflies, peacocks, red admirals, small tortoiseshells and the tame ruffled comma. In 1995 there was a visit by a rare migrant called the clouded yellow. Butterflies have recently become rare due to lack of clement weather, parasites and poor meadow conservation. These areas are now covered in ash trees and brambles.

Among the birds seen in the area, sparrows are rare visitors to the clubhouse, but hedge sparrows or dunnocks, great tits, blue tits, long-tailed tits, wrens, goldcrests, chaffinches, chiff chaffs, blackbirds, starlings, wood pigeons, collared doves, green woodpeckers, song thrushes and magpies are more often seen. In recent years pheasants have visited the allotments and kestrels and peregrines perch on the imposing pumping station.

Foxes, squirrels, badgers, bats, a couple of ponies that are kept in a field near the clubhouse and many plot-holders are among the mammals often seen here!

On the banks of the Chaffinch Brook originates some of the finest honey in the country, free from contamination from rapeseed. Croydon's honey is reported to be the best in England. In 1999 Devon had a bad year for honey and Croydon won the prize, thanks to the practice of John Pearce and Peter Bashford. The honey itself is spun and jarred on the Addiscombe, Woodside, Shirley site and is sold in the trading hut at weekends.

I spent many enjoyable hours as a boy walking up and down the length of the brook in wellies searching for caddis fly larvae and frogs, the former a natural indicator of clean water. Lifting up and turning over every algae-covered stone I could find them surrounded by their own purpose-made home.

I also found enjoyment in racing two or more twigs down the brook to see which one would be the first to the end of the brook not far from the Flower Pot Clubhouse. I would try hard, stopping and starting, to follow them. After heavy rain the brook was known to get quite high and has washed away sleeper footbridges, a shed and bridge combined which was built over the brook; and it is said that in 1966 several feet of topsoil were washed away leaving that year's potatoes high and dry. At the start of the only walled, curving section there is a heavy iron trellis screen, which would become completely dammed up with leaves and branches of trees that had fallen into the brook only to be halted at this point. As much as two feet of water would build up behind this and it only took a hard push with a leg to collapse the iron grid on its face and release a flood of excited water down towards the brick channel.

On occasion this rural location would reveal a slightly gruesome sight of nature when the year's

Peter Bashford with one of his hives, 2002. (B.E.)

Three

Cherry Orchard Road 1847–1939

A Time of Many Changes, by Paul Jordan

In 1847 the main development in Cherry Orchard Road was centred on the junction with Cross Road. In fact, Cherry Orchard Road officially ended here. It continued to the Lower Addiscombe Road as Lees Road (hence Lees Road Cottages). The area mainly consisted of labourers' and artisans' cottages. During the 1850s, Leslie Park Road was developed along with the east of Cherry Orchard Road (formerly Lees Road). This included the building of the Leslie Arms.

Part of the estate was again auctioned in 1876. Leslie Grove was built across the site and the first purpose-built shops in Cherry Orchard Road were constructed (Gladstone Terrace, Nos 135-143) in 1877-78. Leslie Lodge survived until 1900 when it was demolished and the land used for the construction of Alpha Road and the building of a parade of shops in Lower Addiscombe Road.

By 1868 more detached and semi-detached villas had been built on either side of Cherry Orchard Road towards East Croydon Station. From the Census returns the occupants appear to have been retired tradesmen and professionals such as solicitors. Development had also occurred north of Lower Addiscombe Road by this time and the new houses were served by shops in Alexandra Terrace (Nos 45-55 Lower Addiscombe Road) and Devonshire Terrace opposite. Cherry Orchard Road remained predominantly residential.

Major changes took place with the introduction of the electric tram at the turn of the century. The Leslie Arms was rebuilt and four shops were constructed alongside it. During the early 1900s, Leslie Park Villas and Florence Cottages were refronted to form retail units, and finally Leslie Lodge Villa and Leslie Place were demolished and the parade of shops completed. This side remained unchanged until the mid 1930s when Surrey Terrace (including the Surrey Arms) was demolished and rebuilt.

Further along the road near the junction with Oval Road, a number of houses were demolished in the 1920s to make way for two blocks of flats known as Cherry Orchard Gardens. Other cottages and the nursery were incorporated into the United Dairies depot (formerly the Cherry Orchard Dairy) in the 1930s.

The end of the road closest to East Croydon gradually succumbed to industry and some of the villas were replaced by Brown Brothers (motor and radio manufacturers) and Lilico flour producers. Malta Cottage had already been demolished by 1894 and replaced by a coal yard (Nos 74-96). In 1937, more cottages and the Nag's Head public house (on the opposite side to Cross Road) were demolished, and replaced by Ogden Smith's fishing tackle factory. From then until the 1970s Cherry Orchard Road remained largely unchanged.

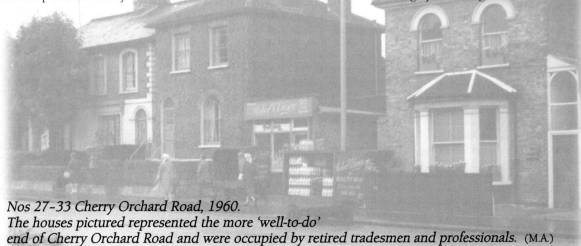

Nos 27-33 Cherry Orchard Road, 1960.
The houses pictured represented the more 'well-to-do'
end of Cherry Orchard Road and were occupied by retired tradesmen and professionals. (M.A.)

THE CHANGING FACE OF CHERRY
ORCHARD ROAD

Aerial views showing the Cherry
Orchard Road, Lower Addiscombe
Road junction in 1868 (based on the
Ordnance Survey Map of that year).
(P.J.)

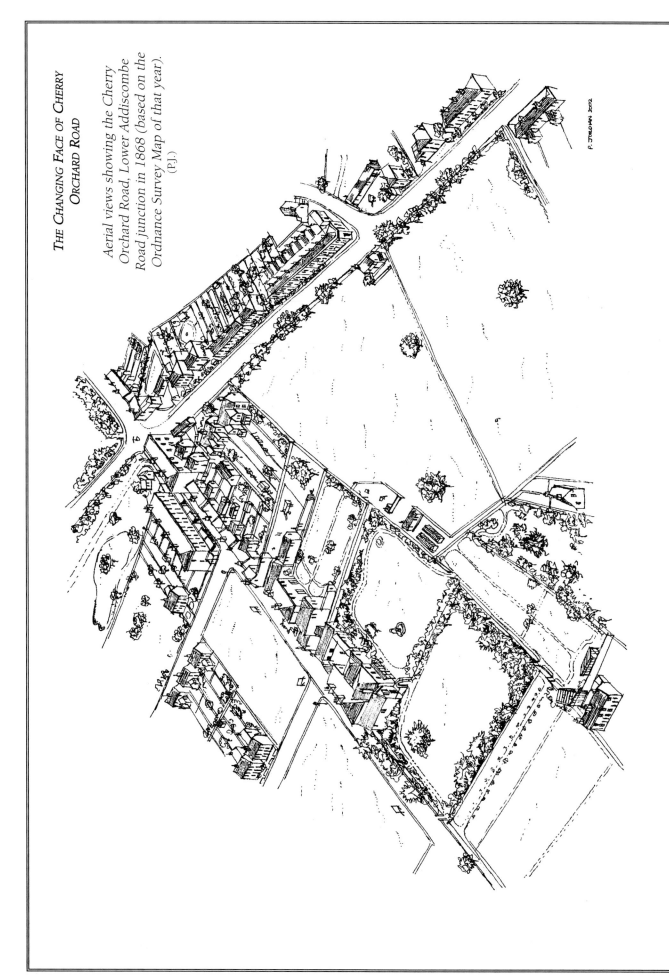

P. JORDAN 2022

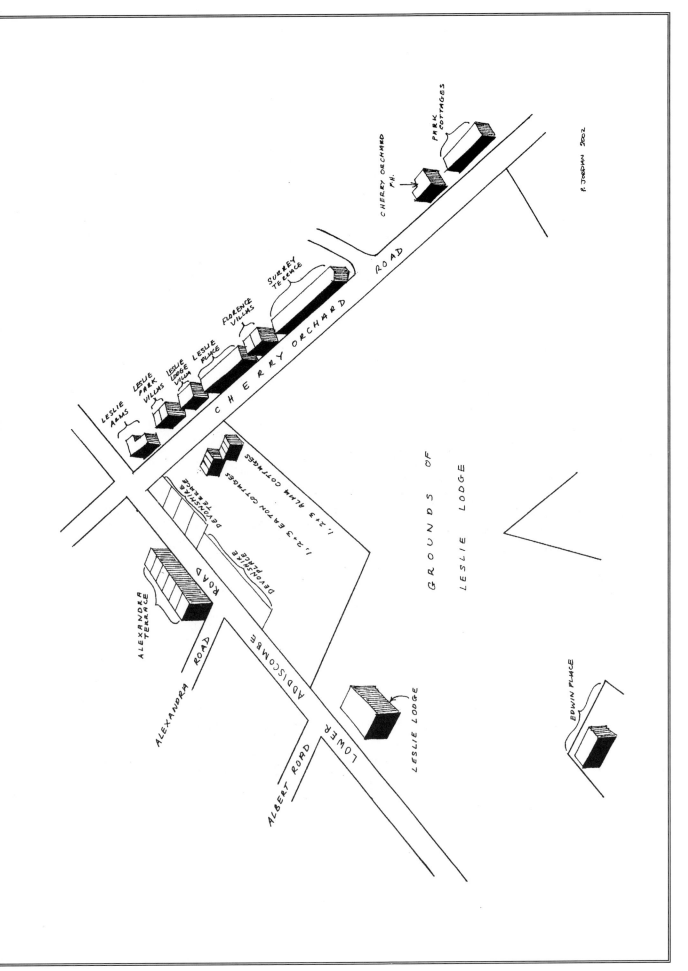

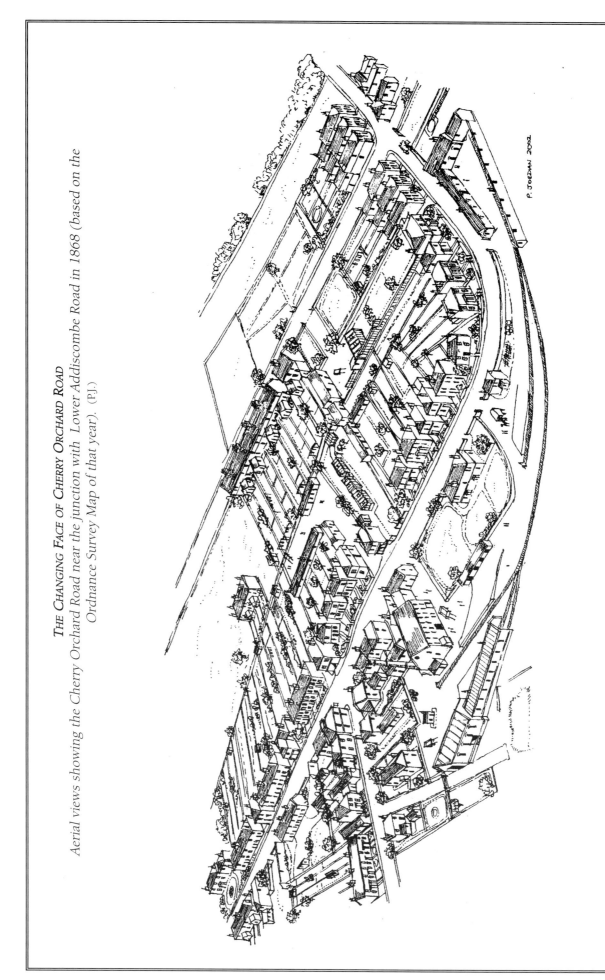

THE CHANGING FACE OF CHERRY ORCHARD ROAD

Aerial views showing the Cherry Orchard Road near the junction with Lower Addiscombe Road in 1868 (based on the Ordnance Survey Map of that year). (PJ.)

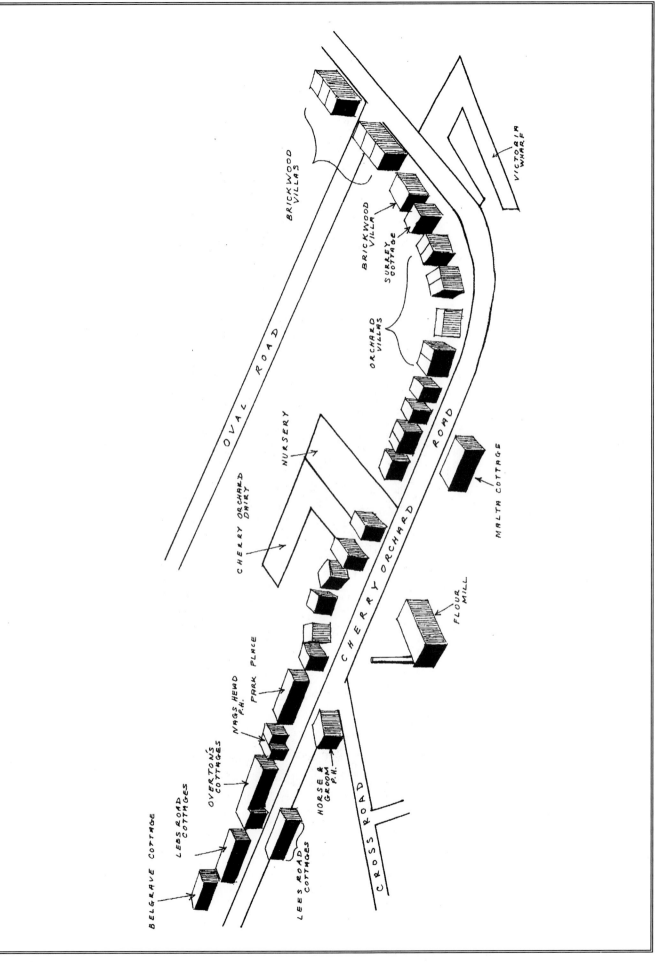

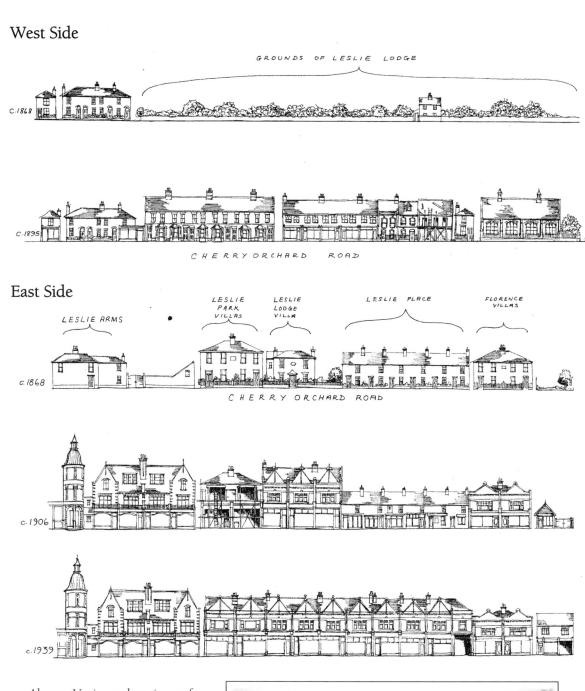

West Side

GROUNDS OF LESLIE LODGE

C.1868

C.1895

CHERRY ORCHARD ROAD

East Side

LESLIE ARMS

LESLIE PARK VILLAS

LESLIE LODGE VILLA

LESLIE PLACE

FLORENCE VILLAS

c.1868

CHERRY ORCHARD ROAD

c.1906

c.1939

Above: *Various elevations of Cherry Orchard Road showing the changes that took place from 1868 to 1939.* (P.J.) *The top two elevations show the west side of Cherry Orchard Road, the bottom three the east side.*

Right: *Leslie Lodge, c.1863. Alpha Road now covers this site.* (C.L.S.L.)

Leslie Place (to left of the horse and cart) shortly before demolition. The rebuilt Leslie Arms is on the left. Fronting the south side of Lower Addiscombe Road was Leslie Lodge (not visible in this picture) a large detached house with extensive gardens and paddocks and a range of conservatories. The grounds also bordered Cherry Orchard Road. In 1851 the estate was sold and some commercial and residential development took place on the junction of the two roads (Devonshire Terrace and Devonshire Buildings). (J.G.)

A slightly later view of the road showing the new shops built on the site of Leslie Place. (J.G.)

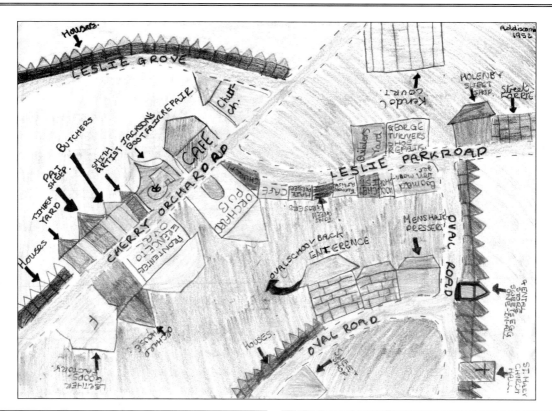

These buildings originally formed a row of six identical houses (Brickwood Villas). The house on the left was refronted in the 1930s. The house on the right, known locally as 'the round house', was said to be haunted. (C.L.S.L.)

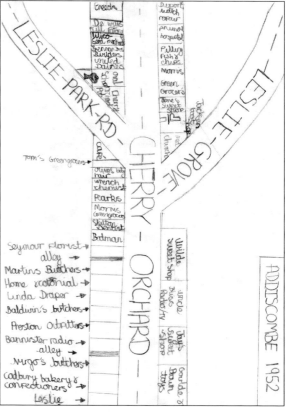

Top and above: *Cherry Orchard Road in 1952, drawn by pupils of Oval Road School.*
(C.H. & C.AB. & N.C.F.)

Left: *No. 98 Cherry Orchard Road, 1933.*
(P. & C.L.)

Four

Along Cherry Orchard & Morland Roads

A Walk in the Past

Lifeboat parade, 1908, at the top of Cherry Orchard Road, after turning out of Addiscombe Road. Behind the fence is the Brickwood estate. On the corner was a natural pond, extending a little way up Addiscombe Road. Later, a skating rink and then Creed's factory were built on the site where Knollys House now stands. (J.G.)

Nos 1 and 3 Addiscombe Road (c.1916) between the station and Cherry Orchard Road, were offices for businesses including Paish, Tyler & Crump, Architects, Surveyors, Valuers and Estate Agents. This was also once the registered offices of Addiscombe Garden Estates. (C.L.S.L.)

The junction of Addiscombe and Cherry Orchard Road, 1964. (J.M.B. & C.L.S.L.)

Between 1913 and 1966, Creed's factory on Cherry Orchard Road occupied the site from the corner with Addiscombe Road to Cedar Road. (C.L.S.L.)

Above and below: *Creed's inspection room and Creed's machine shop respectively during the First World War, when women were brought in to keep the country's economy going while the men were away fighting.* (Both C.L.S.L.)

Houses opposite Oval Road, 1975.
(C.N.H.S.S.)

Left: *'The Farm House' was on the corner of Cherry Orchard and Station Roads leading to the Station Hotel, now called Porter and Sorter, c.1950.* (C.L.S.L.)

Below: *Morland Road, c.1910.* (J.G.)

No. 4 Morland Road. (J.G.)
(See page 49.)

The junction of Lower Addiscombe and Morland Roads, c.1918. The sharp turn out of Cherry Orchard Road sometimes led to the tram becoming disconnected from the wires. (J.G. & P.C.)

Main: *Morland Road at the junction of Cherry Orchard Road, c.1905. Morland Road was named after John Morland who lived at Heath Lodge, which had extensive grounds. The house was between Morland Road and what is now Morland Avenue. After his widow died in 1888, the estate was sold and split up. A Dr Carpenter bought the house with reduced grounds and renamed it 'The Cedars'. Morland Avenue was the first of the roads to be laid out.* (J.G.)
Inset: *A similar view, c.1916.* (C.L.S.L.)

Main: *No. 1 Morland Road, known as 'Glendalough', decorated for the Coronation Carnival in 1902 by the owner, Mr J.M. Hobson, MD, who had a thriving practice here. His surgery was held in the square block to the front, which is now a Co-op supermarket. The practice was subsequently sold to Dr Thompson, who for many years held surgery with Drs Harris and Jones. In 1931 Glendalough was sold to the South Suburban Co-operative Society and the gardens to a speculative builder who put up four semi-detached houses on the former tennis courts and croquet pitch. Dr Thompson had a new purpose-built surgery constructed at the front. This was the first purpose-built GP surgery in Croydon. The new building inherited the No. 1 Morland Road address, and continues to this day as a popular practice. Dr Thompson moved to 135 Addiscombe Road. Surprisingly, Glendalough still exists, since it has the distinction of having been bombed in both the First and Second World Wars. The First World War saw the building being bombed by a Zeppelin which, in the same raid on 13 October 1915, badly damaged the Oval School. The bombing during the Second World War took place in 1941. The whole of the surgery and ground floor of the house are now the Co-op, and the upper floor flats. Although hemmed in by the 1930s building, this important house is still recognisable today. This photograph was taken by Mr William A. Dennis of 101 Alexandra Road.* (C.L.S.L.)

Inset left and right: *No. 1 Morland Road and the GP practice in 2002.* (S.C.)

A Southern Counties touring steam train on the East Kent line photographed as it passed through East Croydon on Sunday 19 March 1967. (GW)

Five

Getting Around

King of the Road, Trains & Addiscombe Station Remembered

King of the Road

Robert Cogger, Bill Maile, Ray Misson & Anne Bridge

For many years the Addiscombe tram line had fallen into disrepair and in the early 1920s there was much discussion locally about whether the track should be repaired, replaced by trackless trams (trolley buses) or given over entirely to the omnibus.

To give you a flavour of the debate, here are a couple of extracts from the *Addiscombe, Woodside & Shirley Notes*, a locally published magazine. On 9 February 1924 an anonymous 'unsatisfied tram user hoping for better means of transport' declared:

Apart from the rough passage one endures on a tram-ride at present, there is the loss of time caused by those irritating waits at loops or behind slow-moving traffic, and the ever-increasing danger of crossing from the kerb to the fixed tram, or vice-versa, to be considered. ... It is quite hopeless to expect the Lower Addiscombe Road to be a quiet residential one; shops are springing up and more are planned, and where there is a shopping centre there must be means of locomotion.

Bill Maile spent 42 years working on the buses. His father before him was a driver on Tillings horse-drawn buses. Bill remembers a ride on one of the Addiscombe trams as a child in 1917:

Aged 12. My first trip to 'Bingham Halt' on the tram from George Street via Cherry Orchard Road. Nothing but loops and stops, quite some ride, not smooth as the main road cars. Pitch and toss, swishing from left to right. More liken to riding a

The number 178 at Black Horse Terminus, an elderly 'NS' type which was followed by a more modern 'L.T.' type, c.1936. (J.G.)

'Bronco'. I was amazed at the number of times that we changed and stopped for other trams to pass. Having arrived there, I wandered to the shops [and] along to a big pub, [the] 'Black Horse'. I noted various names then returned to Croydon. Not to my liking, too slow. Next day I still felt the bruises and aches of that ride. No wonder the bus went along another road.

The editorial of the 10 April 1924 edition of the *Addiscombe, Woodside & Shirley Notes* comes to the following conclusion:

The proposal for the co-ordination of London and suburban traffic has a particular interest for Addiscombe and Woodside in view of the storm that was raised over the trolley trams. ... It appears reasonable to suppose, too, that the question of method – that is, whether the tram car, trolley car, or omnibus – will resolve itself into the simple one, which is best? In that event there is hardly any doubt that popular opinion would plump for 'buses'.

Bring on the Buses

Croydon's prime position on the main road between London and Brighton meant that road-based public transport, in the form of stagecoaches, served the town from the late-seventeenth century onwards. For Addiscombe itself, however, the first operation of what could be considered a local bus service is believed to have taken place around 1866, not long after the opening of the South Eastern Railway's Addiscombe Road Station. In that year a service, meeting most trains, was operating between the station and Croydon High Street.

The first buses were, of course, horse powered. By the early 1900s motor buses had begun to appear and the London General Omnibus Company bought up smaller rival operators throughout London to consolidate a large network of local bus routes. Another famous South London bus operator of the era was the Thomas Tilling organisation. In 1913 and 1914 this company ran the first motor buses in Addiscombe on a short-lived route 55 from Croydon to Shoreditch. In 2002 a reminder can still be seen on the side of many local Arriva buses which carry the letters 'TC' to show that their home garage is the one-time 'Tillings Croydon' base, south of town on the Brighton Road.

On 1 July 1933 'London Transport' was formed to take over, amongst other interests, all the independent bus companies. In 2002, although the 'London Transport' name no longer appears on the side of local buses, this is still the organisation most Addiscombe people would think of as providing their bus services.

Anybody who keeps an ear to the ground on such matters will appreciate that London bus routes can change with alarming frequency. Addiscombe's routes are no exception and there have been countless variations to local services over the years. At the time of writing at least 49 different route numbers are recorded as having been used in Addiscombe at one time or another. Detailing all the changes is far beyond the scope of this book. It does aim to show, though, that despite the frequent alterations, many of the bus services that were started in the 1920s and '30s can still be recognised today.

Cherry Orchard Road routes; the 12 family: Today's 312 service between South Croydon and Peckham is a direct descendant of one of London's oldest and most well-known bus routes, the 12. Those two famous digits first appeared in Addiscombe on 8 March 1922 when route 12A began working every 12 minutes from South Croydon to Charing Cross. The service ran along Addiscombe Road and Canning Road, this lasting until 9 June 1929 when the, by then, plainly-numbered 12 began to serve Cherry Orchard Road instead.

For many years the 12 travelled way up into North London to terminate at Harlesden. However, as the route normally worked in sections, it was a rare sight indeed to see a bus heading through Addiscombe all the way to that far-flung destination. Even so, in 1949, the frequency was such that some 104 vehicles were needed to provide the service on the 12 each day. The 12s' traditional conductor-operated, rear-entrance buses gave way in 1972 to one-person-operated vehicles (still referred to as 'one man' in those less politically correct days). However, at that time the railway bridge in Lower Addiscombe

Road, near Bingham Road, was too low for modern one-man double deckers to fit under (note: this corrects the statement in *Vol. 1*, p.101). Single deckers therefore came to be used on the service which, once again, became known as the 12A. These vehicles would have been totally unsuitable for the very busy Central London section of the route, so the 12A went only as far north as Peckham, overlapping for a short stretch with the truncated, still conductor-operated 12 from its new southern terminus at Norwood Junction.

Although shorn at the northern end, the 1970s and '80s saw the 12A flirting with more southern climes and venturing beyond South Croydon to Purley, Selsdon and Riddlesdown. From 1986 to 1990 there was even a Sunday-only 12B version, giving downtown Addiscombe a one-day-a-week link to Chipstead Valley.

The 312 number was assumed daily in 1990 when modern double deckers appeared after removal of the Lower Addiscombe Road railway bridge to allow for the introduction of Tramlink. At the time of writing the 312 continues to serve the traditional roads from South Croydon to Peckham, although the buses are now of the most modern, low-floor, easy-access design.

Above: *A 'Tilling ST' type on the 12 route by Black Horse Terminus, 1936.* (J.G.)

Right: *Sunday only 12B in Lower Addiscombe Road, 1990.* (R.C.)

Left: *An 'SMS' type on the 12A route by Bingham Bridge, 1977, during the single-deck era. Double decks were 14'6" and were too tall for this route, as shown by the sign on the bridge.* (G.M.D.)

Left: *A 'K' type on the 179 route in George Street, c.1929. The 179 was a forerunner of today's 194 and operated between 1929 and 1934.*
(J.G.)

Below: *An 'NS' type on the 197 route at Woodside Green.*
(C.L.S.L.)

(R.M.)

The 197 family: Another long-standing local bus service is the 197 along Morland Road. This first began on 7 September 1927 between Katharine Street, Croydon and Norwood Junction. In 2002 it ran between the same points although, in the intervening years, the route has been as far south as Caterham and, at various times, has spawned 197A and 197B variations. One-man-operated buses appeared on the route in 1974 and it was at the same time that it started to frequent Cherry Orchard Road, having previously provided a facility to Sydenham Road and Dingwall Road.

For a period in the late 1980s and early '90s the 197's red buses deserted and were replaced by green 'London & Country' vehicles. This was a result of the London Transport bus tendering exercises which

began in 1985 and which have since seen the traditional red London bus joined by a multitude of other colours from a host of independent operators.

The 410: In 1995 Davidson Road was reported to be the longest residential street in Croydon without a regular bus service. This all changed from 9 December that year when the 412 began to serve it on its journey between Norwood Junction and Croydon. The new service was novel in that it was the first to be financially supported by Croydon Council. It proved popular and from 29 August 1998 became part of the more frequent 410 to Wallington, in one of the periodical swap arounds of routes in which the bus authorities like to indulge.

St James Road routes: The first service along St James Road was route 134 in 1927 which ran from Liverpool Street to the Black Horse. In 1934 it became the 133A and then, on 5 January 1938, it was replaced by the 59A. This started at the Black Horse and ran along Lower Addiscombe Road and St James Road before heading north to Camden Town and, later, West Hampstead. It last appeared in Addiscombe on 26 November 1958, having run on Saturdays only since 16 October 1957.

From that date the weekday service along St James Road was provided by route 50. This was an existing 'tram replacement' bus service which was extended into the Addiscombe area, providing a link from the Black Horse to the Victoria Embankment. A Saturday service was added in 1958 and the route underwent many changes over the following ten years until, on 15 June 1968, it was replaced by the new 289 on Mondays to Fridays. Eventually, the Saturday service was also replaced by the 289 from 31 October 1970.

The 289 itself kicked off in a small way between the Black Horse and Thornton Heath, via the length of St James Road. In 1973 it was diverted via West Croydon and, since then, it has grown to its current rather roundabout route from Elmers End to Purley, having ventured as far east as Beckenham Junction between 1978 and 1985.

From 7 February 1987 the 289 was another route to see green buses as part of London Transport's route tendering procedure, but nowadays reds rule the roost once more. Following a decree by Mayor Ken Livingstone all London buses will soon be red again, all new contracts now being let specifying that vehicles must be painted this colour.

The 494 route, from West Croydon to Shirley via St James Road and Lower Addiscombe Road, is a very new arrival on the local scene having only started on 10 June 2000. It was intended to serve as a part replacement for the 54 along Shirley Road (see Addiscombe Road section) and was stated to be experimental for six months. It must have been a success as it is still with us in 2002. The 494 is notable as being the only current Addiscombe bus route never to have been worked by red buses, the blue and yellow vehicles of the Metrobus company having provided the service since day one.

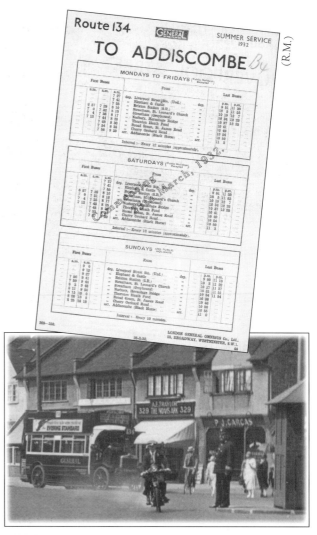

Photographs top to bottom: *The 134 at Black Horse Halt, c.1928;*
An 'RTL' type on 59A route at Black Horse Halt, 1955. (R.M.);
An 'RT' type on 289 route near the Black Horse in 1969, the original shuttle from Addiscombe to Thornton Heath. (G.M.D.)

'SNB' type on 289 route near Bingham Bridge, 7 February 1987. This is an example of the 'tendered' route era, with a green London County (South West) bus with a 'London Regional Transport Service' notice on the front. (R.C.)

Addiscombe Road routes: Many of the bus services along the Addiscombe Road have an equally long pedigree as those serving the 'heart' of town.

One recent loss was the 54. From 10 June 2000 this was curtailed at Elmers End following the introduction of Tramlink. The loss was one of the few negative aspects of the new light-rail system. Prior to this, the 54 had linked the Croydon and Woolwich areas since 1924, at times reaching as far south as Selsdon and to Charlton and Plumstead Common at the other end.

The 194 group: Another very long-standing Addiscombe Road service number is the 194, which, along with 194A, 194B and even 194C variants over the years, has been trundling between Croydon and West Wickham since 1933. From 1936 it ran on to Forest Hill and it has carried on taking this 'long way round' ever since. Until 1996 the service ran across Croydon to the airport and for a period in the 1990s it was unique in London (and possibly anywhere) as the only bus route to advertise two defunct locations on its destination display. Buses would proudly announce they were heading for Croydon Airport – Water Palace. Today's 198 is a development from the 194 group, spawned as a result of the London bus authorities' new-found dislike for suffix letters. In 1963 the 194B was set up to serve the new Shrublands estate. As the 12A eventually became the 312, so the 194B, in 1992, became the 198.

Towards New Addington: The huge New Addington estate was the prompt for the introduction of the 130 route on 5 July 1939, linking the isolated new housing with Croydon and serving Addiscombe Road along the way. Now that Tramlink provides a quick and easy link from New Addington to Croydon it is

easy to forget the efforts that used to go into providing a fast bus service for the outlying estate. From 1955 the corridor was one of the few in London to see regular express buses, the final variant on this theme being the X30 which ran its last on the day after Tramlink opened to New Addington. During the late 1960s and '70s there had been a whole group of different 'C' routes, the C1, C2, C3 and C4, providing the service at different times of the day and week. These were amongst the first ever one-man-operated double-deck buses in London, using the 'farebox' system, whereby the exact cash fare had to be dropped into a sealed container in front of the driver. Unfortunately, they were of little use to Addiscombe residents as they rushed past non-stop. When Tramlink started, the 130 was proposed for complete withdrawal. It has survived so far because of public protest, but it must be the least likely of our local bus routes to still be around if *Vol. 3* of this book is ever published!

The 119 group: The 119 was the last new London bus route to be introduced before the outbreak of the Second World War, starting on 9 August 1939 between Bromley North and Croydon. It has ploughed pretty much the same furrow ever since, with 119A and 119B variations at various times, and ventures north to Thornton Heath, both via the London Road and Purley Way. From 29 June 1996 the route returned to the Purley Way, but this time to the Croydon Airport end, taking over this section of the 194's traditional route. In 2002 it is also another local bearer of the blue and yellow flag, having been run by Metrobus since 29 August 1998.

Clickety Click - X66: The present-day 466 and 367 routes are the offspring of the 166. This had served the Croydon to Chipstead Valley road since 1948, and indeed still does today. In 1970 the 166 was diverted to provide a direct link from the Coulsdon and Purley areas along Addiscombe Road to Shirley, West Wickham and Beckenham Junction. From 1 September 1990 it was withdrawn between Shirley and Beckenham Junction with a new minibus service, the 366, taking over that section from Croydon. More to follow on that shortly. The section of the 166 through Addiscombe was taken over by a new route 466, running through from Shirley to Caterham-on-the-Hill on 29 August 1998. This was later re-routed away from Shirley to Addington. It was intended to be the 130's replacement along the Upper Shirley Road but, as explained above, the 130 has actually carried on running ever since.

Going back to the 366, this was another unusual service. In order to ensure room on the minibuses for passengers at the Shirley end, who had no other bus route options, there was a ban on short-distance passengers using the route for travel along the Addiscombe Road. However, this only applied on the way out of Croydon, leading to much confusion amongst passengers. Thankfully, these arrangements only lasted a short time.

At the same time as the 366 started, there was also a route 367 introduced. This served new ground through the Orchard Avenue area of Shirley. The 366 itself was withdrawn after 13 March 1992 but the 367 survives today, now travelling all the way through from Croydon to Bromley via a plethora of back streets. In its few short years, the 367 has been rather chameleon-like, having seen red buses, green buses, red buses again and finally the present-day blue vehicles of Metrobus.

Nocturnal activities: Addiscombe's first night-bus service began on 12 March 1994 when the N109 service started running from New Addington along the Addiscombe Road to Croydon and up to Central London. The tendering process had seen this route won by the London Central company who didn't serve the Croydon area at all during the daytime. Even more bizarrely, for several years the route provided night-time employment for vehicles used on the company's Docklands Express service during the day. After a night on the town anybody looking up at the enormous logos on the sides of the vehicles declaring 'Waterloo - Canary Wharf' might have been excused for thinking they were getting on the wrong bus. From 18 September 1999 the night service through Addiscombe became the N159, which it remains at the time of writing, although it now runs from the much more local Arriva depot at Thornton Heath.

The Green Line: 1 July 1953 was a notable day for buses in Addiscombe, and throughout the London area. On that day London Transport launched the 725 Green Line. This was a new, limited-stop long-distance service across a swathe of South London, all the way from Gravesend in Kent to Windsor in Berkshire, serving Dartford, Sidcup, Bromley, Croydon, Sutton, Kingston and Staines, including the Lower Addiscombe Road and St James Road along the way.

There were many cross-London Green Line services at the time, including direct links from central Croydon to places as far away as Aylesbury in Buckinghamshire. However, the 725 was the first 'orbital' service which didn't run right through the centre of the metropolis. There have been many variations to the service and route numbers over the years, including, from 21 May 1977, a diversion via Cherry Orchard Road to serve the major traffic magnet of East Croydon Station.

London Transport attempted to withdraw the route in the early 1990s but public protest was vociferous and, eventually, victorious, and the route is thankfully still with us. In 2002 it runs as the 726 on a shorter route starting from Bromley and providing Addiscombe with a very handy direct link to Heathrow Airport. It's no longer known as the Green Line. From 29 February 1992 it became the Expresslink, gaining red vehicles provided by London Coaches. At the time of writing the service is provided by the Tellings Golden Miller company with smart, white, blue and yellow buses.

The future: Today there is still much discussion about the use of roads; which form of transport should have priority on roads; bus and tram-only lanes, infamous fines, cycle lanes and parking restrictions. The main changes from 80 years ago are in shopping habits, relative wealth, prevalence of car ownership and a greater expectation of mobility. Time will tell.

The number 725 from Royal Parade, Lower Addiscombe Road in the mid 1950s, the original Addiscombe 'Green Line' coach. (J.W.)

Above: *Woodside Station. The exit on the left was especially designed for horses because of the proximity of the racecourse.* (J.G.)

Left: *Hayes train seen from Long Lane, 1932.* (G.W.)

Below: *The downside of Bingham Station on its last day of operation on 12 May 1983.* (D.P.)

A Southern Counties touring steam train photographed from a garden in Northampton Road, Sunday 19 March 1967. It left Victoria at 11.05a.m. and travelled to Eastbourne via Selsdon, East Croydon and Woodside. (G.W.)

The down-side passenger steam train clearing Bingham Halt, probably a hop pickers' train, 1931. (G.W.)

Bingham Road Station (also known as Bingham Halt). Peter's newsagent is visible (see section on shops), mid 1950s. (R.K.K.)

Opposite: *Tony Hancock at Bingham Road Station filming the opening sequence of 'The Rebel' in 1960. Alan Pollett recalls this 'famous scene from the film starring the late, great Tony Hancock in which the lead character boards the crowded London-bound morning train by going through an empty train standing at the down-side platform. It was filmed at Bingham Halt. The location was chosen because there was no rail traffic through the station between 10.00a.m. and 4.00p.m. During their lunch break, Hancock and some of the film crew adjourned to the Black Horse pub and I, together with several other avid teenage fans, spent some time watching through the dimpled window glass whilst he ate his lunch. On their return to the station, Hancock and party took a leisurely stroll past the shops in Lower Addiscombe Road.'* (A.B.K)

Addiscombe Station Remembered

Addiscombe Station opened on 1 April 1864 and was rebuilt in 1899. On 31 May 1997 the last train ran from this station, which was closed to enable Tramlink construction further up the line but was never reopened. The fine signal-box was destroyed in an arson attack before it could be listed. Exactly four years after the day of closure, on 31 May 2001, a demolition firm, having installed their heavy equipment, stood awaiting a call on their mobile phone from developers. The moment it arrived, the demolition team set to work pulling apart and knocking down the station. Here are some records of the station at work. We document its demolition and the construction of the first flats. When the developer's on-site sales office opened on 11 May 2002, many homes were sold that day. But... do they know about the ghost?

1986 (J.S.)

DOWN TRAINS. MID KENT LINE. *June, 1878.*

Charing Cross, Waterloo Junc., Cannon Street, London Bridge, New Cross, St. John's, Lewisham Junc., Lady Well, Catford Bridge, Lo'r Sydenham, N Beckenham *ar*, N Beckenham *dp*, Elmer's End, Woodside, Addiscombe

UP TRAINS. ☞ H. VINCENT MOSS, THE COLONIAL STORE, ADDISCOMBE.

Addiscombe, Woodside, Elmer's End, N Beckenham *ar*, N Beckenham *dp*, Lo'r Sydenham, Catford Bridge, Lady Well, Lewisham Junc., St. John's, New Cross, London Bridge, Cannon Street, Waterloo Junc., Charing Cross

SUNDAY TRAINS.—Addiscombe to Charing Cross, 9-15, 2-30, 7-20, 10-0. | From Charing Cross, 8-5, 1-20, 6-10, 8-55.

a Saturdays only.   *b* Not on Saturday.   *c* Mondays and Thursdays only.

1878 (R.M.)

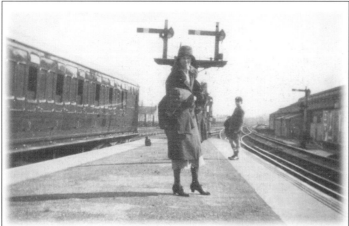

Top left: *1969* (J.S.)
Top right: 1990s (P.B.)
Above: *Mrs Weaver and John Womack, 1932.* (G.W.)
Right: *1969* (J.S.)
Below: *1969* (J.S.)

Main: *The station before demolition.* (P.B.)
Montage this page and opposite: *The demolition and building work under way. John Hobbs donned a German Army helmet to visit the site.* (S.C. & A.B.)

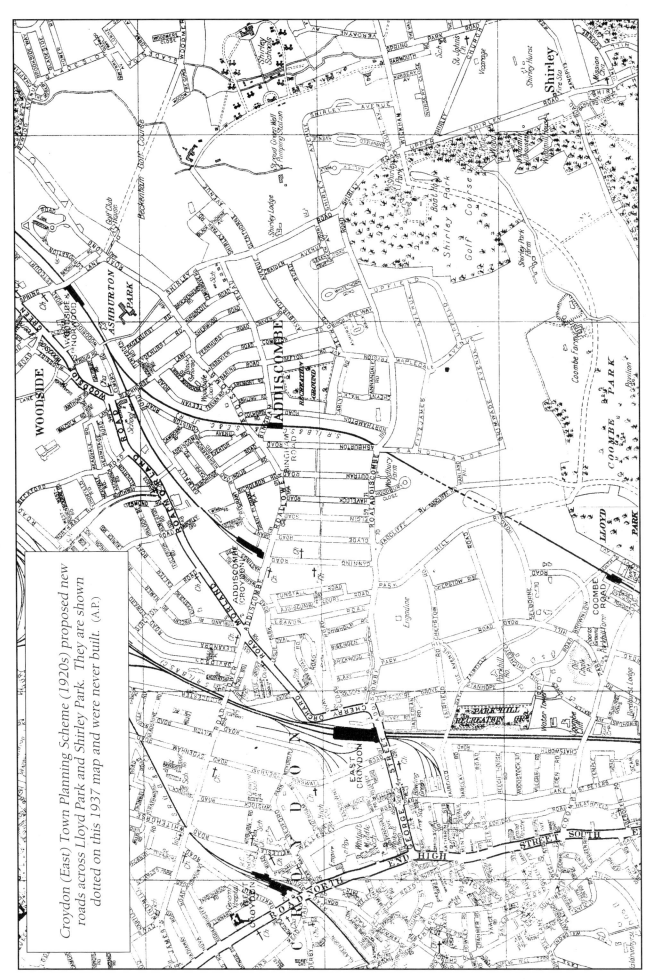

Croydon (East) Town Planning Scheme (1920s) proposed new roads across Lloyd Park and Shirley Park. They are shown dotted on this 1937 map and were never built. (A.P.)

Six

Southward Ho!

Houses Sweep Southwards, Thomas Carlyle & the Ashburtons, The Coombe Estates,
Shirley House, The Whitgift Foundation, Heron's Croft & Town Planning

Houses Sweep Southwards
Tony Stelling (& helpers!)

Until 1910 most of Addiscombe's south-east corner was meadowland belonging to old estates. There were four farms, several estate houses and a few cottages. By 1937 (*see opposite*) the area I will describe was completely developed and indeed is relatively unchanged at the time of writing in 2002.

In this chapter I will concentrate on the area from Bingham Road southwards as far as Lloyd Park and Shirley Park Golf Course. No houses were built in Bingham Road until 1903 and none were built in Northampton Road until 1906; the first houses in Radcliffe Road were built in 1882 and were on a grand scale. Addiscombe Road had no houses further east than Ashburton Road. The area to the north-west – the 'East India Company Estate' – had been developed before 1900; this was described in *Vol. I*. North of Bingham Road was already being developed and to the east there was more open land including the Corporation Waterworks at Stroud Green, and Beckenham Golf Course.

The area was a magnet for town planners. The undeveloped land seemed a challenge to our town managers at the Town Hall (itself only built in 1895), the London County Council (LCC) and the Greater London Council (GLC). Every few years new 'through' roads were planned, but never built. Shirley Park was threatened with another large housing development in 1939 but this did not happen (although subsequently a compulsory purchase order was authorised in 1951 to develop the site for schools and playing-fields, a topic which is dealt with later in this chapter).

Foundations: By 1910 Croydon was already a town of 160,000 people – and it was growing steadily. It had good rail communications and electric trams had been introduced in 1901. The attractions of Croydon's location and infrastructure had already drawn wealthy merchants and bankers away from London into the suburbs and the age of the commuter was beginning – so the clerks and artisans also moved away from the inner London boroughs. During the nineteenth century there was an explosion of houses, speculative and bespoke, for upper, middle and working classes. The large houses had accommodation for servants, whilst the smallest often lacked a bathroom.

The twentieth century saw a sea change to smaller families, and smaller houses with labour-saving features. The First World War and the washing machine did away with servants in a generation! There were government enquiries and reports, and despite the high unemployment during the Depression the days of 'going into service' were over. Locally we had three training centres for 'domestics' in 1914: there was Nonington Hall in Bingham Road, Ashburton Domestic Training School in Shirley Road (previously Ashburton Homes) and the Training Home for Young Servants at 4 Morland Road pictured on page 31. By 1922 all had closed their doors. (The establishment at 4 Morland Road was next door to an 'Industrial School and Detention Home for Boys' – just imagine!)

In 1937 Croydon had a population of 250,000. It was already a hub for the insurance industry. Purley Way was a manufacturing centre and also home to Croydon Airport, London's airport until 1956. Shoppers came from miles around to the excellent shopping centre – with the great department stores Allders, Grants and Kennards. Theatres, cinemas and sporting facilities all thrived. No surprise then that in 1936-37 over 5,000 houses were built in Croydon (East), many of them from local bricks made of Woodside clay.

Our patch: The area that I write about – the 300 acres south of Bingham Road – had been rich dairy country, with cereals and fodder crops. There was some market gardening and a poultry farm near Sandilands. It was truly a rural scene. But change was afoot. Centralised milk processing spelt the end of the small dairy – such as J.J. Parsons at Addiscombe Farm, and Coombe Farm and Oaks

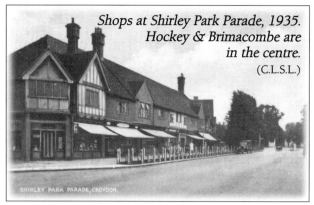

Shops at Shirley Park Parade, 1935. Hockey & Brimacombe are in the centre.
(C.L.S.L.)

Farm (aka Shirley Park Farm).

By 1937 there were two parades of shops, in Shirley Road near to the junction with Bingham Road and at Shirley Park. Most household requirements could be obtained from these shops and delivered if required. There was one church - St Mildreds in Bingham Road - but the Church of Our Lady in Lower Addiscombe Road was only minutes away, with more shops nearby. Otherwise the area was mostly residential. The eight-acre recreation ground had been established in 1905.

The southern edge was (and is) dominated by Lloyd Park and Shirley Park Golf Club. Other recreational and sports areas included Whitgift Middle School (now Trinity) playing-fields and the cricket, tennis and rifle clubs near the end of Radcliffe Road. The bowling club in Mapledale Avenue did not move there from Shirley Park until 1963.

The Ashburton Estate

The Ashburton estate was one of the original estates, along with Coombe, Shirley Park and the Whitgift Foundation. These are visited on the following pages. Ashburton House was an unremarkable - but large - Georgian House on the eastern corner of Addiscombe Road and what is now Northampton Road. There was a path from the house to Shirley Road - sometimes called Lady Ashburton's walk, or Love Lane.

When Louisa, the second Lady Ashburton, died insolvent in 1903, the estates were sold for housing development and the house was demolished in about 1911. For some years it had been a guest-house of the Cooperative Holidays Association - providing holidays for the poor. Lady Louisa Ashburton had also founded 'Homes of Rest for Mothers and Little Children' on Shirley Road. On her death this 3½ acre estate (by Bingham Road) passed to the Shaftesbury Society.

Farmer J.J. Parson, previously tenant of Coombe Farm from 1890, took over Addiscombe Farm on the Ashburton estate in 1894. It is not clear when his dairy farm ceased production - probably in the mid 1920s. He was still living at the farmhouse in 1939.

Below and bottom: *Sketches of Ashburton House in 1868 and 1908 by Paul Jordan.*

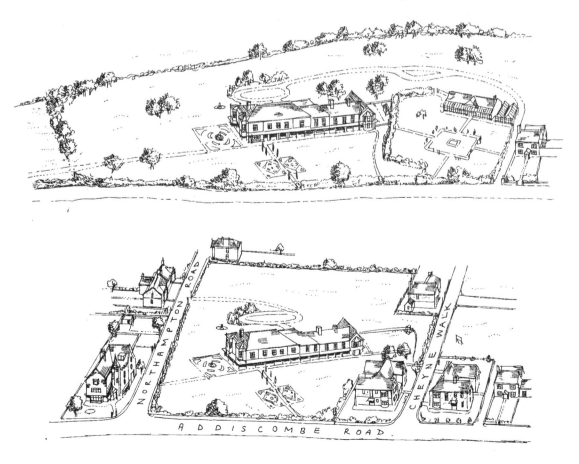

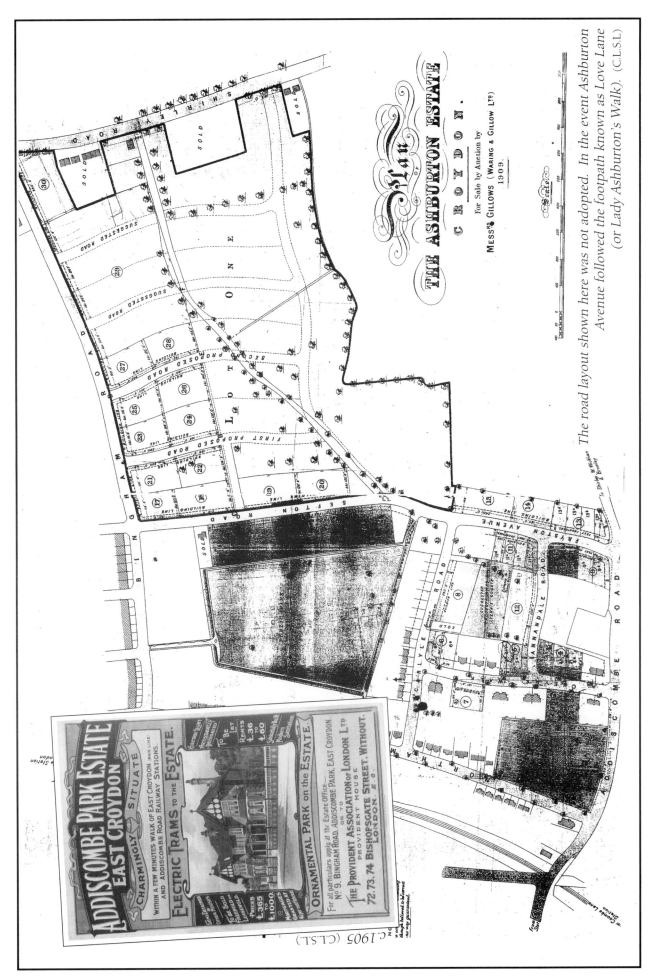

The road layout shown here was not adopted. In the event Ashburton Avenue followed the footpath known as Love Lane (or Lady Ashburton's Walk). (C.L.S.L)

Thomas Carlyle & the Ashburtons
Mary Chandler

Thomas Carlyle was born in 1795 at Ecclefechan, a village in Dumfriesshire, Scotland. His father, James, was a stonemason at the time and had built the house in which Thomas was born. His mother, Margaret, was James' second wife and they had a large family of which Thomas was the eldest. James later became a small farmer and moved several times in and around Annandale.

Thomas was taught arithmetic by his father but apparently learnt to read and write on his own. He went to the village schools but by the age of seven he obviously needed more education than the local teacher could provide so the Minister of the Secession Church gave him private tuition in Latin. Thomas went on to Annan Academy where he received a good schooling which enabled him to go to Edinburgh University in 1809. He was interested in natural sciences, mathematics and, notably, literary reading and, when he had completed his Arts course in 1813, he then continued his studies at Divinity Hall of Edinburgh University part time while teaching at Annan Academy and then in Kirkcaldy. By 1818 Thomas had abandoned teaching and all thoughts of becoming a minister of the Church of Scotland and returned to Edinburgh where he went to lectures in natural sciences and also learnt German. He began to have his own works published.

In 1821 Thomas was introduced to Jane Welsh, a doctor's daughter who lived in Haddington, a three-hour ride east of Edinburgh. Jane was keen to be educated, having studied Latin with her parents, and Thomas tutored her in German, Spanish, Italian and English literature. In 1824 he visited London for the first time and was delighted with the people he met there, especially the writers, but he came back to Ecclefechan enjoying life on the farms and with his parents for a year or so.

Thomas and Jane married in 1826 and for two years lived in Comely Bank, a suburb of Edinburgh, before moving to Craigenputtoch where Jane owned property and land. It was cheaper to live there than in Edinburgh but was very isolated on the hilly moors of Dumfriesshire. Nevertheless, Thomas produced several essays which financed excursions to Edinburgh and London. In the early 1830s he spent many months at a time in London where he felt well received and after another hard winter in Craigenputtoch he and Jane decided to settle for London; in 1834 they moved to Chelsea, to Cheyne Row, a turning off Cheyne Walk.

Over the next five years Thomas both wrote and lectured

Above left: *An advertisement for the Croydon Stock Show, 1900.* (R.M.)
Top right: *Lady Ashburton's Walk, c.1900.* (C.L.S.L.)
Main: *Ashburton House and garden, c.1905.* (C.L.S.L.)

about conditions in the industrial North, comparing the poverty with that in France 50 years earlier. He wrote *The French Revolution* and planned other literary works including a biography of Oliver Cromwell.

Thomas and Jane sometimes went out into society together but on 25 February 1839 Thomas went alone to dinner at the home of William Baring, a member of the banking family and heir to the Ashburton barony. There he met Lady Harriet Baring whom he described as 'one of the cleverest creatures I have met with, full of mirth and spirit - not very beautiful to look upon.' Lady Harriet was the daughter of the 6th Earl of Sandwich and was ten years younger than Thomas Carlyle. She ran a salon at the Barings' London home, Bath House in Piccadilly.

In 1843 Jane was staying in Suffolk with elderly friends, Mr and Mrs Buller, who were expecting their son, Charles, to arrive as soon as Parliament closed. Charles, however, had dashed off to Addiscombe, the summer home of Lady Harriet. Jane was indignant because she was aware that 'Lady Harriet exercised a spell over the best men in London.' In the following few years Thomas often went to stay at Addiscombe, 'the Barings' retreat outside the city' and later Jane too was invited to stay and found 'the Barings' house spilling over with fine company - people whose main objectives were brilliant repartee and the wearing of fashionable clothes.' Jane was not happy there: 'Laying awake - hour after hour - on the throne-like bed of the room to which she had been assigned gave her plenty of time... in which to think.' But Lady Harriet went out of her way to be friendly with Jane who was invited to call at Bath House too.

Early one summer Lady Harriet spent several months at Addiscombe and invited the Carlyles to join her, but Thomas was very busy getting a second edition of *Cromwell* ready for his publishers so Jane went on her own. However, every Saturday Thomas rode out to Croydon and stayed till Monday. Later that summer Jane went off to Liverpool, telling her husband that he could go if he liked to Addiscombe seeing that 'he had established a small permanent wardrobe there - he better use it.'

Twice, when the Cheyne Row house was being re-ordered and the chaos caused by painters and decorators became too much to bear, Jane took refuge at Addiscombe at Lady Harriet's invitation. On several occasions the workmen at Chelsea had fallen through the ceiling so Thomas and Jane decided to accept Lady Ashburton's offer to stay at Addiscombe (Farm), 'beautifullest cottage in the world; the noble owners glad we would occupy a room or two of it in their absence. I liked it much,' said Carlyle.

Lady Harriet Ashburton's health deteriorated and her husband took her to the Riviera for the winter, but on their return journey back to England, on 4 May 1857, she died from a heart attack. Thomas was 'pitched into grief' and Jane too was 'shocked and dispirited'. Thomas was working hard on revisions to the first two volumes of his *History of Frederick the Great* and Jane, who was not well, was having trouble with the servants at Cheyne Row, so in March 1858 Thomas went to Addiscombe to be with Lord Ashburton and 'to find the silence in which to correct his proofs'. Thomas, either with or without Jane, paid several visits to Addiscombe where 'the regime was more relaxed than in Chelsea' and having spent three hours proofreading the rest of the day was given over to riding and 'to idle reading, lounging, smoking'. Thomas had shown great compassion to Ashburton in his loneliness.

In November 1858 Ashburton married again, and his young wife, Louisa, became close to Jane in a way her predecessor could never have been. Even after the death of Lord Ashburton in 1864, Lady Louisa continued to befriend Jane and she sent weekly hampers of garden produce from Addiscombe and from Hampshire to Cheyne Row. In fact, so much fruit and so many flowers were sent that Jane wrote to the Ashburtons' gardener to 'prohibit the hamper! - at least partially; that is two weeks out of the three!' Jane went to great trouble to obtain fresh food to please Thomas' exacting taste; potatoes and oatmeal came from Scotland but groceries and meat, butter and eggs came from local Chelsea shops. Great attention was paid to the housekeeping:

The milkman was Mr Shakespear but the cream had to be got from Mr Wright's cows - and poor stuff it was compared with the beautiful yellow cream from Lord Ashburton's farm at Addiscombe.

Jane died on 21 April 1866 and Thomas spent the next few years writing about their life together and editing her 'Letters and Memorials'. In 1869 he started to get out and about again, visiting Lady Ashburton at Addiscombe because he found 'London and its empty broiling tumult... quite intolerable.' Thomas Carlyle died on 5 February 1881. At first he had been called the Sage of Ecclefechan and then became the Sage of Chelsea; perhaps he might also be remembered as the Sage of Addiscombe.

Shaftesbury postcard of Ashburton House, c.1906. (J.G.)

Coombe Dairy Farm, 1892. (C.L.S.L.)

Above: *Coombe House, 1910.* (C.L.S.L.)

Below: *A garden party at Coombe Lodge, 1934.* (C.T.)

The Coombe Estates

The story of the various houses of Coombe is complicated and intertwined with the nearby estates of Shirley House, Ashburton Park and the Whitgift Foundation. The history of Coombe Lodge, Coombe House, Coombe Farm and Oaks Farm (sometimes known as Shirley park Farm) is described in C.G. Paget's book *Croydon Homes of the Past* (1937). At the time of writing, in 2002, Coombe Lodge is a restaurant, with a motel wing which was built in 1990; Coombe House is Geoffrey Harris House, part of an NHS Trust, while Coombe Farm is a hostel for homeless people. Oaks Farm is a private residence; the Barn is used for civil weddings and receptions throughout the year.

The Lloyds and Lloyd Park Edward Lloyd, publisher, printer and paper maker, started in business at the age of 18 in 1833, publishing and selling 'Lloyds Stenography', a shorthand system. After forays into song books, he moved into the newspaper and magazine trade. His *People's Police Gazette* was the forerunner of the *Illustrated London News*. By 1863 his principal paper *Lloyds Weekly News* had a circulation of 350,000; in 1896 1.7 million copies were sold every Sunday. The main competitor was the *News of the World*.

In 1855 Edward Lloyd installed the first rotary printing machine in England - capable of printing, cutting and folding 25,000 newspapers per hour. In 1876 he bought the *Daily Chronicle* and turned it into an important national newspaper. He also owned a large paper-mill at Sittingbourne in Kent. Business did not take up all his time as he fathered 24 children! In 1857 he moved his family into Water House in Walthamstow (now the William Morris Gallery – as the Morris family had lived there previously). Edward died in 1890 and one of his sons, 36-year-old Frank, headed the family firm. He decided to move to Croydon 'because the new roads opposite the Water House did not provide the right kind of companions for the social life of his growing children.' He purchased Coombe House in 1892 and lived there for 35 years until his death in 1927. His daughter, Mrs J.R. Garwood, carried out her father's wishes by presenting the land now known as Lloyd Park to the Borough of Croydon.

Lloyd Park was opened on 25 July 1931, when the Mayor, Alderman T.A. Lewis, accepted the gift. We twenty-first-century Croydonians have reason to be grateful that Lloyd Park remains intact (apart from recent erosion by Tramlink).

In 1939 Colonel Garwood, then living at Coombe Farm, played a leading role in opposing the proposed sale of the Shirley Park estate for a housing development. Both Coombe House and Coombe Farm became homes and schools for people with cerebral palsy in the 1950s. The Garwood name lives on with the Garwood Charitable Foundation which is still based in Croydon. Coombe Lodge was bought by Croydon Corporation in 1941 and became an old people's home until it was transformed into a restaurant in 1989.

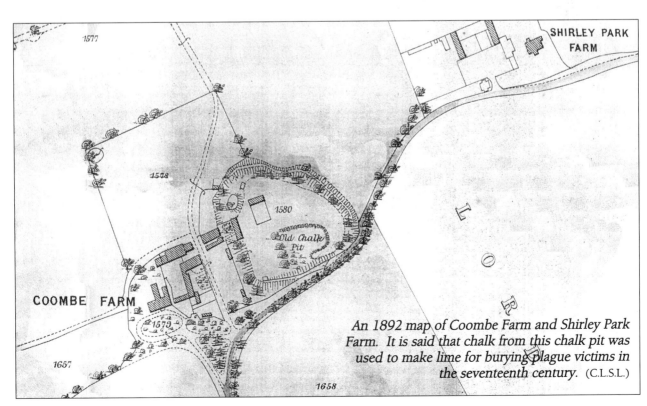

An 1892 map of Coombe Farm and Shirley Park Farm. It is said that chalk from this chalk pit was used to make lime for burying plague victims in the seventeenth century. (C.L.S.L.)

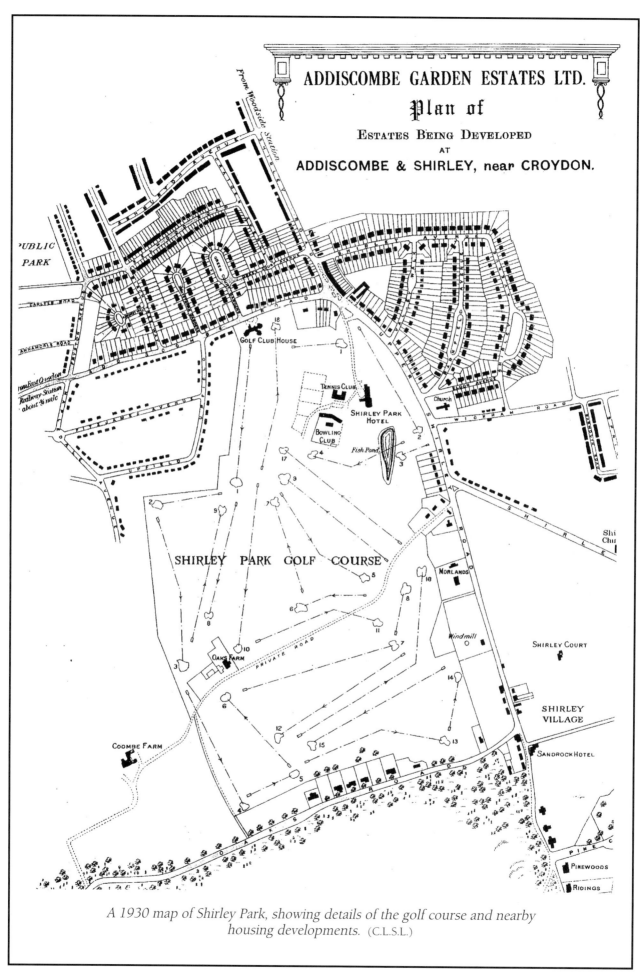

A 1930 map of Shirley Park, showing details of the golf course and nearby housing developments. (C.L.S.L.)

Shirley House

Shirley House was on the site of Trinity School until 1962. It had survived for 240 years - through two world wars and a social revolution. Now, in the new century, it seems unforgivable that only 40 years ago it was bulldozed and destroyed.

In 1649 it is recorded that a brick-built house was on the site owned by the Best family. In 1714 the property was sold to John Claxton and the house was demolished prior to building the mansion called Shirley House in 1721. After various financial vicissitudes, the house passed in 1765 to Claxton's grandson, a barrister in Lincoln's Inn who took up residence in 1779 - and one can speculate how he commuted to the Law Courts before railways!

During the next 25 years Claxton extended the estate substantially, helped by the 1800 Enclosure Act, and in 1812 the property was sold to a banker, John Maberly, who continued to improve the house and bought adjacent land. In 1816 Maberly was elected MP for Rye. About the same time he used devious tactics to get the main road past the house diverted further north. By this time the estate was about 200 acres and the house was a great mansion.

Victorian times: In 1834 Maberly's bankruptcy led to another change of ownership. Samuel Skinner bought the estate and sold it in 1839 to John Scott, the Second Earl of Eldon. His father (the First Earl) had been an arch Conservative Lord Chancellor during the turbulent years of the French Revolution and the struggles between 'property and population' in Britain.

The Eldons lived in Shirley House for about 35 years, whilst Shirley and Addiscombe developed apace. The surrounding areas were still rural. Railway development meant that day-trips from London to Shirley Hills became popular. In 1874 the Third Earl leased the estate to Frederick Banbury, and various tenants occupied the house until 1904.

A London stockbroker and his family (Mr R.H. Simpson) moved from Park Hill and leased Shirley House in 1899. Simpson's mother-in-law was Emily Soldene, a well-known leading lady of the Victorian theatre. Her writings in the first years of the twentieth century show that the family enjoyed their time at the house and in the wooded surroundings. She describes summers, harvests and Christmases. These were the last days of the great estates.

A 1915 map of Shirley Park. The planned housing around the eastern perimeter was never started.
(C.L.S.L.)

Finale: In 1908 the estate was auctioned by the Third Earl of Eldon and by 1914 it had been converted into the Shirley Park Hotel (with golf course, and some housing development). In 1915 the weekly inclusive tariff was £3.13s.6d. The hotel survived for 50 years and in 1917 was used as a convalescent hospital by the RFC, and in the 1940s as transit accommodation for military personnel. It is thought that 'The Manor' referred to in R.F. Delderfield's *Avenue* novels was Shirley House at this time.

The planners and developers had not forgotten Shirley Park. In 1939 an unsuccessful attempt was mounted to plan a large housing estate. In 1951 the Council compulsorily purchased the estate to build schools and playing-fields.

The *RAC Handbook* for 1949 shows that the hotel had 58 bedrooms with a daily rate of 21s. to 30s. including meals (which is probably equivalent to £120 to £180 nowadays)! In 1959 the estate was bought by the Whitgift Foundation and the hotel finally closed in November 1962. Demolition started immediately and continued through the heavy snows of early 1963. There was no substantial local protest.

Whitgift Middle School moved from central Croydon into the new Trinity School buildings on the Shirley House site in 1965. At that time it was a 'direct grant' grammar school but in 1968 it became independent. A more detailed history may be found in *Shirley House to Trinity School* (1999) by Andrew Lamb.

Shirley Park Hotel in 1962, just before demolition. By 1965 Trinity School was on this site. (M.A.)

Shirley Park Hotel, reflected in the lake, 1937. (E.P.)

An aerial view of the Whitgift estate, taken in 1932. Upfield is in the centre and in the foreground the first few houses in Grimwade Avenue have been built. (C.L.S.L.)

The Whitgift Foundation

On 22 March 1596 Archbishop John Whitgift laid the two foundation stones of his Hospital of the Holy Trinity, now the Whitgift Almshouses. This was the birth of his charity, the Whitgift Foundation.

The official residence of the Archbishops of Canterbury is Lambeth Palace but, in earlier times, their favourite house was in the countryside of Croydon, known as the Manor of Croydon. It was a restful place surrounded by gardens, woodland and streams. John Whitgift gave it the name of Palace and relaxed there during welcome breaks from his official duties.

The office of Archbishop produced substantial revenues appropriate to a man with such great responsibilities. Being a bachelor and having no family to support, John Whitgift was able to put aside his personal savings with which he was determined to create a charity during his lifetime. Having developed a love for Croydon and its inhabitants, fortunately for us he chose Croydon in which to establish his home for old people and, soon afterwards, the Whitgift

School in George Street (since demolished and now the George Street entrance to Allders store).

In 1889 the 'Old Palace School for Girls' was founded by the Sisters of the Church and in 1993 Old Palace became part of the Whitgift Foundation – joining the two boys' schools; Whitgift (opened in 1600) and Trinity (1858). Over the years both have been situated on various sites in Croydon under various names.

The income from land and properties that John Whitgift purchased so long ago provides for the care of old people and the provision of generous bursaries and scholarships for the education of boys and girls, still in accordance with his original charity documents and statutes.

The 'Whitgift estate': The Governors of the Whitgift Foundation (GWF) have been managing their properties, which have been situated in many parts of Croydon and elsewhere, for 400 years. Substantial holdings of land were in Addiscombe and Woodside. At the end of the nineteenth century the GWF were selling building leases in the Radcliffe Road area (part of Woodbury Farm), but, until the break-up of the Ashburton estate, the south side of Addiscombe Road (east of what is now Woodbury Close) remained undeveloped. Some of this land was leased to local farms and some used for market gardening. The remainder was used as playing-fields.

It was after the First World War in 1920 when GWF started freehold sales of land at Woodbury Farm and east towards Shirley. By 1930 most of the land between Radcliffe Road and Shirley Park Golf Course had been planned and many houses had been built. Development came to a halt with the Second World War in 1939, but building recommenced in about 1950 and finished when Ranmore Avenue and the south end of Radcliffe Road were adopted by the Council.

Woodbury Farm: In 1871 the 71-acre Woodbury Farm was leased by GWF including 'The Elms' – now known as 'Heron's Croft'. The Woodside to South Croydon railway was completed in 1885, running south alongside Ashburton Road and then in cuttings and tunnels through Woodbury Farm. In 1893 a new 21-year lease was signed by the lessee – Bruce Johnson. It excluded The Elms, which had become a liability. (The Elms was a frequent agenda item at GWF Estates meetings. It seemed to be threatened

with demolition every few years.) The lease included 'resuming' powers to enable the GWF to build a new road in line with Outram Road. (In the event Woodbury Close was built further west in the mid 1920s.) Woodbury's western boundary included the whole of what is now Radcliffe Road, where house building had started in 1881.

Meanwhile Bruce Johnson, cattle farmer and dealer, started sub-letting parts of Woodbury Farm. From 1899 to 1901 sand was taken from a pit at what is now the entrance to Sandilands (hence the name) and Turner Bros' 'Sandpits Poultry Farm' was located there from 1903-25. Many sports clubs rented playing-fields in the area. Mr Johnson died in 1912 after 32 years at Woodbury and the lease was taken over by Charles H. Still. Richard Maidstone had rented The Elms from 1884 to 1908 when it was let to William Woods, a clerk at The Union of London and Smiths Bank (now part of Nat West). After 1918 the freehold was sold to Mr Turner (of the poultry farm).

Woodbury Farm buildings were demolished in about 1925 prior to the building of Nos 82-92 Addiscombe Road in 1927. In the same year No. 100 Addiscombe Road was built for Mr D.A. Lawrence the Managing Director of Allders. In 2002 it was up for sale for over £1 million.

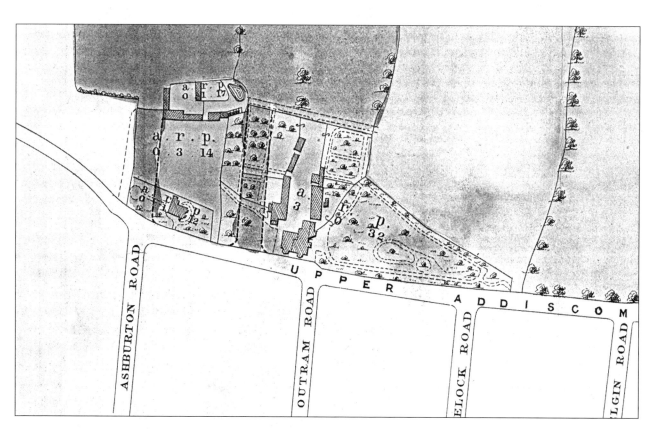

A map of Woodbury Farm buildings, 1871. The Elms can be seen opposite Ashburton Road. The railway came through here in the 1880s. (W.A.)

Heron's Croft
Arlette Beelitz (Our Correspondent from Australia)

Heron's Croft, formerly The Elms, is an ancient dwelling, thought to be the oldest domestic building in Croydon. Of its distant past there are stories but few hard facts. Arlette Beelitz, however, takes up the story of the time when her family lived there:

My grandparents, Mr and Mrs H. Chase Mason, bought 96 Addiscombe Road in the 1930s and moved in with my father, Paul Mason, then a boy who attended Winton House school. There was a very old elm in the garden and the house was originally known as The Elms. My grandfather changed the name... because of the local connection with the Heron family. When the Council wanted the fence put back from the road (to cut off the corner), my grandfather built the low brick wall which is still there today. However, the corner was never cut off and the pavement is as far out today as it was then. My memory is of a rather overgrown front garden, a sort of evergreen jungle (ivy, holly, laurel, I think).

I remember in the fifties that the chimney-stack needed to be repaired; it was then that my grandfather had the little plaque put into the chimney giving the date the house was built [1490s]. When I was young, Heron's Croft was not painted on the outside and there was a blotch on the upstairs wall facing Number 94, where there used to be a window; it had been removed during Oliver Cromwell's time because of a tax imposed on windows.

The hearth at Heron's Croft is original. The bricks are worn away but the cement has not to the same extent, so the cement is higher than the bricks. My grandparents dug up a horse's bit in the garden and fixed it to the mantlepiece. The interior of the house had black beams and white walls.

The land on which 94 was eventually built was part of the land belonging to 96. It was commandeered during the war and an air-raid shelter built. The Air Raid Wardens also used to grow vegetables at the back of the shelter. My mother was in the ATS during the war and Dad in the RAF. I think they met at that military place in Lloyd Park with the ack-ack guns. At the end of the war, the land was returned to my grandparents and the house at 94 was built for my parents. The house incorporated the shelter which sort of became our lounge and kitchen.

I am told you could look out over Sandilands and see horses in the fields even as late as 1947.

Although Heron's Croft was reputed to be haunted, the family never saw nor heard as much as a whisper.

In the gloaming – the Mason family at Heron's Croft. (A.Be.)

Above: *The Elms, c.1920, before its name was changed to Heron's Croft.* (S.R.)

Right: *Addiscombe Road and Heron's Croft in 1947, when the snow stood for weeks.* (A.Be.)

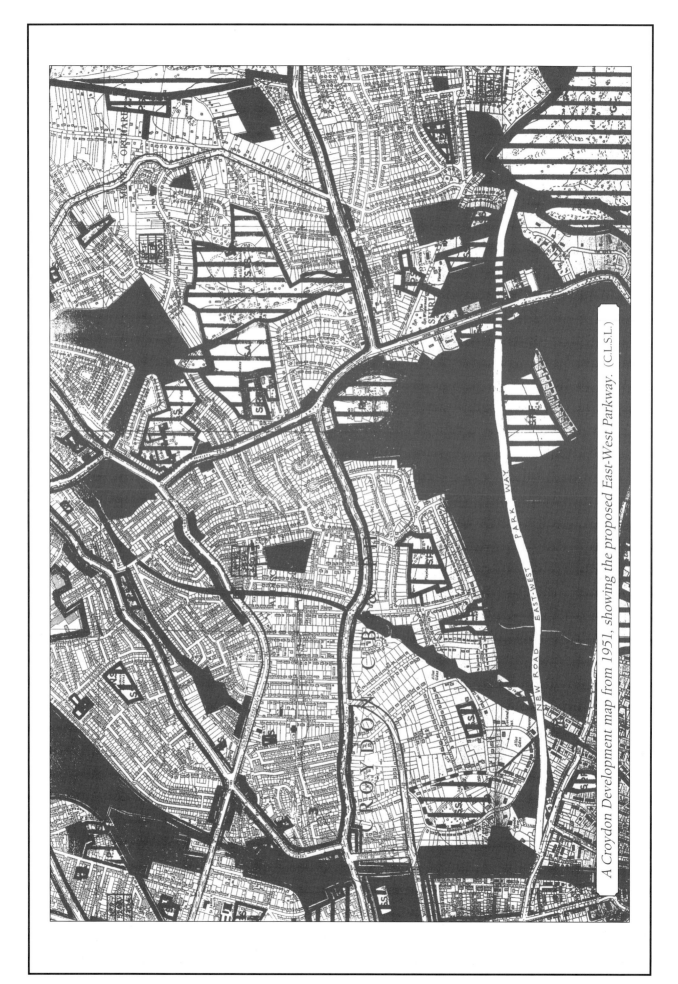

A Croydon Development map from 1951, showing the proposed East-West Parkway. (C.L.S.L.)

Town Planning

If one looks at the main road layout of Addiscombe shown on the 1800 Enclosures Act map and compares it with today's layout 200 years later, very few changes have in fact taken place. Love Lane – from Fryston Road to Glenthorne Avenue - is no more.

Many of the roads were no more than narrow bridleways in 1800 and most were dirty gravel surfaces with many potholes. So what has changed I hear you say! In the 1700s McAdam and Telford brought a revolution to road construction, with stronger foundations and better surfaces. During the early-nineteenth century, railways spread through the land like an enormous spider's web. Personal travel became much easier and the canals, which had briefly reigned supreme for goods transport in many places, were doomed.

Until 1920 Addiscombe had not been much affected by 'The Planners'. Our roads had been widened, realigned and improved; the railways had been built with inevitable effects on nearby roads. However, a visitor in 1920 would have seen few differences in the main thoroughfares since the 1850s.

Croydon has been enlarged with several realignments of its boundaries in the last 100 years. It has to coexist with the other nearby boroughs and in the context of the Greater London conurbation. An industry has grown up to 'plan' our infrastructure to make things better!

Urban renewal, whereby old buildings are superseded, is an uneven but continuous process. Victorian houses are extended and converted into flats. Groups of them are demolished to be replaced by high-density housing, or purpose-built flats. War-damaged houses need replacing. Owners of 'double' plots develop the second plot. Looking around our area one can question the quality of much of the redevelopment, but by and large it provided practical solutions to the need for more dwellings.

The 1920s and '30s: In October 1922 the Governors of the Whitgift Foundation were made aware of the 'Croydon (East) Town Planning Scheme' which designated land use and which areas would be used for housing, shops, recreation, etc. It also specified road-width changes for the main roads. One of the major elements of this plan was to develop New Addington. The most controversial goals included building a network of main roads through Shirley Park Golf Course, Whitgift property and what is now Lloyd Park. These plans bounced around for many years. The first map in this chapter shows the situation in 1937 *(p.48)* with the proposed roads.

In 1939, with war imminent and 'Town Planning Road No.13' still showing on maps, agreements were being made for the War Office to buy certain plots of land for military use. One such site was about two acres of the golf course close to the current bowling club at the south end of Mapledale Avenue (even now there are remnants of concrete from the anti-aircraft guns which were sited there until 1945). The advent of war stopped any further plans relating to our local main roads.

Meanwhile the house builders were having a ball, despite the 1926 General Strike and the recession of the early 1930s. Between 1920 and 1939 nearly 1,400 houses were built in our patch (south of Bingham Road). In 1939 plans were tabled to build 800 houses on 137 acres of Shirley Park. There was a public outcry and 'The Shirley Park Public Acquisition Association' was formed to fight the proposal. The massive opposition, with support from Croydon Corporation and the LCC, halted the plans.

The 1940s and '50s: Before the end of the war, in 1944, the 'Greater London Plan' by Patrick Abercrombie (Minister for Town and Country Planning) was published. Whilst it had no direct effects on Addiscombe, it once again highlighted the need to manage land use, and road and rail communications. The local planners took leads from the report and in 1951 a 'Development Plan for Croydon' was published.

It was no surprise that once again a road across Lloyd Park was specified, this time to start near Coombe Cliff, traverse Lloyd Park and the southerly edge of the golf course, then tunnel under Shirley Road, cross the northern edge of Addington Golf Course and end at the West Wickham boundary near Layhams Road. This was known as the 'East-West Parkway' and would have bypassed our present A232. Once again this plan was not carried out.

This 1951 plan led to the flyover, Roman Way and redevelopment of Croydon centre. The realignment of Chepstow Road provided a route for an east-west bypass of the town centre, which became a reality when Tramlink was built.

In 1951 Shirley Park once again became a contentious issue, which ended in a Compulsory Purchase Order by Croydon Corporation from the owners of 'Addiscombe Garden Estates' who had been managing the property since 1909. The purchase was intended for Council school buildings and playing-fields. In the event John Ruskin School came (and went), and Trinity School was built. The golf club survives with alterations, paying rent to the Corporation. One can only speculate what went on behind the scenes!

The 1960s to 2002: Apart from a minor skirmish (see below), the Planners were quiet until the 1980s, when the 'South London Assessment Study' resulted in proposals for an A23 replacement into London. Various routes were suggested, but there was so much public hostility that the Government dropped the plans. Hundreds of houses would have been demolished and acres of land (including golf courses) would have been affected. By 1990 the scheme was dead.

The skirmish was in 1974 – in Mapledale Avenue. There was a piece of land with a pond (Whitgift Pond) and in 1930 the Whitgift Foundation surveyors decided that (because of drainage problems) it could not be built on. The land abutted Whitgift Middle School's playing-fields and the Foundation offered the land to Croydon Corporation as a gift, presumably to remain as public open space. In 1931 the plot was legally transferred.

Over 40 years later there was pressure from the GLC to find small parcels of land for blocks of flats, etc. for Council tenants. The Mapledale plot matched the requirement and the scene was set for a mighty argument. Croydon Corporation opposed the proposals and the original covenants only allowed single houses to be built. Protest meetings were followed by an inaugural meeting of the Resident's Association. Local MPs were lobbied; questions were raised in the House and reported in Hansard. The plans were dropped, and after establishing that the drainage problem could be solved, Croydon Council sold the land for building the houses we see today.

Tramlink and Red Routes: Many earlier plans affecting our part of Croydon flowered briefly and withered away - but not Tramlink, which was launched in 2000 after several years' work and many years of planning. Interested readers can trace the history through records at Croydon Local Studies Library.

The 30km (18-mile) route, most of it on disused railway lines, links New Addington, Beckenham, Elmers End and Wimbledon through the hub in Croydon. The Sandilands tram stop is actually where the gardens of Woodbury Farmhouse were in earlier times (*see p.60*).

The A232 Red Route traverses our patch along Addiscombe Road and skirts the borough of Bromley in the east to Sutton in the west. Severe parking controls have certainly speeded up traffic flow, but many are puzzled by the vast expenditure on side-road junction treatment. Whilst speed tables have their place in the armoury of traffic managers, it seems odd to put them at junctions where drivers are seldom doing more than 10mph.

The Next 100 Years: We have no crystal ball. The planners will still be planning and advising their masters. The golfers will still be watching the ball. Fossil fuels will be running out. If we are to believe the experts, our climate may have changed substantially. Does anyone out there want to describe how Addiscombe will change over the coming century?

DEVELOPMENT OF MAIN ROADS		
STREET	DEVELOPMENT	NOTES
Addiscombe Rd (north side)	Canning Rd to Ashburton mostly before 1890.	Much renewal since 1950s - purpose-built flats.
	Ashburton to Shirley Road 1906 to 1930.	Mainly 1924-30
		No significant changes since these were built.
Addiscombe Road (south side)	Radcliffe to Sandilands; farm and original 1880s houses now replaced.	Woodbury Farm land (see text). Lynden Hyrst flats (1960s) and tram stop now
	Sandilands to Shirley Park Golf Course 1924 to 1930.	dominate. 'Heron's Croft' still survives, and Nos 84-94 (back gardens were taken by Tramlink).
Northampton Road	Mainly built 1906 to 1909. 6-12 and 29-41 built later.	Tennis Club at south-east corner 1918 to 1932.
Bingham Road	Mainly completed between 1904 and 1916.	Development continued until St Mildred's Church built 1931. Kennards nursery between Bingham and Ashburton Avenue replaced by garage area (access from Craven Road).
Shirley Road (west side)	Ashburton estate (see text) 1906 to 1918.	Named Stroud Green Road until 1908. Lady Ashburton's Rest Homes built 1880s. Shops built 1927 (near Bingham Road junction).
Shirley Road (east side)	All ages.	Was Beckenham Golf Course, Waterworks and 'Shirley Cottage' with some old buildings. Shirley Park shops built 1928.

This image: *Addiscombe Road in 1907 at the Radcliffe Road junction looking east.* (J.G.)
Below left: *A wintry scene in Addiscombe Road, looking westwards from opposite Addiscombe Farm, c.1910.* (J.G.)

This image: *Northampton Road, looking north from the entrance to the recreation ground, c.1910.* (J.G.)
Above right: *A new house after the Second World War. Number 94 Addiscombe Road was built on the site of a public air-raid shelter.* (A.Be.)

Bingham Road, c.1910, looking westwards from near the recreation ground. (J.G.)

Ashburton Avenue looking east towards Shirley Road. New trees have been planted but the road still awaits completion, c.1920. (C.L.S.L.)

Left: *Mapledale Avenue looking south from Upfield junction, c.1934.* (J.G.)

Below: *Looking east along Fitzjames Avenue from outside Number 40.* (C.L.S.L.)

Below left: *Upfield looking north at the junction with Fitzjames Avenue, c.1934.* (C.L.S.L.)

Below right: *Lynden Hyrst has replaced these fine Victorian houses in Addiscombe Road. Numbers 66 and 64 were photographed in 1960 prior to demolition.* (M.A.)

DEVELOPMENT OF ESTATE ROADS

Estate	Dates
Annandale Road	1916 to 1932
Ashurst Walk	1927 to 1930
Ashburton Avenue	1913 to 1916
Birch Tree Way	1927 to 1930
Carlyle Road	1907 to 1916
Cheyne Walk	1908 to 1923
Compton Road	1914 to 1926
Craigen Avenue	1916 to 1927
Craven Road	1926 to 1927
Deepdene Avenue	1950s to 1970s
Fitzjames Avenue	1929 to 1939
Fryston Avenue	1913 to 1926
Green Ct Ave/Gdns	1927 to 1928
Grimwade Avenue	1929 to 1950s
Harland Avenue	1934 to 1937
Harriet Gardens	1970s
Mapledale Avenue	1926 to 1937
(Nos. 12 to 16 built 1970s)	
Radcliffe Road	1876 to 1960s
(north end redeveloped; south end from Harland built 1950s)	
Ranmore Avenue	1950s
Sandilands	1934 to 1938
(north end developed post war)	
Sefton Road	1910 to 1926
Selwood Road	1920 to 1928
Upfield	1927 to 1937
Whitethorn Gardens	1928 to 1930
Woodbury Close	1924 to 1930

The wedding of Emma Roote to Leonard Marlow in 1920, showing most of the Roote family members of that time. (B.R. & C.M.) *Names known, from the back: Arthur, Leonard (Brian's father, standing in front of soldier), Florence (far right, near back with headband);*
3rd row: William Benjamin (far left, moustache), Lilian (small lady by William Benjamin), Dorothy (locket, standing behind bride and groom), William Henry (far right, white tie);
Leonard (bridegroom), Emma (bride) (parents of Cliff), Charlotte (next to Emma).

Seven

❧❦❧

Dynasties

An Addiscombe Family & The Hockeys

An Addiscombe Family

Brian Roote with help from Cliff Marlow

Although their origins were firmly in the East End of London, our family, the Rootes, moved to Addiscombe in 1898 and spent the next 80 years as residents and businessmen. Both sets of grandparents, Thomas and Emma Mary Ann Roote and Benjamin and Susannah Eliza Johnson, were East Enders through and through and it was the marriage in 1883 of their respective children, William Henry Roote (born 1863) and Charlotte Caroline Johnson (born 1863) at St Thomas Church Bethnal Green that started the Roote dynasty. Their first two children, William Benjamin and Florence Beatrice, were born in Holborn and it was this family of four who moved to Alpha Road.

The Addiscombe Connection: All the other eight children were born in and around Cross Road over the next 16 years, the last being my Dad, Leonard Charles, in 1905. William Henry was a journeyman French polisher as was his father, Thomas, but it was son William Benjamin who started the family business at 20 Lower Addiscombe Road in 1921 when his parents retired to Portslade where Charlotte, sadly, died from heart disease within four years.

My Dad and his brother, Arthur, followed in the family tradition and took up French polishing but the other brother, Harold, didn't join them, preferring, it seems, to do a variety of jobs, from being a butler, clerk and decorator to spending time in the Army, finally joining the electricity board as a general labourer. One of Cliff's memories is of seeing Uncle Harold up a ladder in Lower Addiscombe Road cleaning the street lamps. Harold served in both world wars with distinction.

As well as starting the business Uncle Will and Aunt Emily moved their family over the shop with children William, Winifred and Cyril. The space in Alpha Road created by William and Charlotte's move to Portslade was filled by daughter Lilian, husband

Harry Snelling and their four children.

The family had their share of tragedy over the years. A son, Albert Edward Victor, was born on 4 April 1897 but died on 9 September the same year of an infection, which we would now call enteritis. A daughter, Adelaide Alice Ruth, who came into the world on 21 October 1900, contracted pulmonary tuberculosis and suffered for three long years before passing away aged just 17 in November 1917.

Sadly, too, Lilian's daughter, Clarice, died in childbirth aged 26 in 1946. Harold's first two children, twins, died in 1922 at a few months old as did two of Florence's babies. It is quite possible that with today's antibiotics and immunisations none of these deaths would have occurred. Perhaps there is a salutary lesson here for all of us.

Schooling: All of the children went to Davidson Road School before moving up to Oval Road and their children, in turn, followed the same path of education. Oval Road opened in 1873 as a result of the Government Act making school compulsory. As well as losing staff in the First World War the school itself was bombed by a Zeppelin in 1915. Many of the games and diversions the children of that era knew have since disappeared in the wake of more 'sophisticated' interests. Surely we could not have lived together, the children of the 1920s and those of the present time. For the former their simple games and amusements were eminently enjoyable but they were the last to see the carrier's carts and horses as the prime users of the highway. They lived in the last decade in which falling apples could wake a drowsy noon and in which at any hour you could stand, sit or play in the road. All of the Roote children would have known such times around the Alpha Road area.

Cliff remembers that the greengrocers near the shop had a horse and cart for delivery and he often used to help himself to 'fallen' articles on the way to school!

The children were not saints by any means, as testified by the punishment book for the school which still survives in the archives:

May 22 1905: Harold Roote aged 6 of Alpha Road. 1 stroke of the cane for bad behaviour.

March 7 1906: Harold Roote age 7 of Alpha Road. 1 stroke of the cane for bad behaviour.

The saddest entry of all is probably:

December 10 1906: Adelaide Roote age 6 of Alpha Road. 1 stroke of the cane for bad behaviour in an exam.

It is somewhat surprising to realise that very young children, and more importantly young girls, suffered corporal punishment at that time.

Marriages: Several of the family marriages took place in St Mary Magdalene Church in Canning Road and during his youth Cliff sang in the choir. This was probably an early indicator of his musical leanings for he became a successful musician, playing a variety of percussion instruments and the electronic organ which still occupies pride of place in his 'music room'. The photograph on page 68 is of his parents, Emma and Leonard Marlow, on their wedding day in 1920 which, although not taken at St Mary's, is nonetheless priceless to me and cousin Cliff for it shows most of the family members at that time, including my dad. Interestingly this wedding was at St Matthew's Church, situated in George Street. This church was demolished in the name of 'progress' during redevelopment in more recent times.

Business: The Roote business flourished during the 1920s and '30s. Both my dad and his brother, Arthur, worked in the shop although both eventually joined Webber and Harrison whose story is told elsewhere in this book. None of the next Roote generation became French polishers so, when Will reached 'retiring' age, he decided to close the business and at the start of the Second World War the door of the shop shut for the last time. At this point Morland Road became the centre of the Roote empire.

A family at war: Its position on the outskirts of Croydon put Addiscombe in the firing-line during the Blitz of 1940-41 and the following list of incidents shows that the Rootes had their fair share of close encounters as, of course, did many others:

BUILDINGS BOMBED
19 April 1940: 75-77 Lower Addiscombe Road
9 September 1940: 226 Lower Addiscombe Road
16 September 1940: 134-138 Bingham Road
16 September 1940: 19-21 and 43 Morland Avenue
1 October 1940: 6 Leslie Grove

Several doodlebugs also hit Addiscombe and these have been described in the first volume of this series.

Many of the second generation served in the Forces, as did my dad and Harold. Arthur served in the fire service in the London area and must have had a horrendous time, especially during the Blitz; and the bravery of these gallant men is well documented. Only one 'family' member became a casualty: Cousin Vandha Snelling's husband, John David Bylett, aged 27, was killed on 13 March 1941 in Egypt whilst serving with 54 Field Company, Royal Engineers. He is buried in Ismailia War Memorial Cemetery. It seems that the only member of the Roote family not to celebrate VE and VJ Day at home was my dad, who wasn't demobilised until 1946.

The post-war period: The family remained in the Addiscombe area for some time after the war, with Davidson Road, Morland Avenue and Dalmally Road becoming part of the empire. Gradually, however, the Addiscombe presence began to dwindle as the second-generation children moved to take their opportunities in the post-war boom. Harold moved to Brighton, Arthur to Upper Norwood, whilst Dorothy remained in Selhurst. Florence, after living in Redhill for many years, moved back to Selhurst via Sydenham Road. In 1959 William Benjamin died at Morland Road. Cliff's mum, Emily, remained at Exeter Road and was still resident there until she died in 1979. Thus the last connection of the Roote family to Addiscombe was finally broken.

> WILLIAM HENRY ROOTE: 1863-1934
> WILLIAM BENJAMIN FRANCIS ROOTE: 1884-1959
> FLORENCE BEATRICE ROOTE: 1886-1969
> LILIAN ETHEL ROOTE: 1890-1970
> DOROTHY LOUISA ROOTE: 1892-1975
> EMMA CHARLOTTE MARY ANN ROOTE: 1894-1979
> ALBERT EDWARD VICTOR ROOTE: 1897-97
> HAROLD FREDERICK ROOTE: 1898-1972
> ADELAIDE ALICE RUTH ROOTE: 1900-17
> ARTHUR ALGERNON ROOTE: 1903-79
> LEONARD CHARLES ROOTE: 1905-90

The Hockeys
Shirley Roberts

Our branch of the Hockey family originated in a small village called Horsington in Somerset. They came from farming stock and in all the records were classed as yeomen. However, over the years, with very large families to share in the legacies, it became necessary for work to be found further afield. So, in his early twenties, our great-grandfather, Oliver Hockey, rather like Dick Whittington, came to London to seek his fortune, or anyway at least paid

Oliver Hockey, cheesemonger of Fish Street Hill. (S.R.)

his own 'Provision Merchants' at 16 Fish Street Hill, just opposite the Monument. This was a most prestigious position; with the Thames so close he was able to become one of the suppliers of the many ships that sailed up the river in need of victualling. We imagine that Oliver's sons would have learnt the trade in their father's shop.

Oliver and his large family eventually moved to a substantial house in Wickham Road, Brockley and indeed Oliver remained there until his death in 1912 aged 83. When his sons and daughters married, they all seemed to settle in the area close to Wickham Road. Our grandfather, Thomas Hockey, who was always known as 'Harry', met his future wife, Elizabeth Margaret Gill (always known as Lizzie), by way of being friendly with her three brothers. Her father, Alfred Gill, owned an ironmongery business quite close to Oliver's shop in Arthur Street West and could have had connections with the family in business life as well as living in Wickham Road not far from the Hockeys.

employment. Our records don't show where he first found work or indeed accommodation but in 1854 at the age of 24 he married the 21-year-old Emma Brooks and his profession was designated 'cheesemonger'. When their first child was born in 1855 they were living in Brook Street, Bermondsey.

We believe that he and Emma had about nine children and our grandfather, Thomas Henry, was one of the three youngest. Oliver appeared to thrive in business for, by the age of 40 (in 1869), he owned

Harry and Lizzie had four children. Their first child, Harold, sadly died at six months, but they were blessed with three further children – Gladys Barbara, our mother, Kathleen Margaret and a son, Alfred Thomas. They first lived in Harefield Road, Brockley and later moved to Tressilian Road near Hilly Fields. Harry worked at his father's shop, probably as an assistant, to learn the business.

The Hockey family, c.1910. Gladys is pictured on the right and her sister, Kath, is on their father's knee. The baby is Alf, who is one year old. (S.R.)

HOCKEY & BRIMACOMBE
LTD.

POST OFFICE, THE EXCHANGE,
BROADWAY STORES, and
40, LESLIE PARK ROAD,
ADDISCOMBE.

GROCERS and

PROVISION MERCHANTS.

Finest
Quality
Obtainable.

VALUE AT LOWEST MARKET PRICES.

Noted
House
for

Mild Cured Bacon,
Choice Butters,
Cheddar Cheese, etc.

GROCERY HOCKEY & BRIMACOMBE PROVISIONS

Inset: *The new joint venture of Hockey & Brimacombe, 1919.* (S.R.)

Main: *The front of 301 Lower Addiscombe Road. This area was known as 'The Broadway'.* (S.R.)

Left: *'Canning Lodge', 10 Canning Road, where the Hockeys lived from around 1917 to 1922. It has now been replaced with flats.* (S.R.)

One interesting memento of that period of their lives exists in the form of a postcard written by Lizzie in 1908 to Harry at the shop asking him to bring some butter home when he returned in the evening, as she had quite forgotten to ask him in the morning. What a wonderful postal service we had then – for a halfpenny and posted at 11.15 in the morning Lizzie knew the message would reach him in time for him to do what she wanted.

While living in the city, Harry was granted the honour of being made a Freeman of the City of London. This was made during the Mayoralty of Sir Marcus Samuel on the 6 November 1903. I have been told that apart from the honour of being so named, this also allowed the holder to drive his sheep over London Bridge, a pastime that in the twenty-first century is probably not to be recommended.

Following Oliver's death, two of the brothers, Harry and Albert, drew up an agreement whereby Albert remained as sole trader of the shop at Fish Street Hill, buying out Harry who then came to live and work in Croydon. I imagine that they were both very astute businessmen by this time and Harry probably saw the potential of a business in Croydon which was fast becoming an important commercial centre. It also boasted excellent transport connections to London where many family members still lived.

So in 1913 Harry moved into a house in Addiscombe for a short time before moving his family to the house that all his children remembered – 200 Lower Addiscombe Road. This was a fairly large terraced property a few doors along from the junction of Colworth Road; the house is still there today. It apparently had a cellar used for storing coal which was filled from the road by a connecting shute. The family's pet cat lost one of its nine lives when hiding in the cellar when the coalman arrived, but was just rescued in time.

In 1914 Harry first took over Hammonds Provision Stores and Post Office at the Exchange, 6 Lower Addiscombe Road, later to be renumbered 195. Also at this time, at 40 Leslie Park Road, there was a grocers and provision merchants under the name of H.W. Brimacombe. How these two men met and collaborated to form Hockey & Brimacombe Ltd is not recorded. However, as they were both in the same line of business, it is possible that it was through an association or the Chamber of Commerce of which we know Harry was a member.

Apart from their business connection, they became firm friends too. Herbert Brimacombe

Thomas Hockey at the rear of the Exchange Post Office, 195 Lower Addiscombe Road, in 1913.
(S.R.)

became affectionately known as 'Brimmy' by the family. He was a single man and seemed to fit in happily with the Hockey family life, joining Harry and Lizzie on outings and holidays to the seaside. Brimmy lived at 39 Stretton Road, a turning off Morland Road, and was, of consequence, well placed for managing his original grocery store in Leslie Park Road. By the time that Harry and Brimmy had established Hockey & Brimacombe Ltd, Harry no longer served in the shops but ran the company from an office above one of the outlets.

Their first joint venture was a shop further along the Lower Addiscombe Road – No. 301 which was on a parade called The Broadway, quite close to the Black Horse. This shop was called Hockey & Brimacombe and the records indicate that it was managed by a man named M. Gooda. Other managers took over in following years – Messrs A. Wren, G.C. Ross and A. Morley, who was manager from 1946 to 1954.

Harry attended the inaugural meeting in 1917 of the Croydon Grocers' Association and was elected President in 1931. He was also a keen member of the Federation of Sub-Postmasters taking on the role of Treasurer of the Croydon District Branch and becoming President in 1929.

The family lived for about two years on the Lower Addiscombe Road before moving to 'Canning Lodge', 10 Canning Road, in about 1917. This house has now been replaced by a block of flats. It was a spacious double-fronted home which was spoken of by his children in later years with great affection. It apparently had a beautiful garden containing a wide variety of fruit trees and a walnut tree. By that time, Gladys was 15, Kath 12 and Alf 8. All of us in the family have heard stories of the happy times shared there – Alf's dislike of feathers and his sisters' tormenting him with them, the girls sharing a bedroom and being frightened by a door quietly opening in the dark of the night only to be surprised by the appearance of the cat, and watching a Zeppelin during the First World War appearing in the night sky to disappear in flames below the skyline. Harry and Lizzie had been at a cinema when the warning of an air raid was flashed on the screen. They immediately returned home to the family, but thankfully for them all was well.

Gladys and Kath attended a small private school in Elgin Road called Hadley House. This had been started by the Misses Carter in 1889 in a private house at No. 25. According to a report by the

The grocers' outing at the Royal Huts Hotel, Hindhead, 1925. (S.R.)

The grocers' outing to Hindhead, 1925. (S.R.)

This image: *The grocers' cricket match at Addiscombe Cricket Club, Radcliffe Road, 1930s.* (S.R.)
Below left: *Herbert Brimacombe with Thomas Hockey at Margate, 1925.* (S.R.)

The family in the garden of 'Canning Lodge', c.1919. Gladys is pictured on the left, with Kath on the right and young Alf in front. (S.R.)

Inspectors in 1921, this school occupied two rooms of the house, together with three classrooms specially built in an adjoining garden. There were proper cloakroom and office facilities and the fairly large garden was sometimes available for the children's use. It would seem that teaching of reading, speech training and composition with spelling and handwriting was quite satisfactory. According to the report, however, arithmetic was weak which may account for our mother confiding in me when she was over 90 that she was no good at subtraction.

Apparently, the children were taught how to be young ladies and had to practise their deportment by walking around the room with books balanced on their heads. The teaching of geography seems to have been satisfactory, too, for our mother could recite each English county, with its county town and the river on which it stood.

Sport in the form of games must have been part of the curriculum because my sister and I were handed down a hockey stick for use when we were playing that game years later in our senior school. Mother had clearly written her surname HOCKEY on the handle so that it wouldn't be mislaid and we who were using it secondhand were constantly being taunted as to why we had to be reminded for which game it was to be used.

Friends were made at the school and one particular one was Dorothy Kingshott who lived at 29 Elgin Road, a few doors from the school. The friendship remained past the marriage of each of these girls until both their deaths in 1996, aged over 90. Dorothy had married William Secker, remained all her married life in Nicholson Road and played a lasting and valuable role in the life of St Mary's Church.

It is interesting to note that, when the girls were at Hadley House, class distinction was quite common and, as their father was 'in trade', friendships with some of the girls were definitely discouraged.

St Mary's Church played a large part in the lives of the Hockey family. Harry was at one time a sidesman and the girls and Alf belonged to the Young People's Fellowship, enjoying social occasions and playing tennis together. Gladys also taught in the Sunday school and met her future husband there.

In about 1922 the family moved again, this time to Upper Addiscombe. No. 76, or 'Homewood' as it was named, stood almost opposite Winton House where Alf had attended school. Looking from the front-room windows of Homewood gave a clear view down Havelock Road to the Lower Addiscombe Road and when Gladys was courting in 1925 she could watch for Douglas Jarman, her 'intended', walking up from his family home at 172 Lower Addiscombe Road and make sure she was ready for his arrival.

The house next door was built and lived in by close relatives. Harry's youngest sister, Florence, had married Harry Spalding and with their four children they enjoyed many happy family get-togethers. The Spalding family had installed a tennis court in their garden so one imagines the gardens were alive with young people's laughter on hot summer evenings.

The Hockey family was basically a very happy one and family occasions with aunts, uncles and cousins were regularly enjoyed. Lizzie was a very capable hostess and entertained often. The family commonly had evenings when they either played an instrument or sang for the enjoyment of the others.

Harry was quite strict and his rule was law. He wouldn't allow any of the family to cycle on a Sunday but he enjoyed such a ride to the White Bear at Chelsham for a lunchtime drink. He, too, had definite - and I suppose one would say Victorian - views on prospective husbands for his daughters but I know that he was both loved and respected.

In the year 2000 the Hockey and Spalding homes, along with some houses on either side, became victims of the building of the new Tramlink and in fact the Sandilands stop has been installed just where our family home had stood. The Tramlink Company very kindly provided us with photos of the front and rear of the house as it had been prior to its removal, for which we were most grateful.

In 1928 Gladys was married to Douglas Jarman at St Mary's Church in Canning Road with the Revd A. Malley and the Revd J. Wright officiating. Harry gave her away and two of the Spalding cousins, Oliver and Geoffrey, from the house next door were best man and groomsman. Her brother, Alf, played his part as a groomsman too. The reception was held in the beautiful garden of 'Homewood' where a large marquee was erected for the 80 or so guests.

Driving was becoming quite popular at about that time and Harry purchased a succession of cars from Turners, a garage situated at 100 Lower Addiscombe Road. For me personally it is interesting to note that about 50 years later my husband was the sales manager at these premises, the company having been bought by L.F. Dove Ltd.

The Hockey family owned at different times a Morris, a blue Singer and a Clyno. Harry attempted to drive all of these but he didn't much take to this new mechanical invention and so encouraged Alfred, his son, to drive, and he became quite proficient. Kath also became interested and asked Alf to teach her. She picked up the intricacies of motoring with confidence and also drove extremely well. In fact, a decade later during the Second World War she was detailed to drive an ambulance. She and another girl would pick up casualties and take them to the Croydon General Hospital, often driving through air raids with bombs falling around them. She said later that she wasn't scared at the time, it was a job that had to be done so they did it, but she was more anxious when going to pick up a casualty as to how injured they would be and how they could best deal with that person.

In 1928 Harry discovered that a new parade of shops was to be built on Shirley Road at the junction of Upper Addiscombe Road and in the following year Hockey & Brimacombe Ltd added 171 Shirley Road to the three others, 195 and 301 Lower Addiscombe Road and 40 Leslie Park Road. Then in 1930 Brimmy moved to be cared for at a private hotel and the Leslie Park Road shop was sold, with Harry Hockey taking on sole ownership of the businesses.

I can remember the layout of the Shirley Road shop. Through the door one was greeted by counters on each side and, straight ahead, a cashier behind a glass partition. Two chairs were set beside each counter for the comfort of the customer and Gladys, referred to as Mrs Douglas when first married, would visit and spend a pleasant half hour deciding what to order for that week. In front of the right-hand counter were those wonderful boxes of biscuits with glass lids to enable the customer to choose their delights. The last tin in the line was filled with a selection of broken biscuits to be sold at a slightly reduced price. When a customer bought granulated sugar, it was weighed and then put into a cone of blue 'sugar paper', twisted at the base and then folded neatly at the top. Cheeses and bacon were sliced expertly according to customers' requirements and packaged in greaseproof paper with the price written on in pencil.

The smell of sliced bacon, cheese, spices and soap powders pervaded the shop in a way far removed from today's supermarkets awash with their plastic packaging. After the customer had made her order, she returned home to await delivery of her goods right to the door. Sometimes the deliveries were made by young delivery boys but the company also had a smart van with its name on both sides.

In about 1932 the Hockeys moved for what was to be the final time. This house was newly built for them and was situated across the corner of Mapledale Avenue and the main Addiscombe Road. It was No. 130 and named 'Hartgrove', and is still there today – missing its name but looking good with a few extra embellishments.

In 1936 when Alf married Constance Hill he was working in the Penge Surveyors Department. They were married at St John's Church, Shirley as the bride's family were living in Orchard Way. In 1939 Alf joined the Army in the RASC as a 2nd Lieutenant. When the war began he was called up and was posted to France, but having contracted pneumonia there he was sent back to the UK for hospitalisation. He had been due to be posted to another area in Europe but following his return to health he was posted to India where he remained for the rest of the war. On his return in 1945 he was a Major. He continued his

Army service in peacetime in the Territorials and gained the rank of Lieutenant Colonel.

In July 1940 Kath married Cecil Macve whose family also lived in Addiscombe and, like Gladys before her, had the wedding reception in the family home – this time 'Hartgrove'. Gladys was her matron of honour and once again their cousin, Oliver Spalding, acted as best man. Sadly because of so many wartime restrictions, the wedding had to be quite simple but Gladys wrote in her diary that it was 'a very happy and charming affair and a lovely day.'

So the war progressed and thankfully those family members who had to play an active role survived without injury. The three Hockey & Brimacombe Ltd shops continued much-needed trading but of course now had to deal with rationing and coupons.

In 1944 Harry became ill and died in Croydon General Hospital aged 73. His obituary in the local press described him as 'more of a thinker and worker than talker, [who] achieved much success in business life, gave help where needed, and was courteous and considerate to all.' Not long after his death, in the same year a flying bomb fell on the houses opposite Hartgrove and caused considerable damage. So later Lizzie sold the house and moved nearer to Alf and his wife. Following her death in 1961, the shops were all sold. Interestingly, the Fish Street Hill grocers remained in the Hockey name until about the end of the war.

Harry had seen the arrival of J. Sainsbury and he was quite astute in realising that that type of shop could cause the demise of the little local grocery store. I wonder what our grandfather would have thought of the huge supermarkets that open for 24 hours a day where we buy our groceries now, all so very different from the personal attention housewives learned to expect at the time from Hockey & Brimacombe Ltd.

I would like to add a final note that this history of the family is in part taken from local records and has also partly been gleaned by talking to members of the family. I therefore wish to thank Connie Hockey, Hermione Graham, David Jarman and Barbara Mitchell.

The Hockeys' 'Clyno' car, with Alf and his mother aboard. (S.R.)

Above: *Cherry Orchard Road, late 1920s, with Ivy Binstead caught on camera, on the left with plaits.* (I.B.)

Left: *Bill Angell delivering for W.D. Vigar in Rees Gardens, 1938.* (B. & J.A.)

Above and right: *Advertisements from 1938 (C.L.S.L.) and 1940 (K.S.) respectively.*

Eight

ჯ▸◉◂ჯ

Shopping in Addiscombe

Before Fridges & Supermarkets

Contributors include: Evelyn Adams, Bill and Joan Angell, Ivy Ayling, Arlette Beelitz, Ivy Binstead, Arthur Burns, Mary Chandler, Marian Gilliam, John Hobbs, Christine and Peter Lockley, Leslie Lockley, Bill Maile, Cliff Marlow, Paul Nihill, Bill Wood & Anne Bridge

Addiscombe has two main shopping areas. The first to be developed in the nineteenth century was around Cherry Orchard and that part of Lower Addiscombe Road stretching from the Windmill Bridge to the Alma Tavern. The building of shops in the eastern end of the Lower Addiscombe Road (downtown LA) did not begin until shortly after the beginning of the twentieth century. Both ends of Addiscombe were thriving shopping centres and communities. The Cherry Orchard Road area was the first to feel the effects of retail chains and close proximity to central Croydon.

Here is a brief tour of the most remembered shops of Addiscombe. It cannot be complete but we've picked those names that have occurred most frequently. Since until the 1950s fridges and cars were either non-existent or a rarity; most people shopped locally and daily. Here are some memories that span those years.

Cherry Orchard Road

Ivy Binstead (born 1915) has lived in Addiscombe all her life. She recalls:

There was no pre-packed or sliced bread, either a nice crusty cottage loaf, or a coberg bloomer all lovely and crusty on the outside. I often got into trouble for picking bits off the outside when I was sent to buy one. They were only wrapped in a bit of tissue paper. There were no pre-packed biscuits, tea, sugar, dried fruits, etc. Everything was weighed up separately and put into thick blue or brown bags. Sweets were weighed up and put in a screwed-up cone of paper.

Apart from the nice crusty bread from the shop, we used to have a baker call, first with

a handcart and later a horse and cart. The bread and any cakes ordered were brought to the door by him in a big basket. Milk was also brought to the door [on] a cart with a big milk churn on it; the milk was ladled out into your own jug. Eggs were just put in a bag, more often than not some were cracked in transit.

No toilet rolls until the 1930s, unless I suppose you had plenty of money. I can remember my father cutting up squares of newspaper or telephone directory and threading them on a piece of string (I don't think the print came off as it does today). Anyway we survived.

Shops kept to their own things. Butchers just sold meat, grocers just provisions, etc. Newsagents did sell some sweets, confectioners sold tobacco and cigarettes. I can remember that Christmas and birthday presents for my Father were an ounce of tobacco and a packet of paper costing under a shilling or a red spotted handkerchief for 6d.

Kathleen Spalding (born 1920) was born, and raised her own family, in Addiscombe. Kath, Cyril and their three children lived at 154 Cherry Orchard Road above John Preston's, who supplied the Oval School uniform. Kath's children, Jacqueline, Lorraine and Adrian, attended Oval School. Kath did many walks up Cherry Orchard Road taking and picking up the children from school. All the shopkeepers, as you walked by, passed the time of day and had time to talk and everyone knew everyone. At Standens the grocers most people would pay for their weekly food bill on a Friday. Kath's daughter, Jacqueline, can remember paying a weekly food bill for 11s.6d. in the 1950s for the whole family.

Bill Angell (born 1923) has seen many changes. At the age of 14 he went to work with W.D. Vigar, 'Butcher and Purveyor of English and Colonial Meat' at 164 Cherry Orchard Road. The manager, Bill Watts, told Bill Angell that, since there were already two Bills working for the firm, they would call him 'John'. Bill would go around on a delivery bike with a basket on the front. Next door at 162 was Abbotts, a ham and beef shop, and these two originally formed Goddards, the butchers, as pictured in *Vol. I.* Abbotts is fondly remembered. Arthur Burns recalls:

Ham was cut from the bone for each customer as thinly or thickly as required. My aunt lived with us before marrying. She worked for years at Abbotts ham and beef shop from 8.00a.m. to 7.00p.m. (8.00p.m. on Saturdays).

The Home and Colonial, just beyond Leslie Park Road on the right at 146 Cherry Orchard Road, sold saveloys and pease-pudding.

During the 1930s there were nine butchers in the Cherry Orchard Road and this end of Lower Addiscombe Road. These included Bob West (corner of Lower Addiscombe Road and Alexandra Road), across from there a small butchers and the present-day Co-op (which was then a Co-op butchers). On Cherry Orchard Road there was another, Baldwins, at 152, and W.A. Martin at 144. On the opposite side there was a new Goddards at 117 (now an electrical firm). Goddards had their own abattoir in the backyard with a table for killing pigs. To reach it you went through The Cobbles off Addiscombe Grove, opposite the Methodist Church. Mr Goddard wore a Tyrolean hat and buttoned-up collar and was known

to whip the pony he kept along with a trap in the backyard. All nine butchers did a trade and all were friendly. Trade in Cherry Orchard Road died out over a period of 15 years following the arrival of supermarkets. The last butcher left was Bob West.

Bill Maile (born 1905) also remembers the yard behind Goddards. In the late 1920s Bill used to park his employer's van there. He would drive to the end of the yard past stables, coal wagons and oil lamps, parking the van near a gas boiler and billy can. Bill then drained the radiator overnight and filled up with hot water in the morning so that the lorry would start.

In the block of shops nearest Leslie Park Road (in the direction of the Leslie Arms) there used to be cottages with iron railings between the basement and pavement. As children, Bill Angell and his friends would run along and drag something across the iron railings, much to the irritation of the occupants of the cottages. Bill Maile remembers:

On the corner of Leslie Park Road and Cherry Orchard Road was a wheelwright with a little pub (Surrey Arms) next door. I was fascinated watching the wheelwright making steel tyres for cars and barrows. He would take a length of steel, turn a handle and mould the tyre; he got it so lovely.

Main: *Jackson's shoe workshop behind 129 Cherry Orchard Road.* (C.L.S.L.) Inset: *George Turner, who had a shoe-mending business in Leslie Park Road, is pictured in his garden.* (P. & C.L.)

No. 131 Cherry Orchard Road. Jackson's moved from 129 to 131 in the 1930s. (R.S.)

When these cottages were knocked down and the current shops built in 1936, the site of Baldwins the butchers became an ice-cream parlour serving their treats out of the window. The proprietor was Italian and at the beginning of the war was rounded up and sent to the Isle of Man.

Another name that repeatedly crops up is of Pearks grocery shop. Arthur Burns relates:

When purchasing eggs there, which were sold loose only, the customer could see if they were ok by virtue of their being popped individually into a light box. The light was switched on and shone through the eggs, showing up any imperfections.

Other names that crop up are Lovells the greengrocers at 136, Croydon Animal Clinic (121), Pillings fishmongers (123), Bannisters Radios (156) to where people took accumulators and Podmore the draper where Arthur Burns clearly recalls:

... the two elderly serving ladies with their 'One and eleven three', meaning one shilling and elevenpence three farthings, i.e. 2 shillings all but a farthing.

Mr Dumont Smith gave the impression of being an unusual character. He was an art and antique dealer whose sister taught the piano. Christine Lockley (née Turner), living at 98 Cherry Orchard Road, would go there for painting and piano lessons. Christine's father was George Turner who had a shoe-repair business in Leslie Park Road.

By an ironic twist of fate, Christine married the grandson of the owner of the nearest rival shoe shop, Albert Jackson. Albert was a remarkable man who contributed much to the local community. He served the area as a Councillor and Alderman and was very active in the Cherry Orchard Road Methodist Church. Peter Lockley, his grandson, takes up the story:

My mother, Ivy Hilda Jackson, was born on 5 October 1901 at 129 Cherry Orchard. Her father was Albert Jackson (a surgical boot maker and Alderman of Croydon) whose shoe shop was in Cherry Orchard Road close to the Methodist Chapel. At one time before the war he had shops in Hayes, West Wickham and 203 Lower Addiscombe. There was also a second shop in Cherry Orchard for a while, close to the Leslie Arms.

Shoe repairs were done behind the main 129 Cherry Orchard Road shop. My memories of the shop are more of the workshop, where the shoes were made and repaired by mainly deaf and dumb workers. My grandfather took both his Christian and Council duties seriously and this is why he employed disabled workers. He learnt to 'sign for the deaf' so that... he could converse with his workers. In the workshop was the fascinating sight of 'shoe lasts' around the walls for made-to-measure boots, shoes and surgical boots. The surgical boot workshop was a good source of cork for a boy who liked to make models, etc.

Albert Jackson died during the war of natural causes. The shop was taken over by his son-in-law, Norman Baker, but with the emergence of the footwear chains and the fall-off of the made-to-measure footwear market, when the long-time Manager, Mr Tompson, died in 1959, the shop was closed and the premises sold. We both remember Mr Tompson as a very kind man.

Those who remember going into the shop as children may remember the small table and chairs and the rocking horse kept there to keep them occupied... I took [it] off its safety rocker and fitted a traditional one so that it could be used in the Croydon Histrionic Society's production of Anton Chekhov's The Cherry Orchard in the Civic Hall (I was their Stage Manager). After the show it was put back on its safety rocker and is now being enjoyed by Albert's great-great-grandchildren!

Above: *Alexandra Road, c.1911.* (J.G.)

Left: *An advertisement from the 1920s.* (C.L.S.L.)

Lower Addiscombe Road, c.1914. (J.G.)

Lower Addiscombe Road between Windmill Bridge & the Alma Tavern

Boxalls, the greengrocers, has been at 18 Lower Addiscombe Road for many years. The sight of Mr Boxall driving his horse and cart around the area made quite an impression. He stabled his horses under the arches of Windmill Bridge.

During the 1920s a bicycle could be seen in the window of 3 Lower Addiscombe Road. The shop belonged to C.F. Davey and, although it was known as The Addiscombe Gramophone Stores, it also stocked electrical equipment and bicycles. Charles Davey was a renowned cyclist who held several records, including cycling from John O'Groats to Lands End, and represented England in the Olympic Games. He was a founder member of the Addiscombe Cycling Club and a long-term member of the Vegetarian Cycling Club. In the *Addiscombe, Woodside & Shirley Notes* of January 1925, H. Wright, Captain of the Vegetarian Cycling Club, attributed Davey's success in holding three of the classic long-distance cycling road records of the Kingdom to his vegetarian diet!

A little further along at Number 53 during the 1930s was Gunner's fish shop. Cecil Hadfield lived opposite and was impressed by their regular delivery:

I think it was on Monday mornings that a lorry would arrive at the shop loaded with huge cubes of ice. These would be lifted from the lorry by means of a sort of self-tightening claw. A bar would be looped through the claw and two men would each place an end of the bar on their shoulder and in this way would carry each cube into the shop.

Moving along the road and into the 1940s, Cliff Marlow had a part-time job at Harry Leppards, a well-known off-licence store at 101 Lower Addiscombe Road on the corner of Hastings Road. From 1942, at the age of 12, Cliff worked there as an errand boy. The shop was managed by George Head and his wife, Alice, who lived behind the shop. On being given the job Cliff soon learnt to ride the delivery bike in Canning Road. One time the chain came off and he went into the back of a parked car. Cliff earned 10 shillings a week working two evenings and all day Saturday.

There were several regular customers. Mrs Ainslie of 5 Park Hill Rise took a bottle of whiskey each week. The two delivery boys used to vie to deliver to her as she always tipped generously at 6d. A little old lady, who lived in Addiscombe Avenue, worked in the cash office to the right-hand side of the door and, when the errand boys returned from delivering, they gave her the change and receipts.

In those days many bottles were returned by customers to the shop and the deposits refunded to them. At Harry Leppards they bottled their own Guinness and port in the basement. Cliff and the other delivery boy would unofficially work extra evenings there. The Guinness was drawn by a man from a tank into a quart (two-pint) bottle and sealed with a screw cap. One of the errand boys would affix a Harry Leppard label with water paste onto the side and the other boy put a label over the cap.

Morland Road. (J.G.)

Downtown LA (Lower Addiscombe)

The Exchange: Hockey & Brimacombe are well remembered at 195 with the Post Office and also at 301 along The Boulevard. Hockeys was a high-class grocer. It has been whispered that Northampton Road was known locally as 'snobs' alley. A lot of the men worked in the City, travelling up from Bingham Road Station. The ladies of Northampton Road did not think they should be seen carrying shopping so they would walk down to the shops with a basket over their arm, place their orders at Hockey & Brimacombe and the greengrocers, who would deliver their purchases later the same day.

Peter Lockley remembers his family moving to 203 Lower Addiscombe Road in about 1935:

Baldwins the butchers were next door on the corner of Sundridge Road. They had a delivery man who had lost one leg and had a straight wooden leg. This did not stop him from riding his delivery bike which was a 'fixed wheel' with one pedal removed. To see him ride was a wonder.

I cannot remember the business on the other side of us but twice during the time that we were there we woke to find they had done a 'moonlight flit'.

Evelyn Adams remembers that:

Mr Vincent the chemist at 215 Lower Addiscombe Road was a lovely man. Over the shop was a dentist, Charles Ashworth, who was very young then and still lives in Addiscombe Road. Mary Ann, the wool shop, was next to the chemist. Mother and daughter owned it. If you couldn't afford all your wool, they would put it by for you; you could go and get an ounce whenever you could afford it. You don't get shops like that anymore.

Boro Oatmeal Hard Water Soap

Specially prepared for us by Messrs. Price & Co., to overcome the effects of the **Addiscombe Hard Water**.

For Nursery and the Toilet. Per Tablet, **5d.**, per doz. **4/9.**

LILY CREAM, "The Housewife's Friend."

Prevents lined or chapped hands. POTS, 1/- & 1/9.

S. W. VINCENT & CO.
(S. W. VINCENT, M.P.S.)

Family Chemists, ADDISCOMBE.

Left: *Vincents chemists, at 215 Lower Addiscombe Road in the 1950s.* (C. & H.)

Inset: *Advertisment, 1920s.* (C.L.S.L.)

Bottom: *Lower Addiscombe and Ashburton Roads, c.1912.* (J.G.)

Ashburton & Lower Addiscombe Roads.

J.K.Simmons.

The Boulevard: Ladies remember the ladies' outfitters, Jean Leppard, at 237 in the 1930s (moving to 272 by 1960). Ivy Ayling also recalls Claudia Fashions, where there was 'a wonderful little lady' called Mrs Elias, who would tell customers: 'Take the dress home. Try it and, if you like it, come back and see me.' Then there was Irene Newman with her baby and women's underwear shop. She was the first wife of Eric Palmer, who died recently aged 91 and who, as Ivy recalls 'was musical and ran a singing class and put on concerts.' His second wife, Paula Lemoine, had a dancing school and taught Evelyn Adams' daughter.

Sainsburys at 245 (now Alldays) is remembered by Evelyn Adams: 'My husband left school at 14 and went to work in Addiscombe Sainsburys. He left when he was 16 to work on the railway.' Mary Chandler remembers: 'Customers walked into a shop with Doulton tiles on the walls and shop assistants serving behind beautiful mahogany counters'; and Ivy Ayling recalls the 'very tall Manager in a grey coat and apron [who] would walk down the shop and say "Good morning" to the ladies behind the counter.' 'Everything in the shop was just so,' related Ivy. 'You could smell the butter and cheeses. It was quite something.'

Pages at 253 is another shop fondly thought of, a china shop where gifts could be purchased. Ivy remembers her mother admiring a sugar sifter in Pages and she and her sister clubbed together to buy it as a birthday present. Sadly, even as we compile this book, Pages is closing down; it is the end of an era.

At 257 is Gordon's Toys which has always been a book, stationery and toy shop. Nem, who has been the owner for the last 19 years, has an elderly customer who has been visiting the shop for over 80 years. He remembers it as Putt's Library, when the shop was shorter in length. This gentleman recalls sitting outside the shop and being able to see right up to Shirley Hills. Moving on a couple of generations, Arlette Beelitz recalls: 'Putts in Lower Addiscombe Road, a toy shop with every kind of farm animal on display in glass counters, except during October and early November when children could choose their fireworks from the displays.'

The Co-op (now 311–313 Lower Addiscombe Road) originally occupied just 311. It was extended when Holmes, the wet-fish shop, moved.

Left: *Harold Adams on the roof behind Sainsburys, 1932. He has his back to Woodside Grange, demolished in the mid '30s to make way for Woolworths.* (E.A.)

Boulevard Outlets

Jean Leppard
Proprietress: Mrs. W. M. BOSTOCK

Stockists—
JACOLL HATS · CLASSIC SKIRTS · FARADAY BLOUSES
ARISTOC & BRETTLES HOSIERY · BERLEI BRAS & TWILFIT CORSETRY
CONLOWE UNDERWEAR · AERTEX & SMEDLEY UNDERWEAR
MILADI ANNE KNITWEAR · SYRINGA SUITS & DRESSES

272 LOWER ADDISCOMBE
CROYDON
ADD 1514

Claudia Fashions
329 LOWER ADDISCOMBE ROAD
ADDISCOMBE

•

FOR EXQUISITE LADIES' COATS,
COSTUMES, DRESSES, SKIRTS,
AND SEPARATES

•

Stockists of "Hebe Sports"
and Other Well Known Brands

Books! Books! Books!
You are invited to visit
PUTT'S LIBRARY
where you will find the
largest selection of books
in the district at
2d. per vol. Latest 3 days 2d.
Others 7 days 2d.

Fine selection of . . .
Toys, Games and
Fancy Goods.

255a, Lr. Addiscombe Rd.

HAVE YOU VISITED
Irene Newman's
ATTRACTIVE SHOP!

FOR LADIES' AND CHILDRENS' WEAR
CLYDELLA, BRETTLE'S ROB ROY,
MORLEY, MINIMODE, WOLSEY,
AERTEX, TWILFIT
English Rose and Partos

325 LOWER ADDISCOMBE ROAD
(Close to the Black Horse)

ADDiscombe 3369

Below: *An advert for the opening of Freeman, Hardy & Willis on 4 December 1925.* (C.L.S.L.)

All other advertisement 1960s. (P.N.)

An
F.H.W.
SHOE SHOP
239, Lower Addiscombe Rd.,
EAST
CROYDON

Freeman
Hardy &
Willis. Ltd
The Largest Footwear House in the Kingdom

The Freeman Hardy & Willis mosaic. (P.B.)

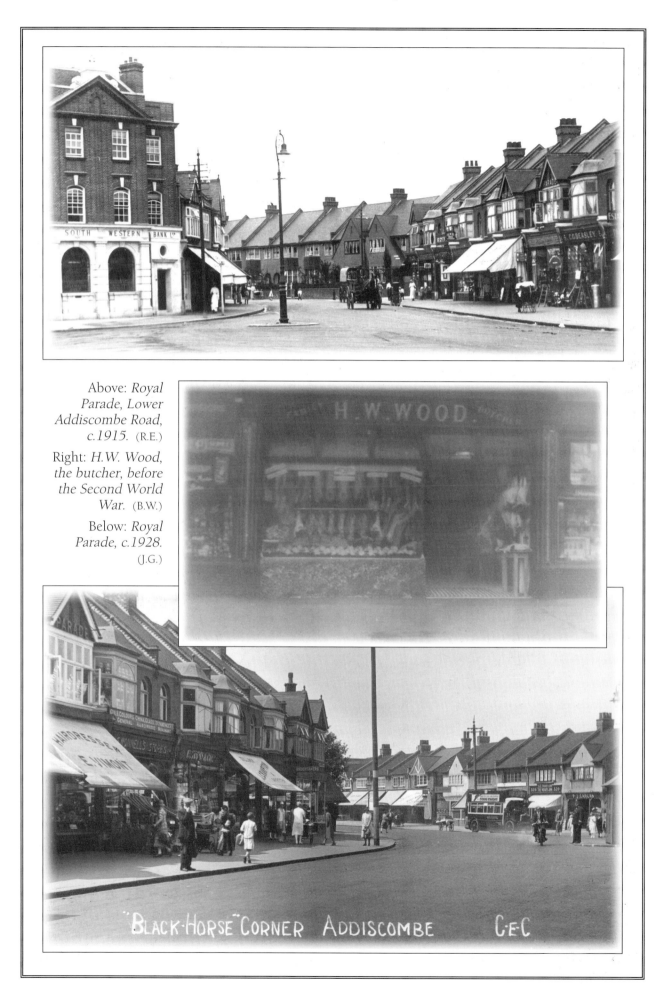

Above: *Royal Parade, Lower Addiscombe Road, c.1915.* (R.E.)

Right: *H.W. Wood, the butcher, before the Second World War.* (B.W.)

Below: *Royal Parade, c.1928.* (J.G.)

Woods in the early 1950s. Left to right: John Crozier, David Moore, John (Jack) Wood. (J.W.)

Herbert Wood (right) with Mr Guntrip, who ran a successful butchers shop by Thornton Heath Pond, 1930. (B.W.)

Regal Drycleaners was located under Bingham railway bridge. Sydney Maizels, pictured here, worked for many years from these premises. (P.B.)

Royal Parade: Back in the 1940s and '50s, the row of shops opposite the Black Horse was a community in itself. Bill Wood's father moved into the butchers at 304 Lower Addiscombe Road in 1923. The living quarters above the shop were reached by passing along an alleyway and up the stairs. At Christmas the butchers boys used to sit on the lower stairs plucking turkeys, whose feathers would waft up to the flat above, much to Bill's mother's annoyance. Bill's brother, Jack, took over the running of the shop in 1945 when he left the Armed Forces. Next door at 302 was Marshall-Woodcock the chemist. An earlier generation and Marian Gilliam, now in her late 90s, remembers the same shop: 'My grandfather had a chemist shop opposite the Black Horse; it's still there. We were enthralled with the nuns who used to come in from where the library is.' Paul Nihill recalls:

On Lower Addiscombe Road, opposite the bomb patch alongside the Black Horse public house, was a shop owned by world table tennis champion, Johnny Leach. Leach, the last Englishman to win the title, was a household name, a far cry from today when you'd be pushed to name a table tennis star. His shop sold all types of sports equipment.

Peters newsagents in Bingham Road under the railway bridge was one of Arlette Beelitz's favourite shops. 'It sold gobstoppers which lasted for hours – 1d. for a large one and a halfpenny for a small one in the 1950s.' Arlette's father, Paul Mason, relates that the rain used to trickle in the shop from the bridge overhead and that the owner got fed up with it soaking his newspapers. Mary Chandler remembers:

There used to be a little sweet shop under the Bingham Railway Bridge run by a very nice man. It was very useful. All the children went there. The shop also served as a newsagents. People could advertise in the window with postcards. The shop was so small that only two people could fit in at a time.

And Evelyn Adams recalls:

The shop in Bingham Road was quite small. It was a newsagents. The gentleman that owned it was a very friendly man. His name was Peter, so the shop was called Peters. He sold newspapers, sweets, cigarettes and ices. It was a very busy shop. Commuters would buy their morning paper to read on the train. Three ladies took it in turns to be in the shop in the afternoon so Peter could go home for a rest as he would be up early to open shop and sort the papers. My two daughters did an early-morning paper round for him before school. Peter owned the shop from the 1940s until he retired in the '70s. The shop was demolished when the railway closed. We all missed him very much.

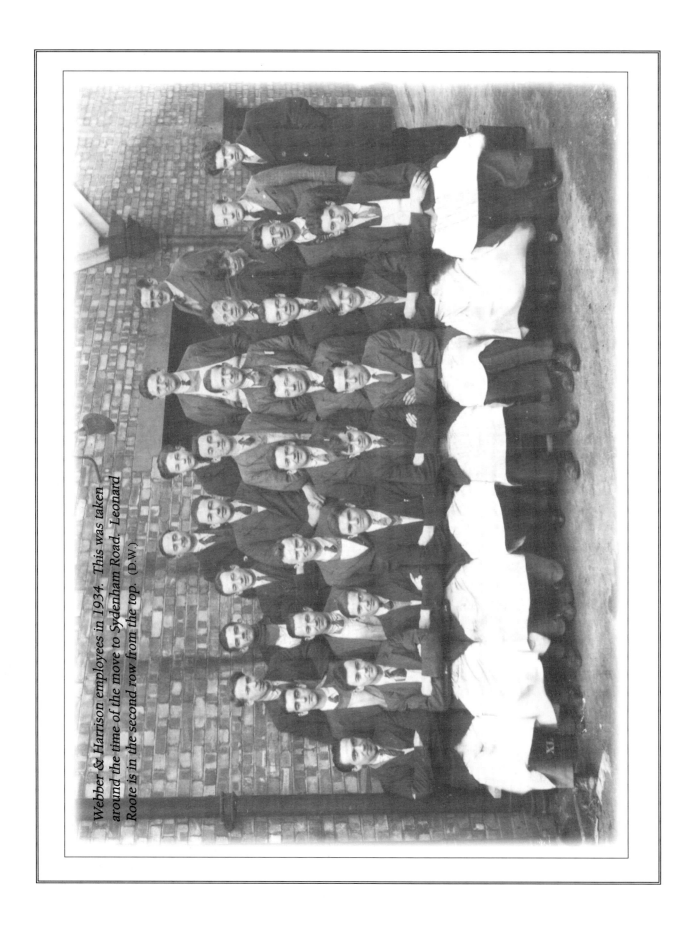

Webber & Harrison employees in 1934. This was taken around the time of the move to Sydenham Road. Leonard Roote is in the second row from the top. (D.W.)

Nine

Local Businesses

R. Whites, The Co-op Dairy, The Inveterate Inventor & Through all the Changes

R. Whites: The Secrets of a Lemonade Maker

Steve Collins, with help from Steve Wickenden & Steve Roud

(S.W. & A.B.)

R. Whites opened their huge bottling and distribution plant at 60 Morland Road in 1897. The site started business life in 1869 as Alfred Ryan's Timber and Mahogany Merchants, complete with steam-powered sawing, planing and milling equipment. In 1874 the business was taken over by Richard Burnham, which shortly after (1877) was taken over by James William Hobbs. As an up-and-coming businessman and local dignitary, he extended the business, and in 1881 provided employment for some 800 men and boys throughout the area.

Hobbs' Morland Road 'steam-powered joinery' became famous. The site expanded, and so too did his influence and business activities. But, as we will discover in Chapter Sixteen, it suddenly fell apart in 1893 and was taken over by R. Whites late in '96 after they had established that they could abstract all the necessary water for the new plant (See Chapter Two).

Robert White was born in 1824 and, along with his wife, Mary, started selling home-brewed ginger beer from a barrow in Camberwell in 1845. From there they went from strength to strength. Trading locally in the Camberwell area they had premises in Albany Road (1870) and then opened their first factory in Cunard Street (1871). In 1880, they were joined by their sons – Robert and John – in the family business, and by 1885 were also trading from Victory Place, Rodney Road, Walworth. By 1887 they also had premises in Neat Street, Camberwell, and their product list included Jubilee Lemonade, Jubilee Ginger Beer, Jubilee Tangerine, Ginger Ale, Pineapple, Cider, Champagne Cider, Orange Champagne, Soda Water, and that after-dinner favourite – Seltzer Water. The Jubilee badge was in honour of Queen Victoria's Golden Jubilee.

A year later they opened a further depot in Gravesend and in 1891 the sons took over H.D. Rawlings – their fiercest competitor (which had been established in the mid 1780s).

The year 1894 transpired to be a good one for business. The firm opened new factories in Camberwell and Barking, became a limited company, and Rawlings was appointed as supplier to the Emperor of France. Whites kept and promoted the Rawlings brand name for this very reason. And that brings us back to 1897 when they opened their Morland Road plant. The area must have resounded to the clip-clop of drays delivering pop to the local shops. Astonishingly, the early bottles were Denby stoneware and disposable (pictured 1901).

It was not until 1914 that deposits on returnable bottles were then charged at a farthing. For a gallon flagon it was one shilling, and for the monster two-gallon, two bob. Returnable deposit bottles continued in use until the 1960s, to be replaced by plastic disposables. It's good to know though that, during that 50-year period, many a child made their pocket money by returning bottles for the refund. Over those years the deposit money rose with gaseous inflation (see Chapter Ten)!

In 1961 the Morland Road plant was modernised and extended. One of the additions was a giant-sized garage with venting fans and automatic temperature control to contain 45 lorries, fully loaded overnight, ready to make the morning delivery to thousands of customers. During the war, this extension had been

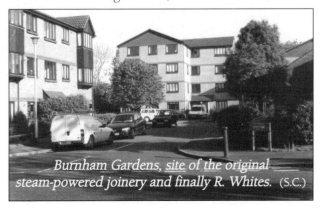

Burnham Gardens, site of the original steam-powered joinery and finally R. Whites. (S.C.)

the site of allotments. At this time, the plant was capable of filling and capping 26oz bottles at the rate of 600 dozen per hour, and for the 4- and 10oz bottles at 1,000 dozen per hour. It employed nearly 200 people.

All of the bottles were carefully washed and sterilised before filling. Four 500-gallon stainless-steel tanks ('boiling pans') held the essences which were mixed, watered, coloured, sweetened, carbonated and quality checked before bottling. If this process seems spookily similar to that of the Leslie Park Road Co-op Dairy plant, then it is basically because it was. One filled bottles with milk, the other pop. Both worked overnight to ensure the morning delivery. And of course, both companies abstracted huge amounts of water from the same luckily-placed geological watercourse. It is therefore not surprising to learn that there was considerable job 'moonlighting' between the two plants, which were separated by just a quarter of a mile.

R. Whites & Rawlings were taken over by Whitbreads in 1969 and the company is now owned by Britvic Soft Drinks Ltd. In 1984 the R. Whites Morland Road plant closed and has since been redeveloped as Burnham Gardens (note the appropriate name).

In researching this story we discovered that records about R. Whites in Morland Road are, to say the least, sparse! For example, it would be sensible to assume that Whites redeployed the Hobbs steam equipment to pump water for their 1897 factory. Why in October 1968 were neighbours up in arms about the area being continually blanketed by soot from the plant – was it still steam driven? If anyone has information about the R. Whites plant then please do let us know. Did you work there, do you have any photos?

The Co-op Central Dairy
Steve Collins

This is the story of a UK and world-standard-setting enterprise. Their mission: to deliver fresh milk that was safe to drink. That might sound simple, but at the end of the 1920s, milk distribution remained haphazard and often unhygienic. The Co-op's aim was to provide the Croydon area with fresh bottled pasteurised milk with a 36-hour delivery time from udder to doorstep. And they did it. Such an undertaking required huge amounts of water for bottle washing, sterilisation and the pasteurisation process itself. Their chosen site was in Leslie Park Road on the corner of Lebanon Road. In September 1930, they sunk a borehole to tap what they suspected would be an artesian well – and they found it - some 390 feet down (see Chapter Two). With pumps, they were able to extract 7,000 gallons of water an hour, enough to meet the needs of their planned plant

The Minister of Health visiting the Dairy shortly after its opening in 1932.
(C.L.S.L.)

which officially opened on 5 March 1932.

Using electric Dando Ferry pumps, the water was pumped to a water tower capable of holding 13,000 gallons. Milk was delivered to the Dairy in huge (1,300-gallon) glass-lined enamel tanks, straight from the Society's creameries. Some farmers also supplied direct in large churns. At this stage the milk was 'raw', and after careful checking and sampling, was poured into the glass-lined tipping tank and pumped direct to the two storage tanks at the top of the building, each capable of holding 1,300 gallons of milk. The milk then passed through a pre-warmer and heated to 50–95°F by means of low-pressure steam. It was then fed to the clarifier, where all impurities were removed by centrifugal force. Then came the pasteurisation process, where the milk is heated from 95–145°F, the temperature being constantly recorded and checked.

Next came the 'first in the world' glass-enamelled compressed-air powered retarder, which maintained the high temperature for 30 minutes, before passing it on to the cooling room. This served to reduce the temperature to 40°F and, via a large trough, was connected directly to the bottle fillers.

There were initially two bottle-filling machines, capable of filling 140 pint bottles a minute. The sterilised bottles were delivered by a conveyor belt, and the whole filling and capping process was automatic. The bottles were then automatically conveyed for crating (from the crate-washing machine) and sent direct to the cold room for storage. In 1932, bottles were washed at the rate of 9,000 an hour. The cold room was capable of holding 7,000 gallons of 'ready for the morning delivery' bottled milk.

The plant was highly efficient and all equipment was maintained by its own staff. They achieved their aim and in 1932 provided Croydon with 57,000 gallons of milk a week.

Ken Hughes of Rymer Road, who worked at the Dairy for 46 years, takes up the story:

I started work with the Co-op working in their butchers shop opposite the Black Horse, which is

This image: *The Dairy was refurbished in the summer of 1965 and became fully automated. But already the introduction of carton packaging and the supermarket boom were changing the pattern of milk-, and other staple-food, shopping habits. The Dairy closed in March 1987, and demolition started in early 1988 to make way for a housing development on the site.*

Far left: *Ken's lorry.* Left to right: *Janice, Lynda and* (front) *Gillian Angell.*
Left: *The Angells lived opposite the Dairy and, as the staff were working year round, invited them for Christmas dinner. This included Ken who took these photos of the children and their friends.* (All B. & J.A.)

now a betting shop. I was then moved to the Dairy in September 1941 as a bottle washer when I was about 15 years old. Later I became a delivery driver, and for many years drove the same Atkinson lorry, its registration number SBY 200.

During the war milk was shipped to East Croydon Station, direct from farms in the West Country and Gold Top milk came from the Isle of Wight. These arrived in huge six-wheel draw-bar tankers at what became known as 'Milk Wharf' at East Croydon and nipped around the corner to the Dairy for processing.

On 19 April 1941 a high-explosive bomb hit Addiscombe Court Road and caused extensive window and roof damage to the Dairy.

The Dairy employed 14 drivers with an 'inside' staff of some 60-70 people.

When Ken Hughes finally handed in the keys to his SBY 200 delivery lorry, with full permission he removed the registration plate and still has it to this very day.

The Inveterate Inventor: Leslie H. Hounsfield
Steve Collins

Leslie Hounsfield was an extraordinary engineer and remarkable inventor. Born in July 1877, he lived and worked at No. 81 Morland Road from 1934 until his death in September 1957. His factory was situated at the rear of 75-77 Morland Road.

From the outset, his preoccupation was with the deployment of the latest technology for the enhancement of people's lives. If this seems too altruistic to be true, then it is clear that apart from his technical talents, Leslie Hounsfield was also a shrewd businessman.

Amongst many designs and inventions, Hounsfield was responsible for the Trojan motorcar, the Safari camp bed and, rather importantly, the Tensometer – an instrument for accurately measuring and recording the properties of materials.

Initially designing and producing pumps, his first major project happened when considering the travel time wasted by his brother, a local doctor with

91

additional locum duties. In the early 1900s the doctor would travel by horse or bicycle to visit patients. Automobile technology was slowly advancing, but only available to the very wealthy. And of course, just up the road at Crystal Palace on 17 August 1896, Mrs Bridget Driscoll, a 44-year-old mother of two, stepped in to the path of a car and the history books to become the world's first road fatality.

In 1904, Hounsfield started designing a 'utility car' and built the first prototype in 1910 which first ran in 1913. It was powered by a two-stroke, four-cylinder engine mounted vertically between the seats and drove the solid tyre wheels through a chain. Despite other engineering jobs, Hounsfield refined the car and built ten pre-production units – all tested over all types of terrain (including railway sleepers). The car was affordable to the middle-class, the engine was long-lived, and although having a top speed of only 50km/h, had the economy of at least 40 mpg and could climb any hill. Because of its capabilities and endurance it was called the Trojan.

But Hounsfield was a precision engineering company – not a car maker. In 1919, Leyland Motors became interested in the Trojan and were so impressed that, in November 1920, they bought a licence to manufacture, and in 1922 production was in full swing. The proven reliability of the engine, the robust chassis and the ease of manufacture were of great appeal. So adaptable was the same basic rolling chassis that it could be turned into a van or a lorry. By this time the engine was a 1527cc horizontal four-cylinder, two-plug duplex two-stroke developing 12bhp at 1,000 rpm and situated under the front seat. The engine was started by pulling an internal lever, the punt-like chassis was pressed steel and the gearbox two-speed epicyclic – the gear pinion wheels, revolving planet-wise around the fixed axis larger central drive wheel. Even though a clutch pedal was provided, it was seldom used, since the driver quickly learnt to just ease the gear into place. The bonnet housed both the petrol tank and the carburettor.

In 1924 the Trojan, designed by Hounsfield and built by Leylands in their Kingston factory, was generally available as both a car and light van. The car was a two-door, four-seater. Complete with hood and sidescreens it cost £157 – about the same price

Leslie Hounsfield, 1898.
(Reproduced by kind permission from *Can You Afford to Walk?* by Rance and Williams)

(£165) as the 1922-launched Baby Austin 7. For an extra £5 the Trojan sported pneumatic tyres, and for £32.10s.0d., a detachable hard top for those winter trips. The small purchase price, coupled with reliability, good fuel economy and the opportunities of different body work, made the Trojan of great appeal to businesses requiring small delivery vehicles. From 1923 onwards, Brooke Bond was one of the largest fleet operators of the Trojans – so much so, that Dinky Toys made a very popular model of the Trojan in Brooke Bond livery.

The robustness of the Trojan was proven. In December 1926, an original solid-tyred Trojan arrived back in London from Singapore after a 15-month and 12,000 mile road trip.

Hounsfield was a stickler for precision measurement: in particular, the behaviour, suitability and endurance of materials used to make things. During the First World War, his firm was engaged in the manufacture of aircraft parts. Testing of the parts was carried out by one London centre and delays of three months were typical. So Leslie designed his own measurement machine so that he could test locally and continue with production, all safe in the knowledge that when the official test results finally came through, they would confirm his own findings.

The machine was portable, simple to operate and gave a complete picture of the mechanical properties of not only metals, but plastics, textiles and films, and was known as the Tensometer.

Because of its low price, accuracy and versatility, the Tensometer took the world by storm. Through many refinements it remains today as the most ubiquitous essential piece of test equipment that has probably ever been designed.

Leslie Hounsfield left Trojan Ltd in 1930 to concentrate on the development of the Tensometer and his rather natty invention – the Safari camp bed. This combined comfort, flexibility, lightness and portability. It was made of high-tensile spring steel and canvas, with special brackets enabling it to be converted to a chair. Originally invented for use at Hounsfield's weekend chalet at Box Hill, from the 1920s it was made and marketed as a sideline by Trojan. Demand for the camp bed was boosted in the 1930s by the craze for the outdoors and with a succession of hot summers became the favourite for campers, back-garden loungers and, subsequently, the military.

Trojan finally gave up interest in the Safari in 1934 and production was swapped to Hounsfield's new house at Morland Road. He was attracted to the property because of its plate-glass windows, high ceilings and garden area that he turned into a huge aquarium. Visitors viewed this by descending steps into an octagonal chamber to see eight tanks built into its side.

Hounsfield's other interests included water-colour painting, ballroom dancing, and a keen interest in the Croydon Natural History Society of which, in 1950, he was made President.

The Safari Bed business was eventually sold to the camping equipment specialists, Black's of Greenock, in the early 1960s. Part of Tensometer Ltd was taken over by Monsanto in 1970 and moved to Andover in 1971. Remaining was Morland Engineering, specialising in the smaller bench-mounted Tensometer that subsequently became Hounsfield Test Equipment Ltd and is now based in Redhill. The company is run by Martin Hounsfield, whose great uncle was, indeed, Leslie Hounsfield.

No. 81 Morland Road became a filling station, appropriately named 'The Safari', and is now a used car lot - a great shame, after all that inventive engineering heritage.

And talking about engineering excellence in Morland Road, just further down, on the other side at No. 176, we had Gowllands Ltd. Known the world over for their optical and medical equipment, they achieved in their field what Hounsfield had done in others. The prominent Gowllands building was demolished on 5 November 2001.

Leyland publicity for the Trojan Utility, mid-1922. The lady driver became a sales feature in the promotional material that followed the 1922 Motor Show. (Reproduced by kind permission from *Can You Afford to Walk?* by Rance and Williams)

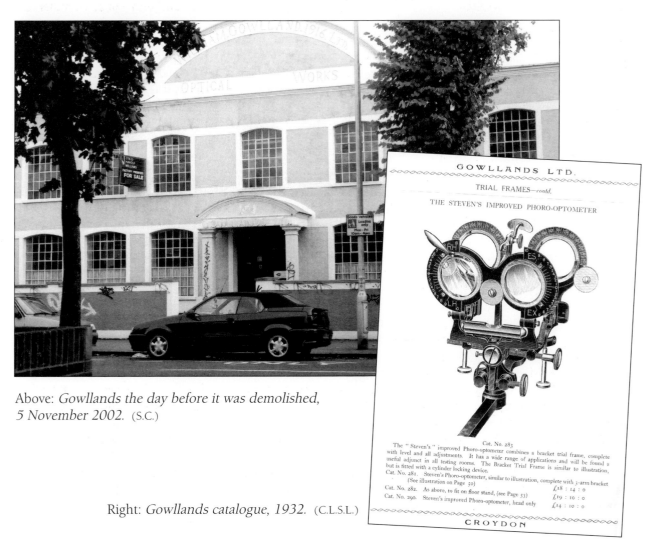

Above: *Gowllands the day before it was demolished, 5 November 2002.* (S.C.)

Right: *Gowllands catalogue, 1932.* (C.L.S.L.)

D.F. Webber & Harrison Webber

Brian Roote with great help from Mr David Webber

The early days: Webbers was started in 1919 by David Frank Webber, the father of the present Managing Director. Leaving school in 1901 at the age of 13 he trained as a cabinet-maker in Drummond Road, Croydon near present-day Debenhams whence the name Drummond Centre is derived. He started a business prior to the First World War but this venture had to close and, as he was medically unfit for the Armed Services, he went to work for De Havilland's at Croydon Airport making airframes for DH9 aircraft. The end of the conflict brought with it a determination in David Webber to start up in business once more and he started manufacturing furniture in a couple of shops in South Croydon in the parade between the Red Deer and Purley Arms public houses.

My mother's family lived nearby in Bynes Road and I will never know whether my father's employment at the firm led to his meeting my mum or whether his meeting my mum led to his employment!

The company was registered in 1929 and continued making the contemporary furniture of the 1920s and '30s but increasing demand for the high-quality goods made a move to larger premises essential and in 1934 the company moved to Sydenham Road where they remain to this day. In addition to furniture some of the first television cabinets for J. Logie Baird also formed part of their output. Sir Malcolm Campbell's house in nearby Epsom was supplied with secure oak cabinets for his many trophies.

Timber goes to war: The start of the Second World War meant that all factories had to go over to war production and Webber's was no exception. Because of the importance of such work many of the workers (my dad amongst them) had their call-up deferred. He finally had the call to arms on 16 April 1942. Because of the gradual reduction in the male workforce ladies were employed as 'polishers' during this period.

During the early days of the conflict, as many readers may recall, even after the siren had sounded it could be some considerable time before any action reached a particular area. So much production was being lost by the employees trooping to the underground shelter and sitting doing nothing that it was decided to set up an 'action watch', whereby two employees would make their way to the roof through a specially-built access hole while the factory kept working. As soon as planes could be seen, the alarm was raised and everyone disappeared. Mr Webber told me that the 'in' joke of the time was that the noise of the two watchers' feet on the wooden stairs when rushing to join their colleagues sounded like

enemy machine gun fire! The underground shelter still exists and is used as a storeroom.

Many different articles were produced at the factory during the war, including ammunition boxes, cases for carrying munitions, and more than a third of the moulds for pouring the concrete for Mulberry Harbours. The premises were damaged in October 1941 when the glass roof of the assembly shop was destroyed by a nearby high-explosive bomb.

Production was only slowed down while staff carried out repairs. More damage occurred in November 1944 when the assembly shop roof and part of the machine shop were destroyed by fire, which caused electric cables to be burnt out leaving many machines idle. Webbers didn't escape the doodlebug menace either as one of these weapons exploded at the junction of Sydenham Road and St James Road in June 1944 blowing off the assembly shop roof.

The Burma War pulled in a lot of orders including one for 338,000 suspension bars for mosquito nets and 500 large cases for flame-throwers. Many of the cases were returned for repair. However, by this time the tide of war had turned and Webbers was helping with bomb-damage restoration work and fitting out Dakota aircraft for VIPs at Croydon Airport. Tents were camouflaged by hand on an adjacent plot of land where the TA building now stands. This was carried out by two ladies wielding nine foot wooden poles with brushes tied to the ends!

The post-war period: Gradually, however, furniture production was restored. The decision of David Webber to concentrate on oak reproduction furniture was regarded with some scepticism by several of the larger manufacturers but that decision has been proved right ever since. My Dad was demobbed in 1946 and started back at the factory. Sadly, modern techniques such as the cellulose spray meant a decreasing need for the skills of French polishing that had been acquired over many years; he decided to try his hand at his own business and left the company in 1949. Ironically, these skills are now in ever-increasing demand and I think he would make a good living in the present-day environment. Today the firm of Webbers Furniture and its 'Croydon' range of reproduction oak furniture is a byword for quality in the trade and it is to be hoped that it will continue to carry the name of Croydon to the far corners of the world for many years to come.

Through all the Changes

Vera King

No matter where you are in Addiscombe you can always meet a friend. It has a delightful village atmosphere and the people really do have a thought for others. I should know, because I have lived here since I was four months old. I had a very happy childhood and I adored my father and mother and sister, Connie, who was a few years older and with whom I shared many secrets. We lived at 206 Lower Addiscombe Road after leaving Dulwich and the house was opposite Sainsbury's - my mother used to boast that she was one of their first customers. We were constantly shopping there and I remember the shop had white slab counters and a black-and-white tiled floor. There was no butchery department early on because there was an excellent family butcher next to Sainsbury's called Heard & Son; in those days shops tried not to encroach on someone else's trade.

One of my earliest recollections was when I was about three-and-a-half years old - Connie and I always had one of the top bedrooms in the front as a playroom, where we saw lots of things happening in the street below, including the old trams which stopped at the bridge at Bingham Halt - and didn't pass the house. About that time my mother was very ill and on her birthday my father took me across the road to a jewellers shop owned by a Mr Tanner. I was fascinated by the eyeglass he wore in one eye (a monocle) and thought it was clever that it didn't fall out. We bought a red-and-clear glass jam spoon which my mother cherished for longer than I can remember.

Next door to Mr Tanner was a Mr Furber who kept an antique business. Later on, around 1945, we had another similar shop on the corner of Everton Road, No. 229 Lower Addiscombe Road, owned by a Mr Turner. Close to Sainsbury's was a baker's shop called Clarke's which also had a small tearoom where ladies would pop in for tea or coffee and cream buns as a break from shopping and, I suspect, to catch up with the local news.

By the time I was four, we moved into a house in Compton Road on the south side of Bingham Road - the Shirley Park area as it is now called. I made very good use of the local park in my schooldays as I was very fond of cycling and loved my 'fairy bike'. The park has always been more or less square, but there used to be a 30" tall iron railing which enclosed what we called 'the ditches'. We had full-time park keepers who mostly wore a uniform - the two I remember were called Fred and George. They kept us all in order but were very kind and our parents felt we were safe in their care.

I went to Hadley House School in Elgin Road, which was later demolished to make room for a block of flats. Whilst I was there it was run by Miss Winstone (known as 'Winnipeg'). We were all frightened of her but she was a good teacher,

getting very good academic results from those boys who successfully passed into Whitgift Grammar School in Haling Park Road, South Croydon, and Whitgift Middle School in North End, Croydon, which was later renamed the Trinity School of John Whitgift and moved to Shirley Park Hotel and grounds - leaving the fine building in North End, which was to be demolished and eventually built up as the Whitgift Centre. My first boyfriend, Peter, was a pupil there and also played the drum in the Cadet Corps - so I bought the piece of music 'Little Drummer Boy' and played it endlessly.

Peter's brother, Bob, was in the choir at the church we attended - St Mary Magdalene (Canning Road) - and apart from a short period when I went to Sunday school at St Mildred's Church I have worshipped there ever since. Dr Budden was the first vicar of St Mildred's in their newly-built church and I recall an actress (Laura La Plante) opening a function there. I went to Sunday school in the now almost derelict church hall next to the park gates - it was pretty old then and is more than ready for demolition now, so I am delighted to know of St Mildred's plans for the future.

Some years later, I think in 1959, Mr Gladwell and I stood opposite our office one evening to wave to Princess Margaret (who sadly died as I wrote this chapter) on her way to the church to attend some dedication service. We waved to her and she waved back. She was beautiful.

At St Mary's Church there was a Youth Club named the '14 to 20 Club' which was formed by three local churches, namely Addiscombe Methodist, the Congregational Church and St Mary Magdalene. A local builder, Bert Berlyn, with offices in Bywood Avenue (near The Glade), led the gym and physical training and the various leaders included the clergy from the three churches. I made many friends there and was always grateful for the help in my early days of Mrs Sunner (known affectionately as 'Sunny') who furthered my interest in the amateur stage. I suppose the '14 to 20 Club' was the real beginning of the friendly connection we had later under the title of the Addiscombe Group of Churches, which now incorporates Our Lady of the Annunciation (Catholic Church) and St Mildred's. There is a strong Christian fellowship between the churches.

With the co-operation of the churches in Croydon, a play entitled A Sword Shall Pierce was written by the Right Revd Bishop Cuthbert Bardsley, one-time Bishop of Croydon, who moved on to Coventry after the war. The production by the Revd Robert Skillern was presented in St Mary Magdalene Church (Addiscombe Parish Church)

Left: *Right Revd Bishop Cuthbert Bardsley is pictured (second left) visiting St Mary Magdalene in 1952. Bardsley Close in Park Hill is named after him.* (V.K.)

Below left and right and bottom: Passion Play, *a production in 1954.* (S.R.)

and was attended by over 1,000 people every night for a week and also for three nights in Beckenham. It was a very moving play in which I also took part. Bardsley Close in Park Hill is named after the former Bishop. Similarly, Fisher Close in Addiscombe took its name from the Archbishop of Canterbury at that time. At St Mary's I was also introduced to Terry Waite who was the late Lord Runcie's envoy, and who later experienced the ordeal of great hardship during imprisonment in the East.

Late in 1940, Mr Algernon Leighton Gladwell purchased from a Mr Albert Holmes the business which was then known as Holmes Co. and it was renamed A.L. Gladwell (Holmes & Co.). The office was then at 289a Lower Addiscombe Road, premises now owned by Graham Murphy under the title Design Lighting. At that time the building was in two halves, one occupied by W.F. Marriott & Son (Jewellers) and the other by Mr Gladwell, together with the flat above.

Vera King with Algernon Gladwell. (V.K.)

Upon completing a two-and-a-half-year Business Course with Pitman's College, I became a Junior Shorthand/Typist with A.L. Gladwell who trained me in all aspects of estate agency which included rent collections, finding my visits to tenants very amusing from time to time, account work on the ledgers, letting of furnished and unfurnished properties and preparing inventories. In fact, all my training came from Mr Gladwell who led me though to the professional career I have today.

He was an excellent businessman - clearheaded and able to tackle most problems. He was kind and thoughtful and made many friends in the profession. The business grew and we had to take on extra staff, and we moved to 299 Lower Addiscombe Road - which was originally Cooper's Toy Shop. There was very little selling immediately after the war - renting was more popular although the Rent Restrictions Act 1939/45 was very much feared by landlords because it gave protection to tenants and rents were controlled. If a house became empty the owners would quickly get some furniture in, with the hope that the local Council would not requisition if it looked occupied. Once requisitioned it was impossible to get the house back for private occupation unless a landlord could prove real hardship.

There was also the Rent Tribunal which operated restrictions on the amount of rent charged for furnished or unfurnished accommodation. I remember one of the first tribunal cases to blaze across the front page of the Croydon Advertiser was one of our own. We let the flat over our old premises to a couple for £4.4s.0d. per week inclusive of rates. Two days after they had moved in (despite having signed a Tenancy Agreement) they applied to the Rent Tribunal and were responsible for the local headlines 'Estate Agent's Rent Slashed to £2.12s.0d'. That flat today (2002) would be let for an average of £500 per month.

In contrast with the Rent Restrictions Act, the various Housing Acts between 1977 and today provide the opportunity to enter into an Assured Shorthold Tenancy, permitting a landlord to let for a certain period (not less than six months) and being assured that he can obtain possession of his property at the end of the period.

I remember that some houses were built under licence with a restriction that they were sold for a limited price. Some were built and sold for £2,500 whereas those houses (greatly improved by extensions) can now fetch nearly £200,000.

The first house we sold for redevelopment was 162 Lower Addiscombe Road - such an impressive property - I was sorry to see the sign outside 'Watch it come down by Syd Bishop'.

With decimalisation in the early 1970s came another change in prices which were almost doubled overnight and there was tremendous competition amongst agents, but we always maintained a good service to our clients. Both Mr Gladwell and I were members of the Croydon & District Auctioneers' & Surveyors' Association (originally founded in 1925) and the aim of the association was to control the behaviour of its members and we all had to abide by the Rules of Conduct. The Association still exists today. I found the meetings with other agents and surveyors most helpful and we all enjoyed a close friendship and business association.

In 1963 I became a Partner with Mr Gladwell and the firm became known as Gladwell & King, and a few years later I purchased the business and Mr Gladwell continued as a Consultant. He maintained his interest in the firm, travelling from his home in Bexhill and working in the office three or four days a week.

In the early 1960s I became a member of the Valuers' Institute and was later upgraded to the

Vera King presenting keys of an ambulance on behalf of the Croydon & District Auctioneers and Surveyors' Association, 1977. (V.K.)

The ISVA by Royal Charter merged with the Royal Institute of Chartered Surveyors in 2000, thereby changing my professional status to FRICS.

I have been asked to comment on the 'changing face of estate agency': suffice it to be said that it is very different from the old days. Our firm has not changed its traditional methods and continues to give personal attention to every one of our clients. I believe that the friendly personal approach is the best way to sell and negotiate, preferably face to face. Computers and internet have become popular, but will estate agency lose its personal touch?

Incorporated Society of Valuers & Auctioneers. For some years I served on the Council Committee of the Croydon & District Auctioneers' & Surveyors' Association and the South East London branch of the Incorporated Society of Valuers & Auctioneers. I learned a great deal from my colleagues in both societies. I was honoured to be President of the Local Association in the Queen's Jubilee year 1977 and enjoyed every moment of my year of office, meeting many important people.

Sadly, Mr Gladwell died in August 1977 having worked at the office until a month before - I was devastated to lose such a close friend and colleague who had given me a wonderful career, but life has to go on and fortunately hard work always helps to bridge the gap. Despite everything, 1977 was a wonderful year.

Five years later, in 1982, I was honoured by my professional society, the Incorporated Society of Valuers & Auctioneers, when I was elected Chairman of the South East London branch. This was an interesting and demanding position working with very experienced fellow ISVA members on the Branch Council. Regular meetings were held with lectures and studying under the society's requirements for Continuing Professional Development (CPD), coupled, of course, with enjoyable social functions over which I presided.

As mentioned, property prices rose in 1970 overnight and they continued to rise until eventually a three-bedroomed house worth £27,000 in 1980 was being sold for £107,000 in 1988, but this sudden price boom was soon to present the ugly face of recession when many young purchasers lost a lot of money. The recession lasted for about seven years and the three-bedroomed houses that were as low as £82,500 then picked up again and are now fetching £180,000 to £220,000 at the time of writing.

Where we are located we are very fortunate in enjoying a friendly relationship with good neighbours - Hawkins (gentlemen's outfitters) at 297 and Vic Gibson (family butcher) at 301 which was once Hockey & Brimacombe, and Leslie (fruiterers) once Foster's at 303. Older readers may also remember: Ernest Todd (corn chandler), Swonnell's Hardware Store, United Dairies, the Express Dairy, the Gas Board, Community Kitchen and The Noah's Ark to name just a few.

Over the past 30 years, we have had an 'all ladies staff', to whom I owe much of my success. Readers will realise by now that I am very attached to Addiscombe and our residents - many of whom are past and present clients - so I like to think that Gladwell & King will go on for many years to come.

Ten

Growing up in Addiscombe

Some Things Change, Some Don't

Contributors include: Bill and Joan Angell, Ivy Binstead, Lynda Blaker, Arthur Burns, Mary Chandler, Peter Crosier, Jan Dyer, Marian Gilliam, David Gowers, Pat Haworth, Gill Hulne, Peter and Christine Lockley, Cliff Marlow, Michael Mead, Paul Nihill, Margaret Robson, Kathleen Spalding and David Blake.

Looking at the experiences of people who have grown up at different times in Addiscombe, from the early part of the twentieth century up to the start of the 1960s, it is interesting to see how the concerns of children stay the same over the years: going to school, having fun in the holidays, going shopping with Mum, making friends and, of course, visiting that favourite sweet shop.

The conditions in which people were born reflect the social diversity of Addiscombe, greater in the past than today. Some were born in comfortable nursing homes like Uplands, 54 Ashburton Road whose Matron was Miss Rust. Other mothers had a tougher time. Kathleen Spalding (now a vivacious 80-something) relates:

Above left: *Uplands Nursing Home, Ashburton Road, with Matron Rust in 1933. The twins in the background are the Jagger twins who later featured in the 'Which one has the Toni perm?' advert.* (M.C.)
Above right: *Henry and Kathleen Huntley in Albert Road, 1924.* (K.S.)

I was born on 29 June 1920 in the Croydon Infirmary, Croydon Workhouse as my mother called it, because she had to scrub all the corridors to earn her keep, as my father had died in Croydon General Hospital in March 1920. My sister was eight years and my brother was two years. When my mother came home with me, the Relief Man came to see her to discuss about help but told her she was young enough to go out to work and put her children in a home. But Mother said never, so she went out to work in local shops, Pollards the dairy and Burrs the baker, both in Lower Addiscombe Road. She worked all her life until she died in 1948 aged 61 years at 154 Cherry Orchard Road.

School Days

Most of us will remember our school, whether we loved it or loathed it. Marian Gilliam, born in 1912, lived the first part of her life in Lebanon Road and attended Oval School. The only teacher she can recall is a Miss Goodfellow, but other memories include 'cold classrooms, small coal fires and desks for two'. Lessons were practical, for as well as maths, history and geography, she recalls sewing, knitting and basket work, which started her off doing handicrafts, which she has continued all her life.

Ivy Binstead, born in 1915, also attended Oval School. Ill health meant that she started late at the age of seven and missed a lot of lessons, but she had a happy childhood and enjoyed school:

On the way to school walking through Cross Road, I passed three sweet shops, two grocers, our boot menders (Mr Duncan) and at the top of the road was the forge. It was fascinating to watch the men at the anvil shoeing the horses. Sometimes this made us late for school.

Ivy describes herself as 'a terrible bookworm':

... so much so that they eventually found out that I

Oval School, 1936. (P.D.)

Morland Road Nursery School, 1946. (M.R.)

Oval School in the 1940s. (M.R.)

Oval School May Queen in 1950, with Jackie Spalding pictured on the left. (J.F.)

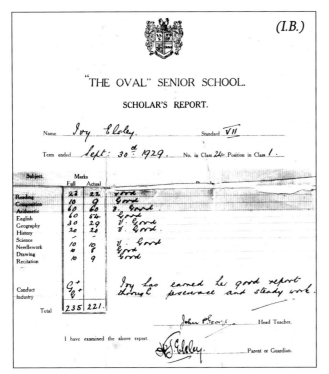

(I.B.)

"THE OVAL" SENIOR SCHOOL.

SCHOLAR'S REPORT.

Name *Ivy Eloley.* Standard *VII*

Term ended *Sept. 30th 1929.* No. in Class *24* Position in Class *1*

Subject	Marks Full	Actual	
Reading	23	22	Good
Composition	10	9	Good.
Arithmetic	40	40	V. Good.
English	60	54	Good.
Geography	30	29	V. Good.
History	20	20	V. Good.
Science	—		
Needlework	10	10	V. Good
Drawing	10	8	Good
Recitation	10	9	Good
Conduct	G+		Ivy has earned her good report
Industry	G+		through perseverance and steady work.
Total	235	221	

John George Head Teacher.

I have examined the above report.

J. Eloley. Parent or Guardian.

was very short sighted and slow at lessons, which improved when they moved me to a front desk in class and fitted me with glasses. To stop me reading so much my mother went to a jumble sale at the Mission Hall and bought me a magnificent dolls' house, dated 1811, that was turned out by Lady King, a member of St Matthews. This did help to keep me from books for a time.

By the age of 14 Ivy had done so well at school that she became Head Girl. This was also the year that she left school, the leaving age being earlier than it is now.

Kathleen Spalding, born in 1920, also remembers the practical elements of school work. She achieved her housewifery certificate when she was nearly 14; this involved learning how to make beds, beat carpets and cook a roast dinner. For boys the equivalent was woodwork lessons.

Cliff Marlow was born in 1929 and at the age of five moved with his family to Lebanon Road. Like Marian Gilliam a generation earlier, he also went to school at Oval Road. He remembers the school day running from 9 in the morning until noon and then from 2 o'clock until 4 o'clock in the afternoon. A quarter of an hour before the start of the morning and afternoon sessions a bell would ring in the belfry, but it was the five-minute bell which would spur Cliff and his friends to hurry so as not to be late. Cliff's school-days were happy. He was taught by Mr George and Miss Huggett, both of whom had taught his mother before him.

Margaret Robson, born in the year when the Second World War broke out, first attended a nursery in Morland Road with her brother John and sister Veronica. Later she also went to Oval School and remembers it as an old building, freezing cold. It certainly would have been cold during the winter of 1947, one of the coldest on record. She was taught by a Mr Cox, who coached his pupils for the 11-plus exam which Margaret passed. Margaret can also recall how her Nan drove a Post Office van and used to pick up the children from school, but they would have to hide in the back under the sacks because it wasn't meant to be used for such purposes!

Paul Nihill (also b.1939), remembers a more impressive method of getting to school for one family:

At the bottom of Grant Road lived a family whose kids were the scruffiest ones around. Their dad was a chauffeur who used to drive a Rolls-Royce. On occasions he would drive the kids to school in Woodside... in the mid 1940s very few people owned cars; so you can imagine the scene when this lot pulled up outside the school in a shiny Rolls-Royce.

Paul also recalls:

At the junction of Lower Addiscombe Road and Morland Road stood a large building that in the war was used as a Civic Restaurant. It catered for workers and families who could not afford too much. At Oval School those children on school dinners would have their meals there. We used to walk in twos from the school down Cherry Orchard Road every lunch-time to get there. There was quite a large overgrown garden out the back and it was possible to gain access to the basement as a further place to play.

Another resident of Lebanon Road was Pat Angell, born a couple of years after the end of the war, so just coming up to 13 years old as the 1960s began. She attended Lady Edridge Grammar School for Girls and remembers life as being 'pretty mundane with me going to school and concentrating on homework in the evenings.' But things were soon to change, when she went to the Fairfield Halls one evening in 1962 and saw a little-known group called The Beatles... more on them later.

Out of School

No matter how enjoyable school is, every child looks forward to home-time and the chance to get out and play with their friends. Marian Gilliam recalls:

There was a children's home on the corner of Cedar Road and we used to play in the fields in Brickwood Road. The games we played were hopscotch, marbles, skipping, hoops and on May Day we danced around the Maypole. Later on I did gymnastics in a hall in Oval Road and joined the Guides. There was a skating rink in Cherry Orchard Road and smithy in Cross Road.

Ivy Binstead says that growing up in the 1920s with money being scarce meant she had to make her own amusements:

Arts and crafts were prominent; knitting, crochet, painting, jigsaw puzzles. I used to make bead flowers and brooches and made quite a bit on the side selling them.

She also spent a lot of time playing happily by herself with her dolls, 'arranging them all out on the sofa and treating them to school lessons.' By the age of ten, Ivy had joined the Bluebells, an organisation similar to the Brownies but run by the Woman's Christian Association. A year later she had become a Guide and remembers her captain, Miss Marjorie Cox:

... a wonderful person; understanding, helpful and encouraging. She lived in a big house in Park Hill Road. We used to go through the alleys from East Croydon Station to be tested for badges at her house. We were not afraid of going alone or in the dark.

Bill Angell, born in 1923, has lived in Lebanon Road for most of his life. He recalls playing in the streets, which were virtually free of cars in the 1920s, although 'the only threat was being run over by Harris and Bailey's coal cart.' Football and cricket were played at the bottom of Lebanon Road.

He also remembers some of the more mischievous antics of his childhood, including the game of 'Tinker Button'. As he explains:

This involved creeping up to a person's lighted window - curtains were naturally drawn - with a large button tied onto a strong pin and long length of string. The pin was carefully pressed into the woodwork and a quiet retreat was performed whilst trailing the string behind. From a distance we could gently pull the string; the button would tap on the window. A well-organised withdrawal was made before the occupier could discover what the noise was.

Another caper involved the Builders Arms pub. In those days the building had two doors to the main front, one on the left which led to the Bottle and Jug where you could buy beer to take away and another on the right which led to the public bar. Both of these doors opened away from each other. The job was to tie the two handles together. You can imagine what happened when someone

tried to exit the pub. Charlie Lambert was in no doubt as to who was to blame and would come haring up the road after us. Because of our youth we were always a little too fast for him. Incidentally in those days Charlie only sold beer and no spirits.

Arthur Burns, a Lebanon Road contemporary of Bill Angell, born in 1925, has many memories of a variety of different childhood pursuits:

Whip tops could be kept going the length of the road by constant whipping, but more expertise was required for the peg tops, which were spun by winding string around them and then throwing them forward upside down, so that when the string was pulled while they were in flight the tops were jerked into the upright spinning position as they landed.

Marbles were very much in vogue at one stage, being launched along the road gutters to hit a marble a few feet ahead that your fellow player had thrown. If your marble hit his, it was yours. White ones with streaks of red were called 'bloods' and were very desirable. I suppose I must have been successful at this because I had dozens and one day I decided I was bored with playing marbles, opened a front bedroom window and flung them all out into the road amongst kids playing there. After the initial surprise, the resultant scramble was something to see!

Very popular for a while were pram wheels - if you could get hold of a single one, through the central axle hole of which a wooden stick was wedged with one end projecting about two inches. A long stick completed this mobile toy, being

Above left: *Lebanon Road, 1919.* (J.G.)
Above right: *St Mary's Boys Club at Ifield Camp near Gatwick in 1940. The usual venue, Fulking in Sussex, was a 'no-go area' owing to possible invasion.* Left to right: *Bill Angell, John Stratton, Sid Simmons, John Fisher.* (B. & J.A.)

placed under the projecting stick, so that it would push the wheel along. I became expert at bouncing the wheel up on the pathway from the road and went everywhere with my 'mobile', shops included.

We had four-wheeled carts that had the sophisticated steering of a bit of string to each side of the front axle. I had one and would take it to the top of the road to then shoot down it at considerable speed. This was normally on the road itself but on one occasion I was on the path when the steering jammed in the left direction whilst on 'my' side of the road, i.e. even numbers side. There was no brake so I shot out on to the road, my head missing by a hair's breadth a window cleaner's bucket which hung beneath one end of his small cart. I shot into the road, across to the other side and crashed into the kerb. Although traffic was almost non-existent then, I remember thinking it would be just my luck to be across the road while a coal lorry was coming down; [I was] so relieved there wasn't one.

Then there were stilts, which were usually two odd pieces of wood, each with a foot 'step' about two feet off the ground. Mr Cole up the road from me made me a pair, one of which was a proper piece of timber, perhaps 2 inches square, the other a rough old bit of fence paling – and I was delighted with them, using them once to go up Lebanon, left into Addiscombe, left into Addiscombe Court, left into Leslie Park and left finally back in Lebanon. Proud? You bet. Mr Cole became Croydon's Mayor. He had three sons, Harry, Ron and John, Harry being the eldest and a friend of mine. I am quite confident that, if presented with these treasures today, I could handle them!

Roller skates were owned by rich kids, i.e. those whose fathers had jobs. I borrowed a pair one day and put them on to roll from the top of Lebanon Road in style – which meant going faster and faster, not being possessed of the expertise needed to apply a 'brake' by dragging one skate sideways behind the other. I became very alarmed, crouched down – and sat down! Can you imagine that? I can feel the impact now!

Arthur can also recall Ron Glaysher, one of Lebanon Road's characters:

He and his mother were two of a kind... I can see (and hear) to this day Mrs Glaysher standing in the middle of the road outside their house calling Ron in to dinner. He would be up by Cedar Road and hear her plainly - we all did - and yell 'OK, Mum' in the same tone and volume. It amused me at the time and it does now to remember it.

Outside Peter Crosier's home at 11 Tunstall Road in 1926. Pictured are Peter's mother and neighbours, Aunty Glad and Uncle Fred Webb. (P.C.)

Peter Crosier, born in 1928, was an only child. When he was quite small he had a blue furry doll called Rosemary. 'I used to tell callers to the house that I had a baby sister in the cupboard (where the doll was kept)!' When he was able to walk he would go from the house in Tunstall Road to the nearby Co-op bottling depot and watch the crates of empty bottles go in for washing and he can also remember his mother taking him to the blacksmith's in Cross Road to see the horses being re-shod.

Cliff Marlow says that the lack of traffic (a few years later in the 1930s) meant that the streets were safe for children to play in. One game involved hanging on to the back of the horse and cart belonging to Boxall the greengrocer. He would drive his cart along Cedar Road and turn into Lebanon Road, hardly stopping. The children on roller skates would wait for him to come out of Cedar Road and quickly grab the cart for a lift up the road.

Paul Nihill recalls from the 1940s:

Geoffrey Stringman lived in Grant Road and was the one person responsible for showing me the 'world'. As six- and seven-year-olds we ventured on our own all over the place ending up as far afield as Riddlesdown and Kenley. Kids wouldn't be safe to travel this far without an adult today but things were different then. I certainly had adventure in me for it wasn't long after chumming up with Geoffrey that I would catch a 12 bus to London and spend the day sightseeing. It cost just 5d. I would visit museums and places like the Tower of London and would be away all day.

Our favourite place to visit was Addington Hills which we always called Shirley Hills. We'd spend hours exploring the hills. Nearby was the bombed-out windmill house, a shell of a very large building which was a popular haunt for all the kids. It stood close to Shirley Windmill which in those days was surrounded by fields.

Local bomb patches were another of our favourite play places. Andrew Bashford and I were a mischievous pair and often didn't return home until dark having been out all day. His mum would sometimes make us take his sisters, Dianne and Caroline, with us, which really cramped our style.

At the top of the rise of Radcliffe Road the surface changed to flintstones and I used to knock the stones together and produce sparks. From this spot on it was mainly open land. On the immediate left was a field where two horses grazed. Bomber and Dodger were their names. I would guess this was round about 1947/48. Me and Andrew Bashford would climb over the fence at the back of the land where the two horses were and battle our way through the thick undergrowth. A little further on was a rifle range and we would spy on the men firing their guns. When they had left the site, we'd go and look for empty shells.

Below: *A high-explosive bomb-damaged site by the Black Horse in mid September, 1940.* (C.T.)

Paul's other interests included sports and he remembers Addiscombe Recreation Ground, which he knew then as Bingham Halt Park:

On this small ground I have played competitive football and cricket, and run races on it. The very first race I ever won was at this park in the summer of 1951. Oval Junior School used to hold their annual sports day there and I was first home in the 60-yard sprint.

Paul achieved an unofficial sporting record aged 13:

In the old days Hastings Road was always considered posher than Warren Road, probably because Warren Road had the most kids in it. Warren Road, when I was a nipper, would have compared with Coronation Street; everybody knew each other and there was a great community spirit. One evening me and my mates decided to see how many laps of the block we could run non-stop. This meant running up Warren Road along a stretch of Lower Addiscombe Road and into Hastings Road, a lap of approximately 500 yards in distance. I carried on running miles after the rest, finally quitting having completed 43 laps. Even then it was not due to tiredness but boredom at running on my own.

These early sporting achievements led on to greater things, for Paul was to win the silver medal for the 50km walk at the Tokyo Olympics in 1964, and in 1976 he was awarded the MBE for services to sport.

This was formerly a farmhouse until the arrival of the railway in 1864. The house remained until the mid-twentieth century in Hastings Road. (C.L.S.L.)

∾ Ashburton Park & Estate ∾

What was known as Ashburton Park lies on the site of a mansion, which was built in 1788 and known from 1869 to 1878 as Stroud Green House. At one time it was owned by the horse-racing celebrity Henry Dorling, stepfather to Mrs Beeton. The estate was acquired in 1878 by Reverend Father Tooth, founder of the 'Community of the Paraclete', and became known as Woodside Convent, with a chapel constructed in the grounds. He established St Michael's orphanage for the sons of gentlemen under the care of six sisters of his community, subject to his own rules, and later for inebriates. Father Tooth had a mixed reputation. Marian Gilliam can remember the sisters visiting her grandfather's chemist shop in Royal Parade. The Croydon Corporation purchased the site in 1924 and the mansion was demolished soon afterwards. The remaining building today houses Ashburton Library. (All photographs J.G.)

Left: Addiscombe Recreation Ground. Originally part of the Ashburton estate, the land was acquired under the 1875 Public Health Act in 1905 and was laid out by 1911. It is also known as Bingham Recreation Ground. (J.G.)

The 56th Croydon Cubs, 1951. (M.M.)

Outside the Co-op Dairy, c.1957. This picture was taken by Ken Hughes, driver. Left to right: *Janice, Lynda and Patricia Angell, Marion Richardson.* (B. & J.A.)

Over in Woodside during the 1950s, Michael Mead was a keen member of the local Cub pack, the 56th Croydon, which was run by the Lovelace and Hollingsworth families from Woodside Green. The group was attached to the Baptist Church in Spring Lane and used to meet in a clubhouse off Cloister Gardens. Like Paul Nihill, Michael had a keen interest in sport, although his father insisted that piano practice had to come before evening cricket or football games in Ashburton Park.

Making your own entertainment was true for Margaret Robson, who played in a skiffle group with some of her friends in the 1950s. They would meet in the basement of the Express Dairy at the top of Morland Road, close to the Leslie Arms, and Margaret would sit on an old wooden chair and play the washboard.

Music played an important part in Pat Angell's life too. A teenager in 1962, she remembers going to the Fairfield Halls with a school friend to see the pop singer Johnny Leyton. Unfortunately he couldn't appear because of illness and was replaced by a little-known group called The Beatles. As Pat says:

My friend and I were suddenly in love [with them] *and from then on life revolved around the group. We went to Heathrow Airport to see them on their return from abroad, once playing truant from school and once getting our photograph in every daily paper out at the time.*

Pat's sister, Lynda, recalls going to a friend's house with a couple of mates: 'We had such fun, dressing up and playing records, pretending to be at the local hop, which of course came later when we were older.' She also used to go to the Oval Road Youth Club with her sisters, where they would dance and put on singing shows.

Another of the Angell sisters, Jan, says that living in Lebanon Road in the '60s was great fun. The family lived opposite the Co-op bottling depot and Jan went with the delivery drivers on their rounds. On Sundays she remembers getting up early and going to Tonbridge, which seemed a very long way away.

Sister, Gill, has a memory of the Builders Arms, a pub which seems to have attracted its fair share of playful youngsters. She and her friends would play on roller skates or bikes. The pub had a first-floor room on the right-hand side, under which the kids used to play. 'It was in effect a tunnel - ideal for skating in and out of,' recalls Jill. This didn't go down too well with the landlady at the time, a blonde woman with a lot of make-up - Gill thinks she might have been the forerunner of Coronation Street's Bet Lynch!

It certainly seems that playtime out of school is remembered as carefree, fun and safe in Addiscombe over the years.

Home & Family

Some of the biggest changes over the last century have occurred in the home: improvements to comfort, with central heating and double glazing; more labour-saving devices such as washing machines and microwave ovens; and the possibility of entertainment in your own home provided by radio, TV, videos and now computer games and the internet.

Things were certainly different in the 1920s, as recalled by Ivy Binstead. She lived at 34 Leslie Grove:

... a smallish house, three bedrooms leading off one another, a small front room, larger kitchen/dining-room and what we called the scullery. It had a walk-in larder next to a coal cupboard and a big stone copper with a place to burn wood or coal to heat the water. Most of this was later removed and modernised by my father, and we had a bath fitted which was covered by a wooden lid. For some years we also had a wooden and iron mangle. Originally we also had an old-fashioned kitchen range, but this was replaced by an open tiled fireplace.

I remember the old gramophone which took pride of place in the front room, along with the aspidistra which my father I think killed, but it was my mother's pride and joy. Anyway the gramophone had a huge horn. We had a good supply of records. My father used to give record recitals, mostly to his gardening club. Later in my teens I had a portable which you could shut up like a suitcase for easy carrying. I had and still have a good many small records purchased from Woolworths for 6d. each.

Above: *In a Selwood Road back garden, 1930s.* (M.C.)
Left: *Ivy's father brought this doll back from France on his return from the First World War in 1921.* (I.B.)
This image: *The back garden of 34 Leslie Grove, 1920s. Ivy's father created an enchanted garden.* (I.B.)

The family also had a harmonium and later 'a pianola you put rolls in and pedalled furiously and it sounded as though you were really playing difficult pieces.' Around 1926 Ivy's father built a crystal set with 'lots of wires and valves and a tiny crystal. You had to adjust the needle - or cat's whisker as it was called - on to this crystal.' She remembers listening to Uncle Mac's 'Children's Hour' through a pair of bulky and uncomfortable earphones while eating her tea and even had her name read out over the air when it was her birthday.

There was no television then and it would not be until considerably later that Ivy first had one. For her though, home entertainment meant:

... a good sing-song round the harmonium and later the piano. We also had evenings with friends when everybody contributed a song, a joke, a poem, charades or games. We amused ourselves very cheaply in those days.

David Gowers also has memories of the 1920s and early '30s, growing up in what was then a comparatively new house:

... 103 Meadvale Road was quite new in our early years, having been built around 1923. It had a living-room, a front room (lounge) and a kitchen downstairs and two bedrooms plus a boxroom upstairs. There was no bathroom or toilet in the house, the lavatory being outside in the backyard - mighty cold in the winter - and except on bath nights we had to wash at the kitchen sink.

He continues:

The kitchen had a cooker in one corner, a copper boiler at the back under a chimney outlet and along one wall, between the sink and the copper, was a huge wooden worktop. This was hinged to the wall and on bath night, i.e. Fridays, it would be raised to reveal a large cast-iron bath. This would be filled with boiling water from the copper and, one after another or sometimes in twos, we four boys would have our baths. We had to stay in the living-room whilst Mum and Dad had theirs, sometimes before and sometimes after ours! As the soap used on these occasions was the standard Lifebuoy or Sunlight 'washing bar' our faces and bodies really shone when we were finished!

With four boys in the family, sleeping arrangements were a little crowded:

The middle bedroom was the main one for the boys and sometimes, especially when we were younger, all four of us would be in the same bed,

top to toe. Later on the boxroom was turned into another bedroom and one or two of us would be transferred there.

David also has strong memories of the clothes they wore:

... usually grey flannel shorts, knitted grey socks, a knitted grey jumper with a wide collar with perhaps a coloured edging to it. Footwear was usually brown sandals or heavy black shoes, very serviceable! Grey wool was in extraordinary good supply, nearly every mother could knit quite fast and all seemed to be using grey. Socks, of course, developed holes very quickly and another skill of most mothers and housewives was to make neat darns to mend the holes.

Home entertainment came mainly from the wireless. David clearly remembers the excitement of the arrival of the first set:

Dad had been to Radio Olympia in London and came back with this intriguing carton. When he opened it, out came a shiny dark brown cabinet with a tree design over a shaped piece of material in the centre of the front, with 'Ekco' in the corner. There was a length of electric wire hanging from it and on the bottom was a turntable. Dad then went to a shelf he had made in the corner of the living-room, about at eye level, and removed the vase which had been on it. He placed the new toy on the shelf and then threaded the lead through a hole at the back of the shelf and plugged it in to an electric socket.

I think I was the only one up and awake at this time but I remember how we all felt when, after a few crackles and other sundry squeaks, a voice came through the material, which I learnt was called the speaker. Dad then turned the wireless sideways back and forth on its turntable until the sound was the best he could get it.

The next day David's father put up a pole in the garden to which a wire from the wireless was attached to make an aerial to improve the reception. David comments:

I remember that the urgency of getting the wireless set up properly was to hear the commentary on an important heavyweight boxing match involving, I think, Tommy Farr. Anyway, I was allowed to stay up to listen. Another important function of the wireless was to keep children quiet. There was 'Children's Hour' with Uncle Mac telling stories, and at tea time on Sundays we would sit around the living-room table to listen to the Ovaltinies programme and decipher the coded message put out for us members of the Ovaltinies Club. Our new wireless made us a very proud family!'

Cliff Marlow has memories of music in the family when he was growing up in the 1930s. His mother could play the piano and Cliff's family would visit his grandmother in West Croydon to have a sing-song. Cliff's cousin, Margy, would also play the piano and his older cousin, Bert, could play the drums. This inspired young Cliff to practise drumming at home with nails on red Oxo tins; he also used to hang up milk bottles with varying amounts of water in them to make different sounds.

Cliff also recalls how homes were heated at the time: 'Central heating in those days was only for the most wealthy. Heating was usually by coal fire in rooms and stone hot-water bottles for beds.'

By the time Paul Nihill was enjoying music in the 1950s and '60s, things had moved on from the days of the wind-up gramophone and crystal set:

David Saunders lived opposite the Harris family in Warren Road. He was the first person I knew whose family owned a radiogram. I loved listening

to music around there. His younger brother, Phil, was lead singer of the then well-known local band, Glenn Athens and the Trojans. In 1965 and 1966 they were voted top semi-professional band in the country.

According to Michael Mead:

... entertainment at this time was what you made of it yourself. The radio was of course important with programmes such as 'Dick Barton,' 'Paul Temple' and 'Journey into Space' most prominent.

Meanwhile the Angell family remember good times in the 1960s, despite Bill having had health problems with both tuberculosis and a heart condition. His wife Joan had to cope with money being in short supply and four girls to look after, but daughter, Lynda, remembers the time with much affection and says that despite their problems:

... it was more than made up for by the amount of love we were given by both our parents... growing up in Lebanon Road was eventful, good fun and very much different from what it is today.

The cadet band on the old Fair Field, 1942. (C.T.)

On the roof of St James Lodge, Lower Addiscombe Road, c.1943.
Left to right: *Claude Glover (guitar), Cliff Marlow (drums),
Stan Woodall (clarinet).* (C.M.)

*James Drasey, cinema
page boy, 1930.* (J.T.)

Left: *A Croydon Empire
Programme from the 1940s.* (K.S.)

came out from Plough Lane to
Brighton Road, Purley and Purley
Fountain by the waterworks. There
we sat for a while and watched the
traffic, people coming home, in cars,
motor bikes, cycles from a day out in
the country or from Brighton. Then
back home by tram arriving home
pleasantly tired, the whole outing
costing just a few pence.

At other times they would go to Park
Hill Recreation Ground to listen to the
band playing. Ivy recalls:

*We would sit on the round seats. Dad might meet
some of his cronies but said his greatest pleasure
was watching the fashions. I suspect though it was
the girls.*

If Ivy's father had had a good week and a little more
money was available, they would travel further afield:

*Sometimes we would go from home right up to
Westminster Bridge and on to Marble Arch, where
we would go into Lyons Corner House where for
about 1 shilling you could have a slap-up tea while
listening to a light orchestra. We would walk back
through Hyde Park to get the tram for home,
arriving very tired but happy.*

For Arthur Burns, cinema was the big draw:

*I went almost always on Saturday afternoons when
it was 6d. for any seat in the house before 8p.m.
Saturday morning was the 'tuppenny rush' at the*

On the Town

Family entertainment did not only take place at
home; there were plenty of other things to do to keep
children entertained. Marian Gilliam remembers the
skating rink in Cherry Orchard Road, later to become
the site of Creed's engineering works. She also did
gymnastics in a hall in Oval Road and joined the
Guides. Sunday-afternoon trips were real treats for
Ivy and her family:

*Sometimes in the late afternoon, we would go for
a long walk or a tram ride - a penny transfer from
the top of the road to West Croydon Station, then
another tram to Stafford Road, then all fields to
Plough Lane. We would walk through Plough
Lane until we came to the spot where the aero-
planes crossed from the hangers to the airfield.
They were only small planes but the exhaust was
dreadful and used to make me feel really sick. I
was glad when we got past there. We eventually*

Empire in North End, which was packed with kids yelling 'Look behind yer' to cowboy heroes about to be shot in the back. I sniffily avoided such low behaviour!'

Cliff Marlow remembers something similar at the Odeon in North End, with children queuing up outside the cinema on a Saturday morning. Once the doors were open, they would clamber over the tops of the seats to reach the front, such was the rush for the best seats. The 'tuppenny rush' was a treat as 2d. was a lot of money for someone of Cliff's age.

Although Cliff's father had a job with London Transport, money could not be wasted and Cliff soon learnt this when he wore a new pair of shoes in the snow. He helped his friends make a snowman, but by the time he got home the shoes were soaked through and ruined. His father pointed out that in order to replace them, the family would not be able to afford to see The Crazy Gang perform at the London Palladium.

However, Cliff's musical talents meant that he was performing himself by the age of 15 to 16, running a three-piece band: alto sax, piano and drums *(see previous page)*. They got local bookings, playing mainly dance music at halls and clubs, although some of the popular tunes were not to Cliff's taste!

At the age of 16, Peter Lockley joined the Sir Phillip Game Boys' Club in Morland Avenue, where he joined the concert party, which used to give shows at the club and around the district for charity. He remembers the concert party being run:

... by an old music-hall trooper by the name of Tom Cooper with his wife, Doris, on piano. Tom wanted to call a show he was writing 'London Pride' and, as he did not have much money, he wrote to Noel Coward to ask if we could use his song without paying royalties. He also invited Sir Noel to come and see the show. Much to our delight 'The Master' gave his permission and accepted the invitation! I still remember him being so pleasant and generous with his praise of our efforts.

Peter can also recall an audition where he saw 'this small kid with large spec's on stage. Tom turned to Peter and said, 'This lad's a natural'. The lad's name was Roy Hudd, star of stage, radio and television, including 'Coronation Street'.

Paul Nihill was also a member of the same boys' club, where he used to box. He remembers two brothers by the name of Brazier, who lived in Windermere Road, coming to the club one day:

No one took much notice of them for neither was what you'd call handy with their fists; but they were keen, being encouraged every minute by

their father. When sparring with them I used to take it easy. It wasn't sporting to take advantage of novices.

These 'novices' stuck with it, however, and became well-respected amateur boxers. David Brazier got a bronze medal in the 1962 Empire Games in Jamaica and won two national titles in the early '60s.

Tony Hancock is remembered by many Addiscombe residents. Mary Chandler, by then married and living in Bingham Road, was one of those who saw him filming the opening sequence of the film *The Rebel* at Bingham Road Station in 1960 *(see page 42)*.

As already mentioned, Bill and Joan Angell's daughters enjoyed going to the Oval Road Youth Club to dance and sing. Jan Angell also became interested in football, but this was mainly because of her fiancé, who was football mad. She certainly won't forget the day she got engaged: 30 July 1966, the day of the World Cup final when England famously beat West Germany: 'Our engagement party turned into a World Cup party as it was the first time England had won the Cup - a great time was had by all.'

Sweet Confections

A lot of the people who have contributed their memories to this chapter fondly recall the local shops of their childhood. Inevitably, the favourite was the sweet shop, as true today as it ever was. Marian Gilliam remembers Whitlock's in Leslie Park Road in the early part of the twentieth century:

What an assortment! Mrs Whitlock was a stern lady but kind. We preferred her daughter serving us. The shop was not very big but we were only interested in the sweets: locust beans which I've never seen again, gob stoppers, cashew nuts... and thick squares of chocolate for tuppence - my treat when I'd done someone's shopping.

Mrs Whitlock had two daughters, Rose and Florrie. Peter and Christine Lockley both remember Mrs Whitlock in the 1930s and '40s:

Christine knew her well and was taught by her to make egg and tea cosies out of scraps of material. They were ruched and stitched onto fabric. Both Mrs Whitlock and Florrie, her daughter, were good at needlework. Florrie made all her own clothes. She also played and taught violin. Florrie and her husband lived with her mother next to the shop at No. 51.

Cliff Marlow also remembers Whitlock's as being full of sweets and cigarettes. He would go in there on his way to school and spend his milk money on chocolate macaroons, being served by Mrs Whitlock, 'a lovely old lady'. Later Cecil Hadfield remembers Mrs Whitlock:

I am proud to say that I knew Mrs Whitlock. My recollection of [her] *was of a housebound old lady with a great sense of fun looked after by Rose and Rose's husband, Leonard.*

Ivy remembers the thrill of having a penny to spend on sweets, 'a big round presence clutched in the palm of one's hand, a source of delightful indecision.' A penny presented one with quite a choice. It could buy:

... a slim bar of chocolate, sometimes from a slot machine on the station platform, a toffee apple, two gobstoppers that changed colour as you sucked them, a comic, a clay bubble pipe, a packet of fizzy sherbet sucked through a liquorice stick, or a bag of chips drowned in salt and vinegar – or a Remembrance Day poppy, a pull on a one-armed bandit on the pier, a long tram ride, one or two small ice creams, a sugar mouse, a pencil, a drawing book, tiger nuts – the choice was endless.

By the 1930s, the favourite sweet shop for Bill Angell was in Leslie Park Road, run by a Mr Law (known as 'Daddy', who lived in Oval Road). There was an area in front of the counter where a bench and chairs were provided:

The lads could sit and talk over the 'business' of the day while eating sweets and taking a drink.

During the colder months Mr Law would keep a kettle boiling to provide hot blackcurrant drinks: 'Warm your hands and fill your belly for 2d.'

Cliff also recalls R. Whites lemonade being delivered on carts to local shops. It seemed as if every sweet shop in the area displayed an R. Whites sign, and Cliff and his friends would receive a halfpenny for every empty bottle they returned.

During the war and for some years afterwards, sweets were rationed, so they became a real treat for children at the time. Although this may well have led to a healthier diet and meant that sweets became more appreciated because of their scarcity, one cannot help feeling that wartime children somehow missed out on one of the pleasures of growing up. Ivy also recalls a time, well after the war had finished, when a shipload of bananas arrived: 'Many of the children did not know what they were.'

Sometimes though, over-indulgence had its consequences. In 1964, nearly 20 years after the end of the war, Lynda Blaker (née Angell) was a 13-year-old. She used to take the family dogs for walks in Park Hill, then an area of large Victorian houses, long since replaced with hundreds of new houses and flats. Along with her sisters and friends, she would sometimes eat fruit from the trees growing alongside the alleyways:

By the time we arrived home we would have eaten so much that we all had tummy-ache. My mum would give me a dose of milk of magnesia as she didn't know what we had been up to and thought that I might be ill – yuk!

Mrs Whitlock and her daughter, Rose Ford, in Leslie Park Road.
(P. & C.L.)

Christine Turner outside her home at 98 Cherry Orchard Road in 1933.
(P. & C.L.)

Cliff Marlow being weighed and photographed in one go in 1936. (C.M.)

Dentists, Doctors & Home Remedies

One other consequence of all that confectionery was a visit to the dentist. Ivy Binstead describes it as 'an orgy of terror', but unfortunately for her, bad teeth were a consequence of a poor diet because of shortages during the First World War. Peter Crosier, born in 1928, says;

I well remember Mr Vincent (with horror), the dentist whose surgery was approached by a steep flight of lino-covered stairs in the row of shops in Lower Addiscombe Road just before the Leslie Arms.

And Peter Lockley, born in 1931, recalls a dentist above a shop in the stretch between Sundridge Road and Bingham Road railway bridge:

He would give children sweets or chocolate if they were good – all good for business! When I was about five years old, I had bad toothache and was taken to this dentist who told my mother: "Take this bloody child away and bring him back when he's stopped crying!"

This attitude did not please Peter's mother, so he was taken to another dentist who had just started practising at the corner of Lower Addiscombe Road and Clyde Road. 'His name was F.W. Lambert, later of Addiscombe Road, a lovely man and good dentist. I continued to go to him until we moved in 1962.'

If memories of dentists are tinged with fear, it seems that doctors are regarded with more respect. Marian Gilliam recalls 'Dr Vance, our dear old doctor in Shirley Road', and Ivy Binstead remembers Dr Thompson, who had the surgery at the corner of Morland Road and Lower Addiscombe Road. The Co-op now stands where the doctor's drawing-room and part of the nursery once stood, but part of the old house remains. Ivy's mother used to work for the doctor, scrubbing the steps every Saturday. In 1915, the year in which Ivy was born, a Zeppelin airship dropped a bomb on Dr Thompson's house and Ivy's father helped dig the locum doctor out from under a fireplace which had collapsed on him. This area was also attacked during the Second War, when the Co-op was badly damaged. Another doctor in the same practice, Dr Harris, had a big house (Bernhard House) on the corner of Ashburton Road and Lower Addiscombe Road.

Until 1948 there was no National Health Service and treatment was not as effective as it is today. Ivy remembers entire families being 'ravaged with tuberculosis and diphtheria... with measles, mumps and whooping cough you had to be in quarantine for three or four weeks.' She also recollects a visit to Croydon Hospital for an operation on her tonsils and adenoids:

... sitting in the waiting room for hours and then being taken, kicking and screaming into a room, laid on a table, face masked [and] clamped down. I was supposed to be doped. It was really frightening for someone six years old.

A variety of home remedies were available to avoid the expense of a visit to the doctor and Ivy remembers quite a few: having an old sock wrapped around her throat for mumps or a sore throat; breathing in the fumes from a tar boiler where the road was being mended to help with bronchial trouble; and taking 'cascara, castor oil and brimstone and treacle [which] worked wonders on the bowels.' The one which she hated most and which was doled out on Friday nights 'was syrup of figs which promptly made me sick.'

Aches and pains could be soothed by a number of unguents, including horse oil, turpentine, lanolin rubs, goose grease (saved from the Christmas dinner), linseed and comfrey poultices, camphorated oil and, as Ivy puts it, 'other nauseous substances'!

Kathleen Spalding, born in 1920, had scarlet fever when she was four and had to go to the fever hospital:

It was Christmas and I wasn't allowed many toys in the hospital, only one toy and an apple and orange. But when I got home the table was filled with toys from my mum and her friends and neighbours, Mrs Hersey and Mrs Heinrech. One toy I can still remember was a small tin pram with a doll.

In 1937 she had to go back to the fever hospital, this time with diphtheria. No visitors were allowed.

David Gowers recalls more home remedies from the 1920s and '30s:

Coughs, colds and sore throats were not uncommon. On such occasions other nightly rituals would be gone through. These involved, with permutations, doses of cod-liver oil (the white stuff - the brown 'and malt' was for sissies), having heated camphorated oil rubbed into the chest (sometimes so hot as to be really painful) and having sulphur powder put into a folded piece of newspaper so as to form a trough, and then blown into one's throat.

In the 1930s, Dr Grassick was Peter Lockley's panel doctor before the start of the NHS. Peter says:

I remember him as a lovely caring man who, whenever he came to see me during a childhood illness, would tell me that his brother, Peter, had the same symptoms as me. I never knew if he really had a brother, let alone one named Peter.'

By the late '50s and early '60s the Angell girls' memories of ill-health are more concerned with their father, Bill, than themselves. Bill was diagnosed with tuberculosis in 1955, at the age of 32, and had a ten-month stay in the King George V Sanatorium in Godalming, Surrey. At this stage lung surgery was beginning to be used to treat TB and Bill considers himself lucky to have been an early and successful recipient of this new treatment. Later he developed a heart condition, but again he was able to benefit from a pioneering treatment, having a successful aortic heart-valve replacement operation at King's College Hospital in the mid '60s.

In the course of a century, things have certainly improved as far as healthcare is concerned, particularly for children. Mind you, the feelings of trepidation at the thought of a visit to the dentist are probably still there, even today!

Working Life

Today's youngsters may be surprised to find that in the early part of the last century there was no such thing as a 'teenager', a concept which did not really take off until the 1950s. Most children left school at 14 or 15 and were expected to start work or an apprenticeship to bring some money into the house-hold. For Ivy Binstead this meant leaving school at the age of 14 and going to secretarial college:

A Mr Porch, who ran a very exclusive college, took two girls each year for training and I was fortunate to be one of them. In return for lessons we made the teachers tea and went to his typing bureau in George Street, where we helped and learnt office routine, duplicating, etc. It was really good training.

A year later Ivy started her secretarial work at a builders merchants in Stafford Road called Wadcrete (Waddon Concrete and Building Materials Ltd), on a wage of 17s.6d. per week. Ivy remembers that out of her first wage she gave her mother half for her keep and used the rest to pay her bus fares and save up for clothes. She was very proud of the first winter coat she managed to buy herself: 'A maroon woollen effort with an imitation red fox fur collar, which cost 39s.11d. (£2 in today's money).'

In the early 1930s, Bill Angell had a Saturday job, working for Percy Pugh, a delivery man for Prices the bakers. As Bill recalls:

... his cart was virtually a box on two wheels pulled along by a horse called Silver. I used to be his

Saturday boy and help him on the round, part of which passed through Addiscombe. During the week I used to meet him during the school dinner break and cycle to the Sandrock in Shirley with a basket of bread balanced on the handlebars. This saved the old horse pulling the cart up Shirley Hills Road. My wages for this were 5 shillings per week, of which I gave my mum 4 shillings, which was a big help financially to the family. I kept the other shilling.

Bill's first full-time job was at the age of 14, when he went to work at W.D. Vigar, 'Butcher and Purveyor of English and Colonial Meat'.

Some means of making money were less savoury. Arthur Burns recalls:

Horse manure was much prized for gardens and of course in those days there was plenty of it! Some boys made money by collecting it off the road and selling it to householders but that didn't include me, and I was horrified one day when the woman next door said she would be asking me to collect a bucketful for her shortly. I scarpered and kept well out of her way for ages!

Arthur also started work at 14, working in the City of London at Anning, Chadwick and Kiver, fur and skin brokers, of Arthur Street, EC4. He was a bit of an exception in having a London job as most school-leavers found work locally in a wide variety of firms.

Mary Chandler started nursing training for two years at the age of 17, the year after the war ended. At this age she was only able to do children's and orthopaedic nursing, but later spent a further two years at St Thomas' Hospital in London. It wasn't until Mary was in her thirties that she realised her academic potential and studied for a London University extra-mural diploma in Sociology, later becoming a social worker.

Cliff Marlow remembers that pocket money was not given as a right, but had to be earned. In the '30s he would help the Co-op baker deliver bread by pushing a cart for four or five hours to earn 3d. In 1942, aged 12, he started working as an errand boy at Harry Leppard's off-licence at 101 Lower Addiscombe Road. Wages were a little better by now – he earned 10 shillings a week working two evenings and all day Saturday. Cliff tells us that, although there was not a lot of spare cash around, the young people did not feel deprived. They may not have got everything they wanted but they did have everything they needed.

After the war, Paul Nihill had a morning and evening paper round for the newsagents shop three doors away from his home in Lower Addiscombe Road. This earned him 15 shillings a week, 'out of

Oaks Lane, Shirley, February 1953. (G.W.)

Far left: Shirley Hills, 1954. (G.W.)

Left: *Shirley Windmill, February 1953.* (G.W.)

Shirley Hills, 1932. (G.W.)

which my mum expected me to buy my own clothes, which not surprisingly were second-hand.'

Michael Mead found that the piano practice which his father had insisted upon when he was a boy proved beneficial to him in the late 1950s. Youth clubs were popular then, but ballroom dancing was also still in vogue. The Unique Ballroom was just over Windmill Bridge in Milton Road and this was Michael's favourite, which had:

... nothing to do with the close proximity of the Windmill pub, although this is where my piano practice came in useful as free drinks were available for entertaining clientele during the interval.

Margaret Robson started working at the age of 16 in 1955 and until 1965 worked as a clerk for BP using punch cards, based at Moorgate in the City of London. She then moved on to become a Holerith punch card computer operator (ICT, later ICL and now Fujitsu). From there Margaret moved to Blue Circle Cement in Victoria and on day-release to Esso where she received training on one of the early IBM 360 computers, a far cry from when Ivy Binstead started secretarial work 35 years earlier.

Finally, one memory that Pat Angell has of her first job in the mid 1960s relates once again to The Beatles, whom she had seen at the Fairfield Halls a couple of years previously when they were not quite so well known. By now she was working at the Odeon Cinema (later demolished to make way for the Whitgift Centre) and she recalls that extra staff had to be hired to cope with the expected rush to see the first Beatles film.

The Day of Rest

Sundays have changed considerably over the last century. Nowadays a Sunday is another working day for many people, or a chance to go shopping or do some DIY, and the concept of a 'day of rest' is gradually diminishing. Shirley Hills (also known as Addington Hills) was a favourite destination of many for Sunday walks. Marian Gilliam recalls walking there from Lebanon Road: 'It was nearly all fields along Upper Addiscombe Road where we walked on Sundays to Shirley Hills. Deans tea shop was opposite Oaks Road.'

Ivy Binstead enjoyed her Sundays. For her, they involved going to morning and afternoon Sunday school and later, when she was older, going to church, sometimes up to four times a day. Sunday school was held at the Mission Hall in Cross Road. Ivy recalls it well:

It was a lovely big hall, with a wood-block floor. Just inside the entrance on each side were two small rooms used for Bible Class and another two at the back.

As a child she can remember returning home after the morning Sunday school when her 'father would be having his usual bottle of stout' and the family would look forward to a roast dinner.

Arthur Burns remembers St Mary Magdalene Church in Canning Road, where he was a choirboy in 1935 at the age of ten. He had to practise on Monday, Wednesday and Friday evenings from 7p.m. until 9p.m. supervised by Mr Dixon-Smith, who was both choirmaster and organist. Arthur recalls:

The two sets of choir stalls were Cantoris and Decani, my location being in the latter and thus under the baleful eye of Mr Dixon-Smith via his mirror above the organ keys. When vicar, James Wright, began his sermon, we all knew we were in for a long session, so I came prepared with a copy of one of the boys' magazines of the day: Wizard, Rover, Champion, Hotspur or Adventure, folded to the point where I had reached, then surreptitiously eased from my trousers pocket as we sat down. My head was thus bowed during the sermon, against everyone else's looking forward, but judging by the glares I received from Mr Dixon-Smith's mirror I doubt if he thought I was meditating.

Arthur has other amusing memories of attending church:

The vicar was as bald as the proverbial coot; consequently he wore a skull-cap which slipped farther and farther back whilst delivering the sermon, so that at intervals he had to make a wild clutch at it to restore it to its proper place on that shining dome.

He also remembers sometimes attending Sunday school at the church:

... after which two or three of us would swing on the bell-rope beneath the tower [believing that] *our puny strength would be insufficient to ring the bell. Perhaps you can visualise what happened: three or four of us swung on it one Sunday afternoon to be horrified by BOOM BOOM BOOM from above. We dropped off the rope and fled – right into the arms of the vicar who had rushed from the vicarage next door. I draw a veil over what was said.*

Cliff Marlow can remember the church hall in Oval Road which belonged to St Mary Magdalene, 'a lovely old wooden hall with a double door'. He recalls Mr Letts, the caretaker of St Mary's who lived in Leslie

Park Road, as a tall man with glasses. On one occasion during a religious get-together at Sunday school Mr Letts came round with a big biscuit tin with bars of Fry's chocolate.

Peter Lockley has family connections with the Primitive Methodist Chapel in Cherry Orchard Road. His mother's maiden name was Jackson. Peter recalls:

My great-grandfather Albert Jackson laid the foundation stone for the chapel. Both he, my grandfather, Albert, and my parents were involved with the chapel. The windows on the Cherry Orchard side were dedicated to the memory of my grandmother, Emma Annie Jackson.

One final connection with churches is provided by Paul Nihill, recalling one of Addiscombe's great characters, Leonard Matthews, a stained-glass artist:

Len, who I knew well, was a bit of an eccentric and I can remember him visiting local shops in his pyjamas and slippers. He was a craftsman and his stained-glass windows are in churches all over the world. I met him through my sport. He was one of the real characters of race walking. In his sixties he had installed a small gymnasium in the back of his shop and exercised every day with weights and pulleys, etc. At the age of 68 he was fit enough to walk 100 miles in less than 24 hours and at 70 walked the famous London to Brighton walk. Len died in Australia in 1984 aged 90. He had returned 'down under' in the 1970s, having first been there 50 years previously. He shocked his friends by marrying his former fiancé of half a century ago.

Fragrant Memories

Sometimes a memory can be triggered by a flavour or a smell, a mere whiff of which can take you straight back to your childhood. So here is a little bit of aromatherapy... Ivy Binstead, recalling Christmas: 'we roasted chestnuts on the open fire and had hot raisins and some other fruit soaked in wine.' On going into her uncle's general store, she recalls 'the wonderful smells that greeted you'. In a shed at the back of the shop, the more pungent things were stored: 'vinegar, paraffin, bundles of wood and small sacks of coal.' Arthur Burns describes how milk was delivered by horse and cart: 'The milk was ladled from the churns directly into housewives' jugs which they brought out to the cart. I clearly recall the sour smell of spilt milk in that cart!' And finally, Peter Crosier:

When I was probably two-and-a-half or three, a near neighbour, a Mr Bravery, put me into his old-fashioned wooden wheelbarrow and wheeled me up to Radcliffe Road on to his allotments at Park Hill. He made me a bonfire of leaves; [this] is the first smell I can remember and I have always loved it.

Above: *St Mary Magdalene Hall, Oval Road in the 1920s.* (S.R.)

Left: *Addiscombe Road at the junction with Radcliffe Road in 1909. 'It was nearly all fields along Upper Addiscombe Road where we walked on Sundays to Shirley Hills. Deans tea shop was opposite Oaks Road.' (See page 65, top two photographs.)* (J.G.)

Eleven

School-days

Woodside School, Addiscombe College & Winton House School

Contributors include: Bill Wood, David Gowers, Michael Mead, Isabel MacLeod, Arlette Beelitz and H. Richard Gilbert, compiled by Anne Bridge with thanks to Leonard Brand.

Woodside School

As with Oval School, the origins of Woodside School lie in the 1870 Education Act passed to provide compulsory education for all children. In 1871 the Croydon School Board was formed. In 1888 a field at Woodside was purchased from the estate of the late W.S. Watton as the site of a school designed for 250 boys, 250 girls and 364 infants. At the time Morland Road started as a road from the Leslie Arms but narrowed into a footpath through fields. The Woodside Board School opened on Monday 19 October 1891 and was known locally as 'the school in the fields'. By the time that our first contributor attended, Morland Road had been extended to run all the way from the Leslie Arms to Woodside Green.

(J.G.)

Woodside Infants, c.1900. (D.D.)

Woodside School, 1947. (J.M.)

Woodside Junior Girls School. Left to right, standing: *Jean Richards, Shirley Nixon, June Grinham, Jessie Carter, Betty Brown, Phylis Turner, Mrs White (teacher), Joyce Francis, Pat Petherick, Joy Everett, Joy Simpson, Freda Bailey, Joan Stevens;* sitting: *Jean Hatton, Audrey Ridge, Miss Delloes (head), Dorothy Pickett, Miss Chaff (teacher), Eleanor Judge, Sheila Thomas, Pam Hudson. This was taken in the summer of 1946 when the school participated in the Croydon Junior School Sports Tournament at the Gaumont British Sports Ground, Thornton Heath. The girls were unable to wear the letter 'W' for Woodside on their shirts as this had already been allocated to Whitehorse School. On arriving, there were remarks made by other competitors 'Here come the losers!' (L), but Woodside girls had the last laugh, as you can see, by winning the tournament.* (I.S.)

Woodside School Athletics Team, 1949. (M.M.)

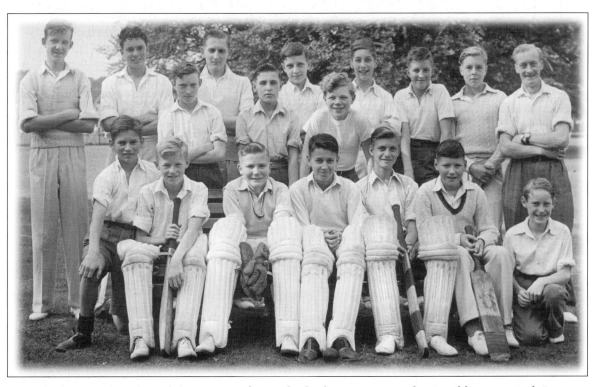

Woodside Green Cricket Club, 1949. Left to right, back row: *Ray Knight, Arnold Varney, Jack Burgess, Harold Stenning, Dennis Skidmore, Eric Crawford, Martin Hart, Alfred Nye (Hon. Sec.);* middle row: *Don Nye, John Arthurs, Geoff Cooter;* front row: *Peter Whiffen, Don Fincham, Ivor Steer, Ron Leard, Ray Beverton, Mick Wood, Alan Nye.* (I.S.)

∾ Bill Wood (1927-33) ∾

On 5 June 1927 I reached the all-important date when all five-year-olds were to be whisked off to school. I can distinctly remember my mother taking me by the hand down Black Horse Lane, Addiscombe over the two railway bridges, passing on the left an open wooden fence and looking down on to Woodside School, then bearing left, walking a few more yards, entering the 'Infants' doorway. I now know I was not in the least bit prepared for school – having had very little to do with peer groups, living behind and over a shop with a busy road in front. Kindergarten, preschool groups, and Sunday school were a nonentity to me. Completely bewildered, I was plomped into a desk seat and left to cry which, if I remember correctly, I did for the rest of the day. From then onwards 'infant' days were a complete blur apart from one when, whilst sitting happily at a little table busily working, I was suddenly removed elsewhere; whether it was promotion or demotion I never did discover – a mystery of one's young life.

The day arrived when I was upgraded to the Junior School and was to go in through the Boys' entrance. On the way I passed the Caretaker's Lodge, turning right under an arch into a (so it seemed) very large playground. I was now to follow in the footsteps of brothers Jack (b.1912) and Ted (b.1916) and [face] the awesome thought, as much discussed in the family, of meeting the headmaster, Mr Lister, Masters Appleton, Simmons, Browning and Miss Crutcher. I can distinctly remember brother Ted, who left Woodside School just after I started, pushing a classmate of mine by the name of Wheeler in a special pushchair from Teevan Road to school, owing to the lad having had serious leg operations from which, I am pleased to say, he made a good recovery – and I knew him for many years afterwards – no Health Service transport those days. My brother, I believe, and a colleague, were considered suitable escorts – if I may say so, well appointed.

In dry weather, children assembled and played in the playgrounds before school and, when an appointed school teacher blew a whistle, we all formed up in our respective classes and were marched to our classrooms. On hot days (and we did have some), especially immediately after the summer holidays, to stand in the sun waiting to march in was, to me, simply awful when I could be doing something more important like out playing.

Classes for those days were quite normal: English, tables, spelling and reading, the latter two on most occasions were done by pupils individually, either standing by one's desk or in front of the class – something I truly hated and virtually quaked in my shoes. On the whole the three Rs dominated – reading, writing and arithmetic (particularly mental, something I have found the modern child without a calculator to be lacking).

Winter heating in the classrooms was by coal fires (nice when they were burning), or even more 'luxurious' were the temporary buildings, if I remember correctly, made of insulated corrugated iron in which the classroom was heated by a coal-burning stove with a chimney leading to the ceiling. This luxury was enhanced by placing, if the teacher permitted, our little bottles of milk on the stove's flat top. If lucky, they were warmed by the break. I have no complaints. It all seemed like good fun. I cannot recall ever being cold in school.

Class discipline was fair but strict. If necessary, one was told to sit upright placing hands in the small of the back or for a change to sit on one's hands. A flying piece of chalk to the miscreant was not unusual.

Highlights include being called (only a few of us) into the playground by Mr Simmons to watch our airship R100 (maybe 101) virtually float over the school with engines running noisily. It looked immense and seemed positively to hover – a marvellous sight. Not that the airship would have gone there but being near Croydon Aerodrome we used to see all the wonderful early airliners, most of which figured on the cigarette cards of that period.

I remember watching what seemed a very senior boy placing an empty pint ink bottle (brown glaze) high on a wall out of the reach of the mischievous youngsters. When questioned [as to its purpose], the answer was to measure rainfall – a science lesson in those days! (I never did work out how rain could enter such a little hole.)

My friend, Bill Holland, upset Miss Crutcher and was hauled to the front of the class and she rapped his knuckles very hard with a thin pencil-like ruler which subsequently broke. Such was her wrath that she then picked up a round ebony ruler about ½ inch thick and finished her punishment on his knuckles. He was a tough lad; he didn't cry but held it back. I don't know what he did to receive such punishment but I, at least, thought he was a hero to have endured it. For an infringement in the playground, knocking a child's tooth out, I was told to wait outside Mr Lister's office after school hours. His office was also in the tin hut, nothing palatial for the headmaster. After hearing my pathetic story, much to my amazement, he dismissed the incident and was quite nice and charming. A child's impression of an ogre was gone.

I would walk to school down Black Horse Lane watching Handley's brickworks erect a new, very tall, square-sided chimney with the word HANDLEY written from the top downwards in white bricks on a red-brick background which, unfortunately, became a good target during World War II and, I believe, was mentioned by Germany's Lord Haw Haw. I also used to watch their steam-driven lorries carting bricks to and from the yard.

Not forgetting the forge near the school at which the local horses were shod – a source of interest for many a child.

For games there was nothing special in the school curriculum apart from physical exercises with balls of different sizes, bean bags and wooden hoops used for various contortions.

The boys on the whole, whilst waiting for school to commence, played with cigarette cards (swapping them), marbles of clay then glass – my father stated 'we' cheated as it was certainly not played like he used to – and the grand game of conkers. All games were played in their respective seasons governed by childish rules which, amazingly, worked. No bicycles, scooters, roller skates (if you were lucky enough to have them) were allowed on the premises.

A feature I never really understood then but naturally do now was that during the summer months several Army-type stretchers were placed out in the playground and certain youngsters were allowed to lie on them and enjoy a rest. [These were for children considered to be of frail disposition and susceptible to tuberculosis who would benefit from the sunshine. The practice was discontinued with improvements in medicine and immunisation.] Very occasionally we were examined by school doctors, dentists, eyesight and head-lice nurses. I did have to visit the school dentist in his surgery in South Norwood which was almost directly opposite the original Lady Edridge School to have a tooth removed using gas as an anaesthetic. It was the most awful experience of my young life. Although supposed to be unconscious, I felt the tooth being extracted and afterwards being barely awake was pulled out of the chair and led over to a sink, told to rinse and in no time handed to Mum. It was a most uncaring, unloving and heartless action. No wonder I have hated dentists ever since.

On the whole I enjoyed my junior schooling. I don't remember much about the actual teaching – what boy did? – but I understand it was as good or better than most. The school is still flourishing. Sister Jean and nephew John also attended Woodside. My two children went there, Michael and Lesley. I couldn't wish for better then or even now – they had a good start in life.

As fate would have it, I had to come back to Woodside School. On 27 February 1940 I took my wife-to-be, Beryl Adams, to a dance in the school hall run by the AFS (Auxiliary Fire Service). Owing to a very enforced blackout all the windows and doors were closed; naturally it was hot. Fortunately the Blitz had yet to start.

Later in the year I used to parade in the school with Dad's Army (Home Guard). In spite of the war I was still learning at the school, this time being taught by World War I men who were to us youngsters kind, very knowledgeable, good instructors, both in drill and arms, as well as being very funny – their Great War sayings are not printable here. Many thanks, if I remember correctly, to Captain Cox and his son, Fred Smith and his father, Fred Watkins, Bernard Pattenden, Sergeants Roper and Paul and many others.

Above: *Woodside School, c.1932. Pictured are Bill Wood (3rd row, 4th from left), Wheeler (front, 4th from left), Lyons (4th row, 7th from left), Bill Holland (back, 4th from left) and Mr Appleton (back, 9th from left).*

Left: *Woodside School, 1920s.* (Both B.W.)

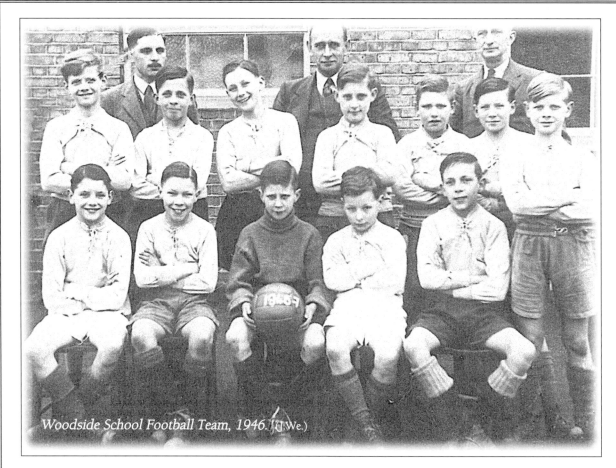

Woodside School Football Team, 1946. (J.We.)

Woodside School Football Team, 1952. (M.M.)

David Gowers (1930–37)

I am the eldest of four boys and we all went to Woodside School, which was only at the top of Hermitage Lane in Morland Road, about three or four minutes' normal walking. Naturally, however, children do not walk 'normally'. It was quite 'normal' for us to play marbles along the gutter, have conker battles or to whip a top along the road, remembering that in the 1930s cars in our side-roads were few and far between. The longest journeys though, were during 'smogs'. These were dense fogs filled with the smoke from countless coal fires, in which it was physically impossible to see more than a foot or so. The only way of getting from school to home was to feel one's way along walls and fences. Given sufficient time, the police would put out 'duck lamps' to indicate where to cross Morland Road, which was a main road and a bus route. These were paraffin lamps with thick wicks about two inches across which burnt through the immediate fog. The first marker, after having crossed Morland Road, was Walker's, the sweet shop which we all frequented regularly. Then it was the fence of the Minatol works, to Alderton Road, cross over to the corner house, follow the fence and wall to the small lane that ran between Alderton and Meadvale Gardens, then follow the fence to Meadvale Road, cross over and our house was nearly opposite. It was some achievement for children of only seven or eight to do this, sometimes on one's own, but it was done several times a year and we thought little of it!

Woodside was, and still is, an infants and junior school. My earliest recollections of school are of sitting with 35–40 others, learning multiplication tables and spellings by rote, using slate boards and chalk.

Each morning we had a bottle of milk containing one-third of a pint. During winter these bottles would be placed around the huge guarded fire to warm but quite regularly there would be a 'pop' when the milk would get too hot and explode through the cardboard cap.

School days were quite interesting for me. When I was in the junior school I developed a liking for numbers and I quite quickly learned all my times tables. This was helped along by my grandfathers and uncles agreeing to pay me 6d. for reciting a table correctly! In 1937 I sat for my 11-plus exams and gained a scholarship to Archbishop Tenison's School in Selsdon Road starting in September of that year.

Michael Mead (1946–52)

I joined Woodside Infants School in January 1946, a term late as it turned out, and stayed until 1952 when I obtained a scholarship to Whitgift Middle School. The teaching at Woodside School was excellent with a total of 37 boys out of a class of 43 gaining places at various grammar schools in the 1952 year.

Having had the honour of becoming School Captain, I spent a lot of time in the sporting side of school, in particular athletics, cricket and football. Geoff Moir was in charge of the football team and organised a strict training programme which included summer holidays, bringing along Doug Flack of Fulham FC as Coach. The 1951–52 season ended with the team winning the league and reaching the cup final. As a reward Geoff Moir took the whole team to the Savoy Hotel for a meal followed by seats at a West End Revue starring Jimmy Edwards and Tony Hancock. Jimmy Edwards' act was based on his 'Wacko' series, where he is a schoolmaster overseeing a class of boys. Somehow Geoff Moir managed to substitute the names of these boys with our own names. In addition he arranged for us to go backstage and meet Tony Hancock and Jimmy Edwards who kindly signed our programmes. Geoff Moir also organised hiking holidays. I personally went on one with the first week being spent walking in the Sussex countryside, the second week hitch-hiking (relatively safe in those days) from Canterbury via the cathedral cities to Truro. The walk to school was not hazardous as there were not many cars either parked or using the side streets, so one's football skills, albeit with a tennis ball, were improved to and from school, unlike the state of one's shoes.

The daily bottle of milk, the all-denomination assembly and the playground whistle are things which are not easily forgotten.

The football team asked Tony Hancock and Jimmy Edwards to sign their programmes in 1952. (M.M.)

∾ Isabel MacLeod ∾
(1959-61 Infant Department)

In January 1959 I started at Woodside Infants School, having been 'interviewed' by Miss Speller, the headmistress, when I went along with my mother to register my name several months earlier. I joined Class 7, already quite large and in the sole care of Miss Morgan. She was the owner of a white bubble car, which used to be parked in the playground near Class 7, a separate building from the rest of the Infants' School.

I do not remember learning a lot in this class apart from doing simple maths exercises with counters. There were toys, a playhouse and a boy called Philip Stamp who got his head stuck in the bars at the back of one of the chairs. I cannot remember how he was extracted from this, but I do remember it caused quite a problem. Each afternoon the camp-beds came out and everyone had to have a rest. This was, I recollect, rather a nuisance and going to bed in the early afternoon was not something I was accustomed to doing.

On the first day of the next school year I had to go to hospital for an appointment, thus arriving late at school and reporting to Class 6 (logically the one senior to Class 7). After lunch when we lined up by the class number painted boldly on to the playground surface, I was removed from the line to join that of Class 4, the one to which I should have gone. It seemed that we had been streamed to a certain extent already even at that tender age. Classes 4, 5 and 6 were middle infants. Classes 1, 2 and 3 were top infants.

For the remaining two years in the infants I was taught by Miss Wilkinson who came by train every day from (I believe) Haywards Heath and later emigrated to Australia. We learned times tables by rote; we read 'Janet and John' books. Everyone in the class wrote to me when I went into hospital to have my tonsils removed. Many of us were off school with measles, mumps and chicken pox - including me. There was also a bout of whooping cough and a large number of children who had to be isolated with scarlet fever.

In the top infants class I was in the Nativity Play at Christmas as Mary, when I had to sing by myself. Being a rather serious and quiet child, I was not naturally a 'performer', but Miss Speller was very kind and made sure I did not take it too seriously and it all went well. I remember particularly the special make-up being put on: I had never worn any before, especially not bright red lipstick. Although why Mary had to wear bright red lipstick remains a mystery to me. That year there was also a trip to Chessington Zoo, where the main attraction even then was the ghost train and other amusements, rather than the animals. There was a hula-hoop craze, with which I could not cope as I was not especially graceful. Maypole dancing was fun, however, and the maypole was moved about either in the hall or outside as required. We were encouraged to 'play' musical instruments, although I never progressed beyond the triangle. Music and movement meant listening to a radio programme for schools and interpreting the commands. Being a tree in the wind or whatever was always beyond me and, I thought, rather pointless... At the end of the summer term there were races, which were much more to my taste. The prizes for winners were cherries.

As a separate school, Woodside Infants was completely self-contained. There were six classes along one side of a corridor and I think some steps at one end led to the head teacher's office. The school hall was on the side of the corridor opposite the classrooms. This was also used as a gym and, I imagine, for school dinners, although I did not stay for those. The playground was edged by a very high brick wall on the other side of which was the railway line. There were very tall hollyhocks flowering in the school playground each summer. They were wonderfully deep rich colours.

(1961-65 Junior Department)

Just before progressing to the Junior Department, we were visited by two teachers bearing recorders for us to try. We were allocated to one or the other and somehow the three classes in the infants became four classes in the juniors. We were also joined by children from Davidson Infants, as there was no Junior Department there. I did not make a lot of progress with playing the recorders, but I remember the taste of the disinfectant to this day.

Throughout Infants School I had had problems with my handwriting. In the early days pages would be torn out of my books for me to re-write in a more legible fashion. Essentially, my enthusiasm was greater than my writing speed, added to which I was left-handed and difficult to instruct. At no time was I ever discouraged from writing with my left hand.

Class 1J in the Juniors, presided over by Mrs Jessop, was situated at the Blackhorse Bridge end of the school, close to the caretaker's house. I think the caretaker was called Mr Nash. He looked very old, and was always called on every time someone was sick in the school, which seemed to be quite often. He would arrive with a bucket of sawdust and a chair to mark the area. Obviously he did have other duties as well! In Class 1J we sat in rows in silence most of the time. During the winter there was an enormous pile of what I was told was coke in the playground. For some reason it had been delivered and just piled up. I had never seen coke before as we used coalite at home and I was fascinated by its irregular shape to the extent that, along with many others, mainly boys, I climbed up on this heap. Unfortunately, we all got very dirty and stained. I did not dare admit to the reason for the state I was in when I got home and pleaded ignorance!

Each summer I got involved with after-school athletics. This was organised by Mr Roberts who later became my form teacher. He was helped by Mrs Ivy Clarke, a former dinner lady. We ran parallel to the railway line – 60 yards in the first year, 80 yards in the second and third years, culminating in 100 yards in the fourth year. We jumped into a sandpit situated on the Morland Road side beyond the long 'new' building, always in my time occupied by third-year classes. Mr Roberts had a box of assorted spiked running shoes to be borrowed. They were all black and if you were lucky you got a matching pair. Each year there was a trip to the Sports Arena in Albert Road for a practice before the Croydon Sports meeting. We walked there, ran a lot and then walked back to school again.

My second-year teacher was Miss Trehearne. She was very strict – quite kind really – but I was never brave enough to admit that I just could not understand long division. I settled for an explanation at home instead. I worked my way through a large assortment of books in the classroom as I usually finished work allocated to me quite quickly. There were lots of Ladybird books, which I found rather boring, but I did enjoy the 'Little Tim' books by Edward Ardizzone. I also discovered Mary Plain.

The third year in the block was followed by the fourth year back in the main building, both with Mr Roberts with whom I learned a lot. We did an Egyptian project which involved building a 3D pyramid constructed from the empty boxes left after the sale of snacks. These had to be measured using proper calculations to ensure the pyramid would stand up properly, and cut to size accordingly. When they had been painted grey and assembled on top of each other, the completed edifice stood about five feet tall. It was, to a

ten-year-old, very impressive. I was so captivated by this exercise that I used to go each Saturday morning to Ashburton Library, which was unarguably one of my favourite places anyway, to make assiduous notes from the encyclopaedia!

Mr Roberts was a very good teacher. He got the balance between education and learning just right. At a time when the process of learning was much more formal than it is now his approach was quite flexible. We were divided into groups according to our ability and the tables at which we sat were arranged in blocks facing each other. To a certain extent, at times when we were working on our own, as opposed to being taught from the front of the class, this meant that it was possible for all children to progress at the speed appropriate to the individual. Although it was only a beginning, we also learned to count to about 44 in French – the reason for this number was that it was the number of children in the class and we all answered to our names with a French number each time the register was called. Strangely for one who has had a lifelong passion for books, I do not have very clear memories of what we read at school – apart from the beginning of Wind in the Willows when each member of the class had to read a little aloud, which was a little laborious.

Mrs Barnett, the deputy head, used to do sewing with the girls. I spent a whole year making a skirt which I never finished. She also accompanied our weekly trips to the Croydon Swimming Baths in Scarbrook Road. We used to go on a dark-green Croydon Borough bus. We would queue up waiting for a previous school class to finish and then get changed in the communal area at the end of the smaller swimming bath. Afterwards, whilst waiting for the bus back to school, we would sometimes peer through the boarded-up former open-air pool, which we were told had been closed because of a polio epidemic.

School trips included the Science Museum and the Ford Factory at Dagenham. There was also a trip to a dairy in Wickham Road. I think we walked quite a large proportion of the way there and back. We were also involved in performing in a music festival at the Civic Hall in Crown Hill, where I was very impressed by the red velvet seats and quite upset to learn that it was knocked down shortly afterwards. We had to go by coach to Gilbert Scott School for a rehearsal – I thought I had been taken right out into the countryside! There was very little obvious preparation for the 11-plus. We sat in alphabetical rows for the couple of days it took to complete. Generally my time at Woodside School was very happy.

Both images: *Pilgrim Fort in Godstone, a former military fort, was bought by Croydon Education Committee in 1921 as a memorial to those who died in the First World War. Pictured are girls from Oval School in 1926.* (I.B.)

Addiscombe College, in the mid 1950s. (A.Be.)

Addiscombe College
(Opened 1918; closed 1960)
Arlette Beelitz

I attended Addiscombe College, a co-ed preparatory school for five- to eleven-year-olds. We wore bottle-green uniforms. The school was situated in Ashburton Road (where College Court now is) and was owned and run by Mr and Mrs Taylor who also lived there. I remember drinking a third of a pint bottle of milk every break time. The older children would have school dinners in the dining-room in the basement with the headmaster, Mr Taylor. He got us to play trivia/educational games while we waited for our dinner. Going round the tables everyone had to name a capital city or river or a proverb or something like that – except when the cricket was on when we had to listen in silence to the radio commentary. After taking my 11-plus I went to Selhurst Grammar School for Girls.

Winton House School
Opened 1917; closed Christmas Eve 1994
H. Richard Gilbert (1952–59)

Inspiration for these notes has come in no small part from my mother's diary entries, which have assisted greatly with providing definite dates. On 5 July 1952 she notes in her diary 'Winton House School Fair, gymnastic display, conjuring, singing, stalls, etc. Mr

Clifton-Everest is Headmaster.' I suspect this was a visit to see whether the school was 'suitable' for me to attend. However, her diary entry for 24 July 1952 reads 'Winton House Sports Day'. Apparently I won the 'bunny hop' and received a box of paints. Whether I was a full-blown pupil at that stage I cannot say. Anyway, it seems I went 'back to school' in September 1952, presumably the start of the new term – possibly my first full term.

Early memories are few, but I remember that the teacher who cared for the 'tinies' in the Kindergarten class was Miss Jupp. I had already been taught to write a little by my mother, but using capital letters only. When introduced to proper handwriting I was confused at first and kept reverting to the use of capitals when in doubt, which puzzled Miss Jupp. She was not nearly as forbidding as she looked.

I don't recall any traumas about going to school, although maybe they have been 'blotted out' over the years. The whole affair was full of surprises and interesting things and I was agog at the new experiences. Inspirational Latin inscriptions on the wall were something rather new to me, as you can imagine.

Speech Day was 24 July 1953 when my mother was asked to provide her services at the piano and received a bouquet of carnations and scabious for her efforts. The second-year pupils were taught by Mrs Pye. Occasional amusing diversions occurred when her son (in his teens, perhaps) would turn up and join us for a few lessons. His party trick was making agonising screeching noises with the chalk on the blackboard, which we thought was hilarious, but Mrs Pye considered unnecessary. I think it was Mrs Pye who normally played the piano for hymns during morning prayers.

On the ground floor were the cloakrooms, toilet and dining-room, along with the Kindergarten and Mrs Pye's class. On the first floor (i.e. level with the top of the flight of entrance steps from the road) was a large room which was used for morning prayers and, initially, as the gymnasium. Clifton-Everest's office was also on this floor, near the front door. Pupils would only enter that office when they were in big trouble or very sick. On the second floor were classrooms for third, fourth, fifth and sixth years. I think I've got that right.

Clifton-Everest held prayers (in the largest room) at the start of each school day, but otherwise left us alone in the early years, as he concentrated on the more senior students. This might have been just as well, as his forbidding demeanour and demand for order might have scared the life out of us younger ones at that age!

I seem to remember that his wife was a tiny woman who helped with administration. School dinners really were nothing to write home about! All the boys had been used to a certain amount of post-war deprivation, but the tasteless (and constant) mince and the unidentified 'meat with pipes in' seemed uncalled for. The rice pudding was a real delicacy in contrast.

School sports was on 20 July 1954. I was winning the 'bunny hop' again, but lost my sense of direction and spilled off into the crowd, missing the winning tape entirely. I remember that event and how frustrating it was at the time. I couldn't keep an egg in a spoon, but I could sure bunny hop and this was a golden opportunity thrown away.

By 1955 I was cycling to school. July of that year was Speech Day - I was in the school choir. Clifton-Everest was very keen on getting the boys to sing and it appeared that I could. In late 1955 the school received a visit from Martin How, Choirmaster at the Royal School of Church Music headquarters facility at Addington Palace. He was picking out potential choristers for his 'headquarters choir' from local schools.

Those of a suitable age were lined up and asked to sing 'la' to a note pitched on the piano. As could be expected, some hit it and others missed by a mile. As Martin went along the lines of boys he made a note of some of their names and hurried past some others. When it was my turn, I was surprised to hear Mr Everest say, 'Now he should sing like a bird!' Apparently I must have done, because I got the job.

On 17 February 1956 I made my first visit to Addington Palace, along with several other Winton House boys, and was made a probationer at the RSCM headquarters choir. I very much enjoyed it and continued to sing there until 1959. We used to go by bus twice a week after school, once for practice, and once for a service of evensong in the Palace chapel with all the other (adult) students that were resident there.

We also participated in various special events at other times, including recording a series of Christmas carols for BBC Radio and singing at such places as Lambeth Palace and St George's Chapel, Windsor. We also had occasional 'chorister week-ends' at the Palace, which were somewhat chaotic (boys will be boys!) but happy times. I will always remember walking down the corridors and hearing the cacophony of two or three pianos (and maybe an organ as well) playing different music in different rooms and echoing round the building. We got jam sandwiches too!

Winton House Sports Day, 10 July 1956, was during the wettest July for 100 years. In December 1956 there was a service of nine lessons and carols held by Winton House School under Mr Clifton-Everest at St Martin's School, Morland Road.

Immediately behind the school was a lawn, on which the grand school photographs were taken. Behind that was the asphalt playground (a perfect surface for grazed knees and elbows) and then a further garden area. At some stage around 1957 the new gymnasium was built on this lower area and this (since it was now the largest room in the school) was also then used for all major functions, including morning prayers.

It was with this new gym that I associate Mr Davies, the very Welsh PT master who was deputy head and who became headmaster in later years, I believe. At the end of PT lessons, while we were changing back into school clothes, he would sing to us - classic Welsh ditties like 'We'll Keep a Welcome in the Hillside', 'All Through the Night' and 'Land of My Fathers', as well as occasional sea shanties. Sometimes he would tell us tales about how awful it was in Wales. We were agog at the gory stories about tragic mining disasters and workers falling into acid vats at steelworks. Why he felt the need to tell us all this is unclear.

Field games and the annual Sports Day were held in a playing-field at the top of Sandilands - a long trek up the hill in a crocodile. This field sticks in my memory because, in the early days, I seem to recall it had a wartime anti-aircraft gun emplacement alongside it, although I think the gun was removed later.

In the third (or fourth) year we found ourselves with a form mistress from the United States. Serena P. Ashley came from Connecticut (tricky to spell and impossible to pronounce the way she did!) and had come to England to see how teaching here compared with that back home. She also wrote articles on her experiences in newspapers on both sides of the Atlantic, I think. She was well liked and somewhat of a novelty; most of us had probably never met a real American before – I certainly hadn't.

In February 1958 my mother notes that I had a lot of homework around this time, including such delights as an essay on 'An Interview with Shakespeare', another on 'The Papists in Elizabeth's Reign' and studies on the work of Grinling Gibbons.

We had occasional visits from local firms who explained about their products and how they were made. Sometimes we got free samples. The Marley Tiles visit was interesting, but the Fry's chocolate project was much better! By this time we were being groomed for the 11-plus exam and considerably more time was spent with Clifton-Everest – indeed he was our form master in the sixth form. He kept a tight rein on us all. I was spanked once in his office. I can't remember what it was for, but I do remember him saying 'I don't know whether you did it or not, but I'm going to cane you anyway to make up for the number of times you've got away with it in the past!' Fair enough, I thought, and bore no malice. He also told me, on joining the sixth form, that I could not become a prefect because my Latin was abysmal. I don't remember losing any sleep over that either.

In December 1958 my mother notes: 'A formal notice was given to Winton House for the choice of future schools – Selhurst Grammar, John Ruskin or Archbishop Tennyson.' Exactly who gave notice of what to whom is not clear, but maybe this was my parents' order of choice for my onward schooling.

I sat the 11-plus on 13/14 January 1959. My last day at Winton House was 24 March. On 28 April my mother records that I received confirmation of passing the 11-plus to go to Selhurst. In fact, it had already been decided that I would be admitted to Pilgrims School (boarding), Seaford, Sussex, a special facility for asthmatics. My mother wrote:

Commendation is deserved, and should be expressed, for Winton House Preparatory School, Addiscombe Road, Croydon, under Mr Clifton-Everest. The boys received a very creditable grounding in education, learning good grammar, and the Headmaster was aware of the need for religious upbringing – witness his attachment to the Royal School of Church Music Addington Palace ... I remember a text fixed to the wall of the main room 'The fear of the Lord is the beginning of wisdom', which immediately created the school's atmosphere. Mr Everest was eventually ordained.

In the diary for 1972 there is a death notice, probably from the *Daily Telegraph*, which reads:

Clifton-Everest – On December 18, at Severn Stoke, Worcs, the Rev Leonard Cecil Clifton-Everest, Priest-in-Charge of St Peter's, Birchen Coppice, Kidderminster since 1968, aged 59.

Being an incurable hoarder, I still have my school cap, tie, scarf and blazer badge, in the startling purple that was so unique to Winton House. By the sixth form we were permitted to wear a grey jacket and long trousers, a welcome concession!

Winton House School, 1957. Richard Gilbert is circled. Staff, left to right: *L.C. Clifton-Everest (Scottish), Mrs Hancock, Mr Lester, Miss Jupp (juniors), Mrs Pye.* (D.G. & R.G.)

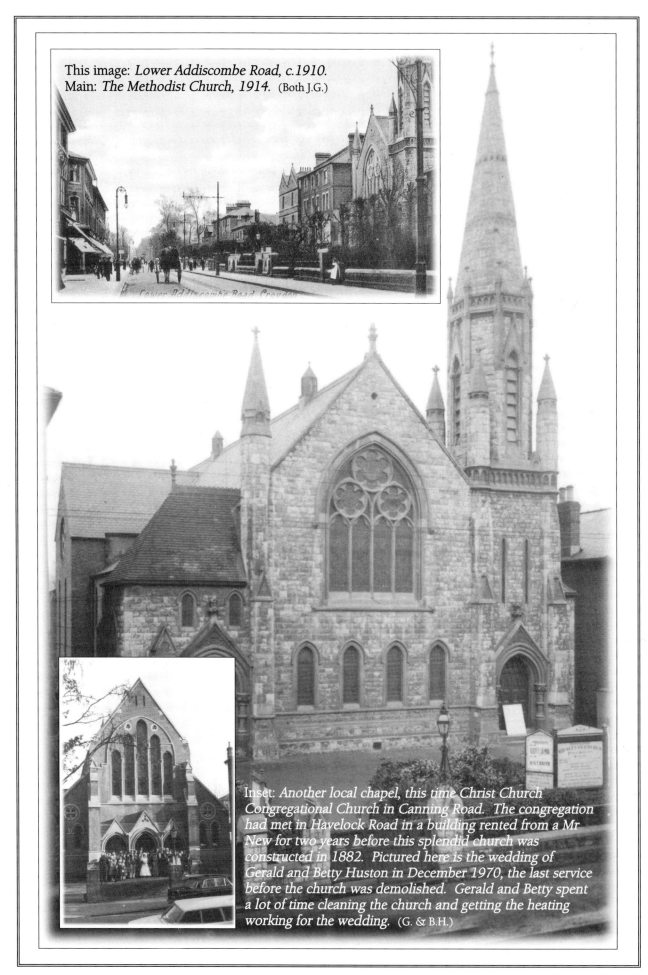

This image: *Lower Addiscombe Road, c.1910.*
Main: *The Methodist Church, 1914.* (Both J.G.)

Inset: *Another local chapel, this time Christ Church Congregational Church in Canning Road. The congregation had met in Havelock Road in a building rented from a Mr New for two years before this splendid church was constructed in 1882. Pictured here is the wedding of Gerald and Betty Huston in December 1970, the last service before the church was demolished. Gerald and Betty spent a lot of time cleaning the church and getting the heating working for the wedding.* (G. & B.H.)

Twelve

❦

Churches

Wesleyan Methodist Church, The Catholic Parish of Our Lady of the Annunciation & St Mary Magdalene

Wesleyan Methodist Church
An Edwardian Cameo by Veronica Hickox

The 1895-1914 Minute Book recording the meetings of the Trustees of Addiscombe Wesleyan Church, supplemented by personal reminiscences, provides an overview of the place of this church in the community of Addiscombe during the early years of the twentieth century. Gladys Hammond, who died aged 96 in 1988, was interviewed shortly before her death. Her family moved to Stretton Road in 1897 and her father James, a solicitors' managing clerk and later a Croydon Councillor and Alderman, soon became involved in the affairs of the church. Originally founded in 1869, by the turn of the century the church had occupied its fine stone building for nearly 20 years and had over 100 members. It offered a range of activities and was becoming a focus of social and community life. Miss Hammond remembered the 'good PSA', which was particularly known for its orchestra. 'Pleasant Sunday Afternoons' were started by Nonconformist churches in the 1890s to encourage people to find their Sunday entertainment at church and not at new attractions such as museums, parks or the music hall.

Church Accounts for 1896 show receipts from a Women's Dispensary, a Young Men's Club and 'Slate Clubs', which were savings clubs, traditionally recording their accounts on slates and enabling their members to save small amounts of money each week to withdraw when necessary, most commonly at Christmas. In 1904 a Literary Society, Boys' and Girls' Gymnasium Classes, a Boys' Social Evening and Young People's Evenings were making contributions to church funds. At their meeting on 1 March 1904 the Trustees set up a committee to organise a sale of work, for which the Women's Sewing Meeting would also be preparing. A tea and public meeting for the church anniversary were arranged and a request for 'the use of the School room to hold an entertainment in aid of the Children's Band' was con-

sidered. This was to be permitted, 'provided the entertainment was conducted without anything objectionable being brought in.' On 8 December 1905 an application to use the Lecture Hall 'for a concert on behalf of the unemployed (local)' was agreed, with the proviso that the 'programme must be suitable for the occasion and surroundings.' In October 1913 Mr Hammond brought to the Trustees Meeting:

... an application from the Ratepayers' Association for the use of the School-room for a public meeting to be held for the purpose of considering the possibility of acquiring the remainder of the Morland Road Estate as a public space and the house standing in the grounds as a Museum.

The Trustees agreed to this unconditionally, but nothing further was recorded about such a meeting taking place, or about the proposed public space.

A church choir flourished, with weekly practices and so many choristers that in 1911 the choir requested 'additional permanent seating accommodation' in the church. It held annual social evenings, occasional choir outings and in 1914 was complemented by the formation of an additional boys' choir. The highest standards were expected: in 1913 one member of the Trustees Meeting 'mentioned that he did not think the Choir were doing their best and that the organist was not doing justice to his position.' Investigation revealed that the choir felt that at their practices 'they had not sufficient work, that the members would not turn up to run over a few hymn tunes which were well known.' In addition:

Mr Hammond mentioned that the organ blower had been with us for many years, that he was paid £5 a year, but would never work for any other than the Sunday services, and at the Communion Service it was always necessary to get someone else to blow.

Remedial action was swiftly taken, with the

authorisation of expenditure on an electric blower for the organ, the offer of a harmonium and the appointment of a new choirmaster.

Miss Hammond remembered harvest festivals when 'as young teenagers we pushed a barrow up to Addington Palace and filled it with bracken for decorations in the church.' She described how 'the church was decorated with all sorts of produce' and 'on the Monday the produce, etc. was sold.' In 1909 the Trustees decided to celebrate harvest festival with a 'Church Social Gathering, with music and refreshments' and 'to have a Flower Stall and also to sell Fruit and Vegetables.' Usually at harvest festival the Sunday school held a Sunday-afternoon flower service.

Miss Hammond remembers Sunday school clearly:

We sat on forms, and alternate forms had swing backs. It was rather noisy because there were no dividing curtains between classes. Our excursions were to the fields on Addiscombe Road belonging to Mr Parsons, the dairyman, also by coal cart (cleaned up) to Wandle Park.

In November 1911, Sunday-school children held an eisteddfod, and the following month a 'Scholars' Exhibition' was mounted. However, the children were not all as well behaved as might have been hoped; in 1909 the Trustees had to deal with 'a complaint received from Mr G.J. Hazelman as to annoyance and damage to his premises caused by lads from our Sunday school and Band of Hope.'

There were also frequent difficulties with the gymnasium clubs. In 1913 there were complaints about 'the disturbance caused by the girls running about the passages whilst classes were being held.' Mr Hammond had reported in 1911 that, although the Boys' Gymnasium had not paid the allotted subscription to the Trust, 'it was decided not to insist upon payment as it was considered the Gymnasium

would have to be given up.' The following year one of the Sunday school lads wrote to the Trustees requesting that the Gymnasium should be restarted, and reference in August 1914 to a gymnastic display given by the combined Girls' and Boys' Gyms shows that this request was granted. This display led to concern about the Girls Gym, one of the Trustees reporting that 'the dancing performance by the young lady leader was very objectionable and should not be allowed to be repeated on future occasions.' A letter to this effect was to be sent to the club's organiser. His reply was read to the October Trustees Meeting and shows the impact of events on the national and international stage. He wrote:

... owing to the great upset through this lamentable war, I do not feel disposed to accept the financial responsibility of the Girls' Gymnasium Class again this season... At the same time, I should be very sorry if it were given up, and I certainly think that the time has arrived when the [Sunday] school might well assume responsibility for both this and the Boys' Gymnastic Class.

Throughout the Edwardian period, church activities had continued to expand. In 1912 Mr Hammond drew the attention of the January Trustees Meeting to the probability of a cricket club being formed and 'asked if the Trustees would grant the occasional use of a room for business meetings', and also ' if there would be any objection to the Club being known as the Addiscombe Wesleyan Cricket Club.' No objections were raised, and the club soon had regular practice sessions at Wandle Park and a full fixture list. A match programme for 1914 has entries recording the results of matches up to the end of July – perhaps the outbreak of the First World War brought the cricket season to an early end, as it indeed ended this chapter in the life of Addiscombe Wesleyan Church.

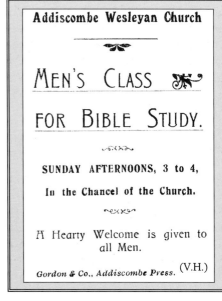

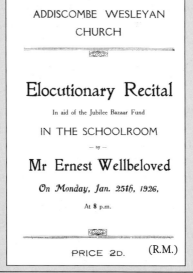

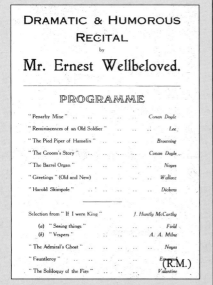

The Catholic Parish of Our Lady of the Annunciation

Paul Moynihan

Most parishes begin in a small way and then slowly, through the years, build up into something far beyond the vision of their original founders. The Catholic Church in Addiscombe is no exception. It began life in a hall built for the Primrose League on the left corner of Brockenhurst Road and the Lower Addiscombe Road [on the site now occupied by Sidda House] in the early 1900s and was later converted into a button factory during the First World War.

The building was purchased for the Roman Catholic Diocese of Southwark for £3,000 in 1925 through Fr Henry Prince, then parish priest of St Chad's, South Norwood and was first used for worship on 11 October that year. Initially there were two Masses on Sundays with a congregation of 170. This is a far cry from the present six Sunday Masses attended by 1,450 people and a boundary encompassing most of Addiscombe, Shirley and Woodside.

Apart from the first 18 months when a Fr Moor was resident priest, Addiscombe was served until 1939 from St Chad's with priests coming over to conduct services as and when necessary. At the time of the outbreak of the Second World War Fr James Barraud was appointed as resident priest-in-charge of Addiscombe. He took up his duties on 5 September 1939, living in a rented house opposite the church at 393 Lower Addiscombe Road. There was then a congregation of 266 and a debt of £2,400.

On 6 September 1940 just before 2a.m., the church was hit by a high-explosive bomb which did a great deal of damage. However, everything necessary for Mass was recovered and on Sunday 8 September Mass was celebrated at 8a.m. and 10a.m. in the church hall alongside, adapted for use as a chapel. First-aid repairs were carried out in 1942 and this enabled the church to be used. In September 1942 Dr Ernest Wake took over from Fr Barraud and he continued at Addiscombe until December 1944. He was succeeded by Fr John McKenna who celebrated his first public Mass here on Sunday 1 December 1944. Fr McKenna had been a student at St Joseph's College, Beulah Hill and had served as an Army chaplain. He was one of the thousands of British troops evacuated from the beaches of Dunkirk in 1940.

At the end of the war in 1945 a third Mass was added on Sundays to cope with the increasing numbers. The repairs to the church were still of a temporary nature and as yet nothing could be done about the sanctuary owing to the critical shortage of materials and a long queue for war-damage licences. With the appointment in 1947 of a curate or assistant priest and with four Masses on a Sunday, Addiscombe began to take shape as a growing parish. Numbers reached the 500 mark. It was now vital to find a presbytery to replace the rented house in the Lower Addiscombe Road as this was not large enough for two priests. The house at 147 Bingham Road was for sale and it presented itself as highly suitable, but the owners were only prepared to sell provided that the two adjoining detached houses were included in the transaction. This was agreed and the three houses and the surrounding grounds were bought for £6,000. With the purchase of this property completed, the priests took up residence at 147 Bingham Road in November 1949. These houses had been built in the 1870s by Lady Ashburton to train orphan girls for domestic service and were used for this purpose until 1909.

In 1949 the war-damage repairs were begun and were completed by October 1950. These repairs, together with a number of alterations, now gave the church a new sanctuary, two confessional rooms and a Lady Chapel. A choir gallery was added in 1952 with the result that there was seating accommodation for 270 instead of 140. By 1955 Mass attendance was nearly 1,000, not including 150 Polish people who, from 1949, came to their own Mass here from various parts of Croydon.

Further progress in the parish was made in October 1957 when work began on the building of a church hall in the grounds alongside the priests' house. The hall, costing £12,500, was opened by Bishop Cyril Cowderoy in June 1958 and proved a great asset in the building up of the parish.

Meanwhile, parishioners from Addiscombe and South Norwood campaigned for a Catholic primary school in the Addiscombe and South Norwood district. After much disappointment their untiring efforts were rewarded when Croydon Education Committee agreed. A site was acquired in Birchanger Road, between the two parishes, and the St Thomas Becket Primary School subsequently opened on 5 April 1967. Around the same time the Daughters of Mary and Joseph transferred Coloma Convent Girls School from its former home in Tavistock Road, West Croydon to new premises in the Upper Shirley Road. This religious order was not new to the parish as its sisters had already been involved in taking children for religious education at weekends for over 20 years.

In September 1962, the architect T.J. Denny [who designed the church hall], designed a new church – seating 450 people – on the Bingham Road site. Costing £60,000 to build and furnish, the new church was officially opened on 8 December 1964 and consecrated by Archbishop Cowderoy on 2 October 1975 once the final debts had been paid off. Fr McKenna remained as the parish priest until his death on 2 February 1978. The stained-glass window depicting the Annunciation was erected by the parish as a memorial to him.

The Catholic Church of Our Lady of the Annunciation

Left: *The old church of Our Lady of the Annunciation in Brockenhurst Road, 1925–64.* (P.M.)

Below: *The church was hit by a high-explosive bomb on 6 September 1940 which exploded in the boiler-house wrecking the sacristy and sanctuary. The tabernacle was overturned but undamaged, the altar crucifix was battered but whole, and the Lady statue only chipped.* (P.M.)

This image: *The extension to the old church.* (N.S.)
Below: *The new church of Our Lady of the Annunciation in Bingham Road.* (P.M.)

Opening of the new church in 1964. (C.T.)

The dedication of the new church in 1975. (C.A.)

St Mary Magdalene
The Young Uns by Elsie Pamphilon & Bill Angell

Over many years dedicated clergy and volunteers have contributed much to the life of our community by expending large amounts of time and energy on young people. Here are memories of two people who themselves benefited from this, then in turn as adults provided activities and support for younger generations. First we hear from Elsie Pamphilon:

All my life from... the age of seven years has been centred around St Mary Magdalene Church and for many years the happenings in the Oval Road Halls. An early memory is of collecting farthings to help build the tower which was completed in 1928. My next memory is the St Mary's Gym for Girls. In 1930 I won the medal. I have it still, a small bronze object with a wreath of leaves and the inscription 'St Mary's Gym 1930' on one side, and on the other my name, E. Hillman.

Of course the Sunday school played a large part in our lives also. The very young met in the Small Hall, the others in the Large Hall. I have in my possession the Roll Book dating from 1932 until 1950. Very interesting. Classes were segregated, boys' classes on the right side of the hall and the girls on the left. At Christmas there was a large tree full of presents. On high days and holidays

we would have the Revd Wright and some older ladies sitting on the stage watching us! Once a month we all walked in crocodile fashion round to the church and joined up with what appeared to be a service for other children. I believe these were the children of families that were not allowed to join the 'hoi polloi'.

I belonged to the Brownies [whose] meetings [were] held in the Small Hall, but when it came to the 'flying to the Guides', I had to join the Baptists at West Croydon. St Mary's Guide company was not started until I was an adult. As I grew older, the Church Army Captains played a great part in our lives. I remember joining 'The Better Britain Brigade'. We had a uniform of red jumpers which we knitted ourselves.

Around 1935 or 1936, I was prepared for Confirmation by Mr Arthur and his wife. I remember making myself a white dress and the church supplied us with linen veils. On the great day, before we entered the church, Miss Wright (the vicar's daughter) looked us over. We were sternly admonished for showing our hair, hastily made to straighten the veils and told that we were not 'brides'!

Around this era there was a great deal of activity for the boys: gym, cricket club and the boys' club, culminating in a camp every year at Fulking. Many of the boys of that time, on becoming adults, then became the leaders of the

Revd James Wright (seventh from the right, front), 1940s, *did much for the people of Addiscombe during his tenure from 1918 to 1945. He was instrumental in building the tower and encouraging work with children and young people.* (V.K.)

❧ St Mary Magdalene ❧

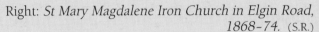

Left: *An early design for the St Mary Magdalene Tower, taken from the Addiscombe Parish Magazine, January 1918.* (S.M.M.)

When the church was first built in 1868, there were not sufficient funds to build the planned tower. In 1926 plans were set in motion to raise money to construct one. There were many fund-raising events including garden parties and an informative history of the church, written by Revd James Wright. In January 1928, Hall & Co. of Cherry Orchard Road donated 1,000 bricks to be sold at the Bazaar: 'One shilling a brick, with the purchaser's name pasted on, and the undertaking that it will be built into the Jubilee Tower!' On 31 July 1928 the Jubilee Memorial Stone was laid in the Tower, an event reported in the Daily Telegraph. The tower was completed in October 1929 and dedicated in January 1930, along with a bell, Gabriel.

Right: *St Mary Magdalene Iron Church in Elgin Road, 1868–74.* (S.R.)

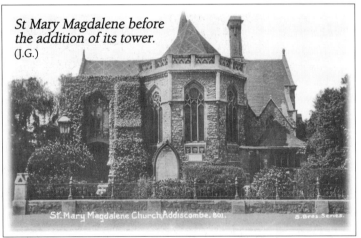

St Mary Magdalene before the addition of its tower. (J.G.)

Right: *The tower in 2002.* (A.B.)
Below: *The tower under construction, 1928.* (E.M.)

Bottom right: *The vicar, Revd James (Jimmy) Wright (with characteristic skull cap), Mr Gillespie (churchwarden), Revd Brian Aldis, Mr Fretwell, Mrs Gillespie and Miss Dorothy Wright (vicar's daughter), 1942.* (V.K.)

future. It was widely known that Captain McKinney, who helped in his time with the camps, would fumigate his tent with 'Flit'; he couldn't abide creepy crawlies. Captain McKinney married a young lady from this area and one of their sons, Mervyn, was our previous vicar for ten years.

Another organisation around the years before the war was the YPA. This was a mixed group, as far as I remember, meeting in Oval Road Hall and going for long hikes on bank holidays. Some time around 1937 or 1938 the 14 to 20 Club was started in conjunction with the Methodist Church. This was very popular with the young people with all kinds of activities which went on during wartime as well. From the period of wartime until the 1960s I would say that St Mary Magdalene Church was still the hub of activity for the young.

St Mary's eventually had Scouts and Guides, Cubs and Brownies. I can only speak for the Brownies and Guides. By the 1950s there was a need for another Brownie pack. Sunday school had spread to Beverley Hall in Grant Road so in 1955 I started a second Brownie pack, the 8th A. This is still running. Eventually my oldest daughter was running the Guides and my sister-in-law was running the Cubs.

There was a youth club named the Juventas, a thriving drama group and a marvellous choir. However, starting in 1952 were the wonderful mixed summer camps of boys and girls from 11 to 16 years of age, started in the Revd G. Strutt's time, under the auspices of Graeme Spears, the Curate. It was a mammoth operation. The organisation was terrific. Cooks, tent headers, medical officers etc., etc. As a family I might add that our own

holidays had to be arranged around church camps and Guide camps. Then, when the family grew older, they in turn became leaders, as did others, and thus continued the cycle.

Another mention should be made of the Christmas Carol fortnight. A mixture of youth and other church members took part. This was initiated by an enthusiastic bell-ringer church member who started bell-ringing classes. It culminated in the fortnight before Christmas, trying to sing and collect in every road in the parish. This was no ordinary group. They sallied forth with a fire in a brazier, a large banner, masses of lanterns, a team of handbell-ringers and an enthusiastic band of singers. The work that went into this was unbelievable. All lanterns had to be repaired every day, the fire had to be lit in good time, the banner primed, and leaflets put into every house being visited that day. For years this went on and folk looked forward to hearing the Christmas message and making a contribution to the work of the Children's Society.

Above: *St Mary Magdalene Brownies, Elsie Pamphilon is top right outside the Beverley Hall, 1963.* (E.P.)

Left: *St Mary Magdalene Oval Road Sunday School, 1943.* (V.K.)

Above: *St Mary Magdalene Boys Club at Fulking Down in 1934.* (E.P.)

Left: *The fête at St Mary Magdalene, 1949.* (V.K.)

Below left: *Mr Frankham. If any reader knows what he is actually doing we would love to hear from them!* (V.K.)

Below right: *Farewell to Mr Ayers.* (V.K.)

This comes from Bill Angell:

As a youngster I virtually grew up with St Mary's. In the early 1930s I took my Confirmation Class there and was confirmed into the Church of England at the Croydon Parish Church in Old Town in 1934. Also during this time a club was formed for the youngsters of the parish. It started with the name of BBBs, translated into 'Better Britain Brigade' from I know not where. Somehow this name did not go down too well. It was later changed to St Mary's Boys' Club. The club was held weekly in St Mary's Church Hall which was situated in Oval Road, just up from Leslie Park Road on the left-hand side where the actual 'oval' begins. For some reason the church sold the hall (I believe it was in a bad state of repair) and now houses stand on the site. The Boys' Club was run by a very dedicated member of St Mary's congregation, Mr John Stratton. I remember running without stops with John to Shirley and back. He left me standing. Well, after all he did stand about six foot six tall and with strides to match and, me, I was only a small 'un'. A number of activities were enjoyed and entered into by the lads including a gymnasium, table tennis and a form of handball. Very often the evening began with the more energetic lads doing a certain number of laps around the Oval at the double.

At this time there was a Church Army Captain attached to the church. I simply cannot remember his name but I am fairly sure he was a jovial and very nice Irishman. Whenever he was at the club, he would get involved with our activities in no uncertain manner. In his own way, deep down, he was a 'toughie' and would show no mercy, nor expect any. He entered with gusto our wrestling battles. He may have 'spared the rod' but he certainly didn't spare the child!

During the summer a camp was held at Fulking below the South Downs (John Stratton again). This was real camping, sleeping on the bare ground on a groundsheet and in a homemade sleeping bag of blankets. The days were spent exploring the countryside, playing games and even helping on the farm whose field we stayed in (a Mr Brown, I think). In the evenings before bed we sat around a roaring camp fire singing songs and telling jokes (all clean). Wonderful times!!! All the cooking was done in the open and no sign of 'jippy tummy'. The worst chore was

when your name came up on the duty rota for fetching water in the morning. It involved trudging across the fields with buckets and billycans to draw water from a public fountain on a wall on the corner of the road. The fountain was outside a public house called the 'Shepherd and Dog' (both are still there today). Many very tasty Cornish pasties were washed down with lemonade. (In those days youngsters were not allowed inside.) Sunday mornings was a wash and brush up and a hike through the country lanes to attend a church service at nearby Poynings.

My first suit, which was a dark blue pinstripe affair and also included my first pair of long trousers, was given to my mother by the Vicar of St Mary's, at that time a Reverend 'Jimmy' Wright. Sometimes life in those days could be a bit of a problem and I remember the suit was far too big but mum had it altered to fit. Yes, I with other young lads and lasses could spend as much as five nights a week at the Church Hall, which I did. Just think - no TV, no computer games, no clubbing and for many no holidays...

Over the course of time from the success of the Boys' Club other activities evolved. The Young People's Association (YPA) was formed for mixed membership, run almost like a parliament. I remember I once held the position of Prime Minister. Two badminton nights were run, one for boys only and another which was mixed. Also a special gymnasium night took place which was also mixed. I never made the church choir - music and singing never has been my strong point - but I did attend the Bible Class which was held in the Crypt. After a time it changed to a debating class in religious subjects, one for example being 'Does science contradict religion?' I can remember one evening being in the hall during an air raid when a bomb landed nearby and the roof and walls literally shook. However, the hall survived and my own four daughters enjoyed going there in their young days after the war.

The carol singers of St Mary Magdalene, c.1960. (G.W.)

The Crescents, photographed at Homelands, Spring Lane, Woodside in 1907. (D.D.)

Bingham Athletic FC, 1958-59. Left to right, back: *Mr F. Payne (Chair.), Bill Angell (Hon. Sec.), Les Clack, Les Steadman, Doug Smith, Tom Evans, Brian Tweddle, Les Knight (trainer), Jack Payne (reserve); front: Tony Ward, Ivor Steer, Les Broughton, Ray Smith, Tim Gadd, Harry Peckham. This photograph was taken at Selhurst Park on 4 May 1959, when the club beat High View FC by 4-1 after extra time, to win the Croydon League Senior Cup final. The club also won the Premier Division League title to achieve a notable double.* (I.S.)

Thirteen

Sport

It's a Goal!, Addiscombe Rifle Club & Playing the Tables

It's a Goal!

Bill Angell, Geoff Green and Michael Mead

There have in the past been several football clubs with close links to our parish. Those that come to mind are Addiscombe United, Addiscombe Swifts, Addiscombe Celtic and also Clyde Athletic. A junior side existed between 1949 and 1954 called Oval Old Boys, closely made up from ex members of Oval Road School. On one occasion, while playing in the Croydon Minor League, they won their Division Cup and also in two other seasons clinched the Division and the Cup double.

Bingham Athletic (Bill Angell): In the early years of the 1950s it was the 'done thing' on a Sunday morning for many lads to congregate at Bingham Road Rec. Ground for a 'kick around'.

Sides were organised and, depending on the number who turned up, the games would comprise anything from nine-a-side to fourteen-a-side. The goals consisted of piles of coats and, as there were no lines marked out, the entire Rec. would become the pitch. Of course there was no referee and it is not known who supplied the ball, but a game could last all morning and only ended when the lads were too tired to carry on, or when they were called for dinner.

Many had spent their school-days at Oval Road School and were firm friends and ten or twelve of them actually lived within a mile or so of each other in roads such as Oval Road, Leslie Park Road, Leslie

(I.S.)

Oval Old Boys who completed a League and Cup double by defeating Strathyre Rangers FC by 9-1 in the Croydon Minor Combination Cup final at Selhurst Park, 28 April 1952. Centre forward Bill Prior scored six of the goals. The club had already won the Division and League title. Left to right: Ken Cross, Ron Smith, Ivor Steer, Bob Taylor, Laurie Montague, Melvyn Williams, Terry Gee (mascot), Les Broughton, Tom Evans, Mike Burrow, Doug Smith, Bill Prior.

Grove and Cherry Orchard Road and about four or five in the Davidson Road, Freemasons Road and Little Road area. Little Road (running off Lower Addiscombe Road by Windmill Bridge) is long gone.

There came a time when it was decided that Bingham Road Rec. was no longer big enough so the Sunday-morning venue was changed to Ashburton playing-fields. Some time in late 1952 or early 1953 a number of the 'Sunday Morners' got together and decided that they would form their own football team and apply for entry into the Croydon and District Football League. A name for the team was discussed and, in view of the area in which they had enjoyed their football, it was decided that they would call themselves Bingham Athletic. A Club Secretary was elected and Ray Reed became the first of only three people to hold this position. Ray Smith was chosen to become team captain and this pair were joined by Tommy Payne and between them they formed the Selection Committee. Meetings were held at Ray Reed's home to decide upon team formation. Fathers were asked to become involved and Mr Fred Payne took up the position of Club Chairman. From a photograph taken in 1954 it appears that Mr H. Smith accepted the job as trainer. Mr Vic Baldwin, who lived in Little Road, also joined to help in the development of club and team. Application to the Croydon and District League was successful and entry to the Third Division was made.

In the early days fixtures were played on various grounds. Pitches would be hired from the local Parks Department. The club went for Lloyd Park, Pitch No. 2 at that time and it virtually became our home ground. Of course they did not supply us with goalpost nets although the club was able to purchase a set and with a happy arrangement with the two park keepers, the nets were erected and taken down for us. They made tea for us at half time and along with sliced oranges it became very professional.

The 1953-54 season in the Division Three proved to be a very successful start to the club's introduction to organised local football. Not only did they win the divisional championship, they also completed the 'double' by winning the Croydon District Football League 'Challenge Cup' - Junior Section. To the delight of the club they were presented with a Certificate for Sportsmanship and with it promotion to the Second Division.

The following year was, again, a very successful one for the club and team, as they won not only the championship of their new division but also the Surrey FA Lower Junior Cup. The team beat opponents St Johns FC. The game was played on Banstead Athletic ground but regretfully the score has been lost through time.

By the 1955-56 season (now in Division One), the team was entering into the Senior Section of the League and continuous strong and entertaining football brought more awards. The Divisional Championship and the Senior Challenge Cup earned them another 'double' and again a Certificate of Sportsmanship, which was the second one in three years. The opponents were Bailemeta Sports FC, the venue Selhurst Park and on the final whistle the score was 4-1 to the club and automatic promotion to the Premier Division followed.

The 1956-57 season saw the team facing some very good opposition but playing their own style of football as from the start. Once again they won the award for the Division. You can imagine the feelings of the club members after coming top club in the League. There were of course a few big heads around, as Hon. Secretary none bigger than my own, but who could blame us as after all it was some achievement.

From their formation in 1953 the club had not failed to win a Divisional Championship. They did, however, achieve runners up to Coulsdon Athletic in

Addiscombe, also known as Bingham, Recreation Ground, c.1922. (J.G.)

Bingham Athletic Football Club, 1954. (B. & J.A.)

the 1957-58 season. They also took the Senior Section Cup for the second year running. It was played once again at Selhurst Park. The opponents were Croydon Gas FC – a very close game and the club emerged winners 1-0 with the goal being scored by Alan Ward of Tunstall Road.

The season of 1958-59 was the last to be played in the League. Regaining the number-one spot in the Premier Division the club was awarded the trophy for the second time in three years, in addition to which they once again won the Senior Cup making it a hat trick. Selhurst Park was becoming familiar and our opponents were High View FC. After an excellent match the score stood at 1-1 and therefore went into extra time. Bingham Athletic appeared to be the stronger team and eventually emerged the winners 4-1. In the same season the club participated in the Surrey Junior Charity Competition winning through to the final which was held at the Leatherhead FC's ground against Westfield FC. After extra time the result was 4-2 against the club.

The Bingham Athletic line-up for the cup final in 1958. (B. & J.A.)

As previously stated, the club did not re-apply for entry into the League and perhaps there was nothing more to prove at this level after having gained a record five Divisional Championships, one runners up, three Challenge Cup awards for the Senior Trophy and one for the Junior Cup.

During this five-year period the club had also run a second eleven which did not achieve the same success but which did win the championship of the League's Fourth Division.

Participation during the two years played at this level of the Surrey Intermediate League Division One (1959-60 and 1960-61) brought only moderate success. Memories of this period are somewhat blurred. As far as can be ascertained, in the first year the club finished third and then fifth in the second year. Travelling to away fixtures was carried out by hiring a coach from Paynes Coaches whose owner was none other than Mr Payne who ran his business from his home in Leslie Park Road. The meeting-place for team and supporters was the saloon bar of the local, the Leslie Arms, whose proprietor was the late Mr Ernie Hudson who became a very faithful supporter of the club. One wonders if this was because of the many glasses of liquid refreshment that used to be consumed there.

At this stage the original team had undergone some changes due to club members having other commitments, whilst travelling arrangements were becoming difficult as well. It was agreed to go back to local football and we were accepted into the Thornton Heath and District League.

The 1961–62 season in the Premier League proved to be a little disappointing. Although still a strong team, we finished fifth. The following year provisional improvement was achieved ending in third place. This was to be regretfully the last year of competition for the club with the last game ending in victory. Woodside Albion were our opponents in the final of the Senior Cup and again at the end of 90 minutes the score was level at 2-2. Extra time saw us win the game 3-2, Gordon Wren scoring two goals and one coming from the penalty spot by Alan Ward.

After eight years as Secretary of Bingham Athletic the author of this piece was forced by serious ill health to give up this position and lost all touch. When the club closed, it could congratulate itself on a fine record over the ten years of competition.

After Cyril Smith left the club he went into refereeing, eventually making it to the FA Supplementary Division, going on to be linesman for two international games, Italy v West Germany and Wales v Scotland.

In addition to football the club also ran a social evening. A room behind the Cherry Orchard Pub (as it was called then) was hired out and on a Monday evening members would meet for a pint or two or three - and also to be able to play a game of darts, table tennis, cards, etc. Table tennis teams played matches throughout the borough and in the summer months a cricket eleven enjoyed playing too.

Oval Old Boys: This club included Ivor Steer (who now lives in Colyton, Devon), George Austin and Ernie Drew (now in Tonbridge). George Austin, born in Cross Road in 1912, is the oldest known former member of the team. He attended Oval Road School in 1917 and while a pupil played for the school team run by Mr Emerson who was later to become the headmaster of John Ruskin School. George played for Oval Old Boys in 1934. He recalls a very sad occurrence. After one game an 18-year-old, Ron Griffith from Tunstall Road, died after being hit in the stomach by a ball during a game played at Duppas Hill

The club ceased to exist after 1954 following a number of successes. They were joint winners of Division Four in 1950-51, winners of Division One and the Cup in 1951-52 and again in 1952-53. The Croydon Minor Football Challenge Cup Final was played on 21 April 1953 against High View at Selhurst Park. After a 'good-luck' telegram from Doug Lishman (Arsenal forward), to Terry Cowles, (Oval Old Boys' left back), the team went on to an impressive victory. Les Broughton, who also played for Fulham's nursery team, scored two goals and P. Tubbs one. Ken Cross and Ivor Steer in defence were described as outstanding. The final score was 3-1 to Oval Old Boys.

Oval Old Boys, 1953. Left to right, back: Melvin Williams, Ernie Drew, Terry Cowles, Mike Burrows, Reg Brown, Dennis Pink; front: Ken Cross, Ron Pugh, Ivor Steer, Pat Tubbs, Les Broughton (who now runs a pub in Portugal). (B. & J.A.)

Clyde Athletic (Geoff Green): Clyde Athletic team was made up from all members of Oval Road School football team. Geoff recalls:

The school team at that time was run by Mr Amoss, the art teacher. When we all left school in 1947, Joe Challenger's Dad and Uncle formed Clyde Athletic. His Dad was also called Joe Challenger. I only knew his uncle as Mr Constable. Both lived in the first house in Clyde Road on the right from Lower Addiscombe Road end.

We were in the Croydon Combination and won the League once. I left Clyde in 1950 to join Sutton United. I think Clyde packed up in 1951 when most of the lads were called up for National Service.

Clyde Athletic's home ground was Bingham Park. We used to meet Thursday evening for the picking of the team in the room behind the Enterprise Café next to the Alma Pub. Joe Challenger (junior) went into the Army in 1951, became a PTI, came home one weekend in 1952 and died on the Friday night aged 19. I think that was the end of Clyde. His Dad then decided to call it a day. I think that the few lads that were left joined Bingham Athletic. Members were: Doug Smith, Brian Baily, Geoff Bushel, Jackie Paine, Bob Cox, John Sprigall, Geoff Green, Don Reed, Joe Challenger, Patch Purnell and David Voot.

Addiscombe Boys Club FC (Michael Mead): Michael Mead joined the club for the 1956-57 season and played for four years until he moved on to West Wickham. He relates:

At the time I joined Addiscombe Boys Club it was run by a Mr A.W. Halliday (known widely as 'Doc') who lived in Spring Lane. The club evenings were held at that time in Ashburton Junior School in Long Lane and all training was in the gym or in the playground. At one time these sessions were taken by Marvin Hinton (ex Chelsea, Charlton and Woodside School). Most home games were played either at Ashburton playing-fields or Lloyd Park depending on availability.

The highlight of the season was a match against Crystal Palace Juniors at Selhurst Park under floodlights, generally on a cold November evening with an attendance of about 50 people. We normally lost but the experience was very useful. The other 'personal highlight' was my selection together with another player, Bernard Brennan, to represent Surrey in the NABC Club Championship in 1957-58.

Although only a small club in those days with limited resources and few members, owing to the enthusiasm of Doc Halliday it was very successful in a number of sporting fields. Members from the club were selected during three seasons, 1957-1959 for the Surrey Cross Country Team and there were various selections for the Surrey Boys Club Cricket XI culminating in a fixture at the Oval against Young Surrey where we had four representatives on the team.

Addiscombe Rifle Club
Tony Stelling

The club was one of those formed in response to Field Marshall Earl Robert's brief at the end of the nineteenth century. Lord Roberts of Kandahar VC had trained at the East India Military College in Addiscombe in 1850-51. He had an illustrious career in the Army and was made a freeman of Croydon in 1902. Sir Frederick Edridge and General Wm Gordon CIE were founder members and invited Lord Roberts to open the club. In his absence, the first shot was fired on Easter Monday, 20 April 1908, by Major Morrison Bell, Scots Guards, the organising Secretary of the Society of Miniature Rifle Clubs (now the National Small-Bore Rifle Association). Lady Edridge presented the prizes, and Sir Frederick became President in 1911.

In 1910, the local police started to make use of the range. Records show that 30 officers from Metropolitan Police 'W' Division used the ranges. At that time the range was set up for both rifle and pistol practice.

During both world wars the range was taken over by the Army; the Second World War saw two remaining civilian members, Mr F.W. Privett and Mr D. Tilling, becoming official instructors for the Army, as they were over the age for military call-up. They trained hundreds of men who were given their first experience of firing rifles. An indoor range was added and officially opened in 1964. Carrying on the family tradition, the club's President in 2002 is Mr R.V. Privett, son of F.W. Privett.

Over the years the club has had many competitive successes. In 1934 Henry Longhurst won the World Prone Rifle Championships, held in Granada, Spain with a new world-record score of 396 (out of 400!). Approaching its centenary, the club is still one of the UK's leading competitive clubs.

Invitation to the club opening in 1908. (A.R.C.)

ADDISCOMBE RIFLE CLUB.

The Officers and Committee desire the pleasure of the company of

Stanley Just Esq & friend

at the Official Opening of the Rifle Range, on Easter Monday, by Major A. C. Morrison-Bell, Scots Guards Organising Secretary of the Society of Miniature Rifle Clubs. (representing Lord Roberts.)

OPENING CEREMONY AT 3 P.M.
Entrance to Range—Selbourne Road, Top of Park Hill Rise
A reply will oblige to A. T. Ashwell, Hon. Sec., 80, Alexandra Road.

Above: *Addiscombe Rifle Club range, c.1922.*

Left: *Opening the new indoor range in 1964. The inaugural shot.*

Below: *Three target riflemen, 1930s.* (All A.R.C.)

Playing the Tables
A quick match with Johnny Leach by Steve Collins

Johnny Leach was probably one of our most successful local sporting heroes – his game was table tennis. Born in 1922, 20 years later he was an ordinary club player. Four years after that in 1946 he made the world rankings list. In 1949 he won the World Singles title – and, in 1951, went on to win it again! During the 1942–49 period, Johnny was coached by Jack Carrington, himself a distinguished player. Jack was an English international from 1939–49 and in 1950–51 was doubles champion of England, America and Ireland. He went on to be coaching director for ETTA and National Instructor to Sweden, Denmark, Finland and Ireland. Jack said of Johnny:

Many reported that his game was incapable of winning World Singles, because he was such an all-rounder. He could defend or attack on both wings from any position, but none of the shots were especially severe, drop shot ordinary, and footwork slow by world standards.

Clearly, Jack's message got through, because he later reported: 'On the great occasions, Johnny's wonderful temperament stood up to all the tests. Speed came to his feet and fire into his drives.'

Apart from winning the two World Singles titles (and being semi-finalist in 1947), Johnny was a great doubles player and amongst others reached the Men's Doubles final in 1947, partnering Jack. He was also a runner-up in 1952 and 1953, including mixed doubles in 1952.

The 17 March 1951 *Croydon Times* reported:

Croydon's international table tennis star, Johnny Leach, who has a sports outfitters shop in Addiscombe, regained for England on Sunday in the World's Championships in Vienna, the table tennis singles honour he won in 1949.

In the final he beat Ivan Andreadis of Czechoslovakia... sheer determination allowed Leach to tame the attack of the man fancied to win the title. Varying his tactics and speed, Leach unsettled his opponent's defence, which in the opening games was magnificent.

The same report commented on the fact that Johnny, partnered by Diane Rowe (one of the famous Middlesex table tennis twins), was beaten in the Mixed Doubles semi-finals. The twins (Rosalind and Diane) did, however, win the World Women's Doubles title (against Rumania), and were due to provide their many fans with an exhibition match at the Central Baths (Scarbrook Road) the following Monday.

Basically, Johnny Leach claimed victories over every known international champion and in 1950–51 was American, French and Welsh National Champion. In the early 1950s he was a national hero, household name and made table tennis the cult game of the times. Throughout the land, dining-room tables took on a new purpose!

His sports outfitters shop was at 272 Lower Addiscombe Road, opposite the Black Horse Co-op, at the time of writing the disused Abbot Heating Bathroom Shower & Kitchen Centre. Although most sports items were available, the emphasis was of course on table tennis equipment and clothing – the fashion for which was going through a major overhaul. Until the early 1950s, competition rules laid down that 'the lower part of the clothing should be grey flannel trousers for men and a grey flannel skirt or shorts for women.' The tops were even worse, stipulating a sweater and a shirt of the same colour. All of this was overhauled in the 1950s; men were allowed to wear shorts, and Johnny and his shop provided the new garb.

Johnny frequented the Addiscombe Table Tennis Club at 160 Lower Addiscombe Road. Now redeveloped as three houses, next to the now Lonsdale Hotel, 160 retains its original coach-house. And talking of coaching, Johnny encouraged many local people into the sport. In April 1959, Johnny Leach made his 150th and last appearance (against France) for England. He was the first Englishman to hold the world title since 1927 and still remains the only Englishman to have won the World Table Tennis Championship twice. In recognition of all of this, he was awarded an MBE in 1966. Good on yer Johnny!

Johnny practising, c.1947. (S.Re.)

John Surtees
John Blunsden

And talking about MBEs for Addiscombe sporting personalities, apart from Paul Nihill and Johnny Leach we have John Surtees. Uniquely amongst motorsport personalities, having reached the pinnacle of achievement as a racing motorcyclist, he proved able to move seamlessly across from two to four wheels, and again reach the very top of his sport, this time as a racing driver – true versatility at the highest level. The bare statistics say it all: 350cc World Champion in 1958, 1959 and 1960; 500cc World Champion in 1956, 1958, 1959 and 1960; then Formula One World Champion in 1964. Add to that his innumerable individual race victories on two wheels and four, his brilliance as a driver of sports-racing cars, and his human and technical versatility which, quite remarkably, enabled him simultaneously to combine the roles of designer, production director, team manager as well as driver of his own Surtees racing cars, and it is clear that he has left an indelible imprint on the motorsporting world.

Already a Crystal Palace favourite and a multiple winner and lap record-breaker, Surtees brought an exciting new high-pitched sound to the circuit in 1956 when, as a new member of the Italian MV Agusta works team, he raced this four-cylinder 500cc machine. (J.B.)

Most of John's greatest racing achievements were on the international stage, but closer to home, too, he was a star of the racetracks. In his motorcycling days he rarely went to a meeting at Crystal Palace without winning every race in which he was entered and setting a new lap record in each of the classes in which he was racing. He competed on no less than nine different makes of machine, although it was as the leader of the Italian MV Agusta team that he scored his greatest successes.

Turning to cars in 1960, he immediately matched the pace of the current stars in Cooper and Lotus single-seaters, but his 1964 World Championship came at the wheel of a works Ferrari, a success which he achieved against all the odds. Then two years later he turned his back on the Italian team when he discovered that he was being treated unfairly by them. A

Cooper-Maserati followed, then he drove for Honda and BRM, and had a short spell with his own McLaren-Ford pending completion of his Surtees-Ford cars.

Always a strong character, with a clear understanding of the difference between right and wrong, John has consistently been prepared to speak his mind, and if necessary to ruffle a few feathers when he felt it was justified. It is likely that he inherited this trait from his hard-working father, Jack, a tough but fair man, who knew all about the privations of the 1930s as he strove to support a family while trying to establish a motorcycle business as well as compete (very successfully) in grass-track events with a combination, a sporting endeavour which clearly inspired John and ultimately set him on the path to fame.

His mother and father had no home of their own when John was born on 11 February 1934; instead, they were living temporarily at John's aunt's house in Tatsfield. But Jack Surtees soon started a motorcycle repair shop in Tamworth Road, West Croydon, and when this was relocated to Elmers End, he and his family, which by now included younger brother Norman, were able to occupy the flat above it.

Shortly after the start of the Second World War, Jack Surtees was posted to Catterick to train despatch riders in the Royal Corps of Signals, and the family, with the recent addition of John's new sister Dorothy, were relocated into a council-house in Homer Road, Shirley. But when a bomb dropped in their front garden and they were covered in debris whilst taking cover in their indoor shelter, Jack hastened to move them to Yorkshire, initially into a tiny flat opposite the barracks and later into a pair of cottages which had been joined together on the moors near Huddersfield. It was here that John's great love of the countryside and his distaste for inner-city urban life was born.

A move back to the South seemed sensible, and as the repaired Homer Road property was now occupied by others, an alternative was found in near-by Mardell Road, conveniently close to Monk's Orchard Primary School, where John was educated until 1946, when he transferred to Ashburton Secondary Modern School in Long Lane. Shortly afterwards came another move, this time to Palace Green, Old Addington, where a garden shed became his hobby headquarters in which he made modifications to his pushbike, built model aircraft and inevitably graduated into motorcycle parts 'liberated' from his father's premises, now located in Sunderland Road, Forest Hill.

It was there that John first became a wage-earner after leaving school at 15, becoming his father's 'gofer' while he gained a feel for the business prior to taking an apprenticeship with motorcycle manufacturers, Vincent, at Stevenage. Soon his own prowess in the saddle was to become apparent, and what started off as a leisure activity was quickly transformed into a profession.

With the successes came financial security and this gave him the opportunity to enjoy the fresh air of country living as well as to build a property investment business. For a time he and his first wife lived in the family home in Purley; then they moved to Limpsfield. The next change of home was to South Godstone, and ultimately to a manor house near Edenbridge, where John spent years meticulously restoring the building in which he now lives with his second wife and their family.

Team Surtees, his racing-car construction business, was also based in Edenbridge, but eventually it was to be closed with just one spot of unfinished business: although successful in other single-seater racing categories, a Surtees car failed to win a Formula One Grand Prix, although John's great friend, the late Mike Hailwood – another convert from two to four wheels – came close when he finished runner-up in the 1972 Italian Grand Prix in one of John's cars behind the Lotus of the newly-crowned World Champion Emerson Fittipaldi.

Today, John Surtees is still to be seen around the racetracks, usually at historic meetings, where his collection of beautifully maintained motorcycles from the past are always in demand, or like those other famous contemporaries, Sir Stirling Moss and Sir Jack Brabham, taking guest drives in the sort of cars which decades earlier took them to fame. Like them, he is one of an elite bunch of the sport's elder statesmen, still close to the heart of decision-making, where their experience and connections are so often in demand. It is a role John Surtees clearly enjoys; indeed, throughout his half century of involvement with motorcycles and cars travelling unusually quickly, his smile has probably never been quite as broad as it is today.

In July 1990 John Surtees sampled the power of a supercharged 1939 Grand Prix car when he was invited to demonstrate this restored V12 Auto Union at the first Christie's Historic Festival at Silverstone. He was both amazed and delighted by the experience. (J.B.)

The arrow-like front end was a familiar trademark of the Surtees Formula One car. Somehow, John managed to combine the roles of designer, builder, team manager and driver, but outright victory in a World Championship race was to elude his team, which he operated from 1970 to 1978. (J.B.)

THE DORAN SCHOOL OF DANCING

Principals : The Misses Dorothy and Joan Lintott

Phone : ADDiscombe 1878/2598/1863

A.R.A.D. Advanced Certificates
L.I.S.T.D. Stage Branch
F.I.S.T.D. National Movement Branch

M.I.S.T.D. Ballroom, Operatic
National and
Historical Branches

SPECIAL FEATURES

BABIES FROM 2½ YEARS OF AGE

Coaching for—
R.A.D. GRADE EXAMINATIONS   R.A.D. MAJOR EXAMINATIONS
I.S.T.D. NATIONAL MEDAL TESTS   I.S.T.D. TAP MEDAL TESTS
GIRLS' and BOYS' BALLROOM CLASSES

SCHOOLS VISITED

Dances and Ballets arranged and taught

Apply for full particuars to :

"HIGHLANDS," 257 ADDISCOMBE ROAD, CROYDON

CLASSES AT

SHIRLEY PARISH HALL   ST. MILDRED'S HALL
81 WICKHAM ROAD   and   BINGHAM ROAD
SHIRLEY   CROYDON   CROYDON

PRIVATE LESSONS

"DOVERCOURT," 1 NORTHAMPTON ROAD, CROYDON

Above: *The Owlers Concert Party were a well-known local troupe who performed many concerts for charity.* (B.B.)

Left: *1960* (P.N.)

Mrs Winifred Salusbury Tardrew receives a bouquet at St Mildred's Hall in 1956. (B.B.)

Fourteen

Music & Dance

Let's Dance, Addiscombe Record Shop & Beat That

Let's Dance

Dorothy Anglers, Barbara Broughton,
Arthur Burns & Anne Bridge

One's feet never needed to stay still in Addiscombe. From the 1930s to the early '60s there was a choice of dance schools just in Addiscombe: Doran School of Dance, Paula Lemoine, Lonsdale School of Dance by St James Lodge, Lower Addiscombe Road, George Holden School of Dancing, not to forget the impressive sounding Progressive School of Music, Elocution and Dance.

Arthur Burns remembers the George Holden School of Dancing, Lower Addiscombe Road, almost opposite the end of Leslie Park Road:

My sister, Sheila, learned to dance there, attending three or four times a week, at about 2s.0d. (10p) a lesson. She is an excellent dancer, so it was money well spent.

Barbara Broughton attended the Progressive School of Music, Elocution and Dance run by Mrs Winifred Salusbury Tardrew, a lady dedicated to the young people she taught. The school was based at Alverston House, 155 Lower Addiscombe Road where the east part of Academy Gardens now stands:

It was a fine house with a flight of steps leading up to the main floor. On the right on entering the house was the large room known as the studio, which was used for ballroom, ballet and tap-dancing classes.

At the end of each term a 'Studio Concert' was held when the piano, singing and elocution pupils performed in front of their parents and a collection was made either for King George's Fund for Sailors (a charity which is still in existence) or for the Church of England Children's Society, now known simply as The Children's Society. Shows were also given at the Civic Hall, Croydon (where Littlewoods store is now), St Mildred's Hall, St Peter's Hall and numerous other venues including

old people's homes. Most of these shows were in aid of the same two charities.

Dorothy Anglers and her sister taught at the Doran School of Dance, a highly successful school between 1932 and the early 1960s. 'Doran' was an amalgamation of their two names, Dorothy and Joan. It was a truly family affair with Dorothy and Joan's parents playing an active role, father laying the wooden floors and mother making the tea. A brass plaque outside the house in Addiscombe Road, on the corner of Ashburton Road, bore the name Doran School of Dancing. The ground-floor studio had a beautifully laid wooden floor that was perfect for dancing. The school attracted so many pupils that Dorothy's father laid the floor upstairs for the upper studio. During the Second World War around 300 pupils a week would dance in one or other of the studios. Classes were also held at Shirley Hall and St Mildred's Hall. Many of the pupils came from the Sandilands area. Pupils could begin as early as two-and-a-half years. The house was eventually sold in the early 1960s so that Dorothy and Joan could look after their parents well in their old age.

By the 1960s formal dance training had become less popular. New ways of dancing had arrived and increasingly young people preferred just to rock!

1960 (P.N.)

153

Addiscombe Record Shop
Paul Nihill & John Hobbs

Paul Nihill recounts:

At Number 235b Lower Addiscombe Road were the Addiscombe Music Stores, situated virtually under the now demolished railway bridge just a short way from Bingham Road Station. This store must have been the smallest record shop in the world yet they seemed to stock almost everything and - don't forget - in the mid 1950s we are talking about cumbersome 78s (a 10" gramophone record). Unlike today, where you pay for anything to do with a pop star, in those days you could collect, free of charge, no end of photographs of your favourite recording artists. The store even had a 24-hour service where they would despatch an LP record anywhere. The wonderful shop where I used to buy my Frankie Laine records has been closed for many years and the shop itself has finally disappeared to make way for the new tramway.

John Hobbs:

Every morning from August 1959 after getting off the No. 59 bus at Bingham Halt I had to walk under the bridge in Lower Addiscombe Road stopping at Pete's shop under the bridge to buy a paper, pausing at the record shop to look in the window to check the latest charts and turn into Pavement Square where I worked at Fernhurst Precision Tool Co.

I was the youngest lad in the firm so was often sent out shopping for the whole firm to get rolls, etc. which meant the shop would be open and I used to pop in for a quick look around. I got caught by the foreman more times than was good for me.

The owner, Ralph, and his assistant who was very tall and wore thick black horn-rimmed glasses were usually at the door. Ralph was often smoking a cigarette; he wore thick gold-rimmed glasses and had a moustache, and was usually wearing a cardigan. He knew all the local shop owners and was very friendly.

He knew our boss and would often pop his head around the door of our workshop to get a little job done; he would say 'It's only a small job, could someone make this or that up for me? I've seen the boss.'

I had a passion for all the latest records and come Thursday lunchtime having been paid I would make my way to see Ralph in his super record shop to see what new releases were out. Rarely would a week go by without a purchase, although I was only an apprentice toolmaker, and often got my leg pulled by my other workmates saying, 'If you stayed out of the record shop you might have some money to last the week.' Over the next seven years or so I spent many an hour and pounds in Ralph's shop building up my record collection.

As to the records I used to buy, it was the early 1960s and I liked traditional jazz, Acker Bilk, Chris Barber and anything pop, Bobby Darin's Mack the Knife, Beyond the Sea, Elvis Presley; I even liked Cliff Richard in those days. The early Stones were great plus The Beatles, who I saw live at the A.B.C. cinema, and The Animals. There was just so much good music in that era. It was great to have lived through those fab times.

I was a real cool-cat. I remember Sonny Boy Williamson, a blues singer. He used to appear live at the Star pub along with Yardbirds. No wonder I never had any money left.

Beat That
A Musical Rock & Roll Around Addiscombe by
Steve Collins & John Hobbs

Over the past 50 years, Addiscombe seems to have begotten and attracted many talented - some now famous - musicians. We'll start with Cliff Marlow (see Chapter Ten). Born of a musical family, he remains an accomplished drummer, keyboard and vibraphone player. During 1945-46 he ran a three-piece band, playing locally in Cherry Orchard Road and the Leslie Park Methodist Club. He well remembers a 1946 gig for the Women's Unit Air Corps when he had to wait until enough men had arrived to lift the grand piano onto the stage. The music of the time was very much dance music. Having listened to the likes of Ambrose and Glen Miller, Cliff was well equipped to entertain. After leaving the Air Force in 1951 and living in Dalmally Road, he formed another three-piece band (drums, guitar, piano) which gigged extensively throughout South London, and was later a regular feature at the new Arnhem Gallery.

In the early 1950s we also had Margaret Robson (see Chapter Ten) playing skiffle - tea chest, and washboard stuff - in the basement of the Express Dairy, then next to Dr Thompson's surgery at the corner of Morland and Lower Addiscombe Roads.

In the early 1950s we still had food rationing, were recovering from war, had a baby boom, the new National Health Service was proving itself, and there was great enthusiasm for a new lifestyle. This was

Cliff's music room above the shop at 157 Portland Road, 1986. (C.M.)

Left: Cliff Marlow at the Downham Tavern, 1975. (C.M.)

Above: *Cliff Marlow on the roof of St James Lodge, Lower Addiscombe Road, c.1943.* (C.M.)

nies were prepared to gamble on promoting new artists with their new style of music. And so pop music was born, and the kids tuned into Radio Luxembourg to hear the latest. If they liked it, then (in Addiscombe) they rushed to Ralph's record shop to buy it.

The growth in record sales during the early '50s was phenomenal. As a marketing wheeze, the competing record companies thought it would be a good idea that the public should know each week's most popular record (by sales), and turn it into a kind of competition. Thus, on 14 November 1952 the Charts began - the Top of the Pops! In fact, it started life as the Top Twelve (pre-decimal!), and the No. 1 was 'Here in My Heart' by Al Martino on the Capitol label.

The 1953 Charts were dominated by the likes of Guy Mitchell, Frankie Laine, David Whitfield, Perry Como, The Stargazers (regulars on the Billy Cotton Band Show) and, cutely, the cerebral '(How Much is) That Doggie in the Window?' by Lita Roza... all sing along please.

At the beginning of 1954, amongst others, the Charts figured Eddie Calvert (on trumpet) with 'Oh Mein Papa', Doris Day with 'Secret Love', Johnnie Ray with 'Such a Night' and Frank Sinatra chucking 'Three Coins in the Fountain'. The Top 20 began on 1 October 1954 and was dominated by Winifred Atwell and Vera Lynn. In 1955 the Charts included Jimmy Young, Dickie Valentine and Alma Cogan. All of this music was basically 'light listening' and echoed back to dance music. Ballroom dancing was very popular at the time and the music was designed to match it.

On 25 November 1955 everything changed. Bill Haley and his Comets hit No. 1 with 'Rock Around the Clock'. On 6 January 1956 Lonnie Donegan was top of the pops with 'Rock Island Line', and rather importantly in May 1956 Elvis Presley had No. 1 hits with both 'Heartbreak Hotel' and 'Blue Suede Shoes'.

Rock was here to stay and the kids wanted to be part of it. Throughout the land bands were formed, in youth clubs, church halls, schools, front rooms, bedrooms and back gardens. Using the new electric guitar, anywhere close to a plug would do! At all times of day and night, the sound of guitars, drums and singing could be heard. Nothing was going to stop these youngsters achieving their aim of fame.

Astonishingly, the whole musical spirit of the time was identified by BBC TV. On radio, 'Auntie' did not figure 'pop' music. But someone on the TV side thought it would be a good idea. Until 1955 there had been just one mono 405 line channel, and the number of sets were few. Programme material was sparse (it drifted off into potter's wheel interludes) since all of the programmes were live.

Until 1957 a closed period of television between 6-7p.m., called the 'Toddlers Truce', was in place.

particularly so for the then teenagers; a teenager had not existed before, kids leaving school instead at 14 for a job or getting called up. Now there was more leisure time, and as music has always been the food of love, the boys in particular went for it in a big way!

Methods of recording music were going through major and innovative changes. In 1948 Columbia Records demonstrated 12" unbreakable vinyl disks that could play about 25 minutes of music a side at 33$\frac{1}{3}$rpm. Victor soon countered with its own microgroove records - 7" vinyl discs at 45rpm - which could hold as much music as the then 12" 78rpm shellac (rigid) records, but of course were smaller, lighter and unbreakable. By 1950 the pattern had been set - 12" 33$\frac{1}{3}$rpm for albums and 7" 45rpm for singles. Later, extended play (EP) 7" 45s were also developed and were particularly popular in the early 1960s.

As pressing and distributing vinyl records was a much cheaper process than with 78s, record compa-

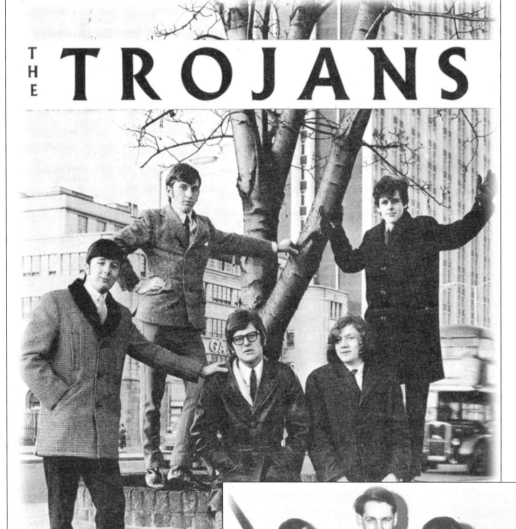

THE TROJANS

Left: *The Trojans outside the Fairfield Halls.* Left to right: *Tim Guest, Mike Roberts, Phil Saunders, Derek Needham, David Little.*
(M.Ro.)

Below: *Society Five.* Left to right: *Mike Roberts, Derek Spiller, John Wallace, Matthew Fisher, Mike Shun.*
(M.Ro.)

This basically meant that there was nothing on! This was famously and formally ended on Saturday 16 February 1957 at 6p.m., when the BBC televised a five-minute news bulletin, followed by, as they announced, 'a new programme aimed at young people, featuring live music and a live audience'. And so the Six-Five Special was born. It made both television and rock 'n' roll history – just think of it as a really live current-day 'Top of the Pops'. Your chance to see the hit makers of the day.

The first intro and outro Six-Five Special theme music was played by Kenny Baker and his Jazzmen. Michael Holiday sang songs such as 'Hot Diggity', and the rock was provided by Bobbie and Rudy and the King Brothers. The first show was introduced by Pete Murray:

Welcome aboard the Six-Five Special. We've got almost a hundred cats jumping here, some really cool characters to give us the gas, so just get on with it and have a ball.

Intended to run for just six weeks, the Six-Five Special was an instant hit and rocked and rolled on. It showcased the likes of Tommy Steele (our first native rocker), Jim Dale, Marty Wild, Lonnie Donegan, The Mudlarks and Don Lang and the Frantic Five (who recorded the excellent theme tune). It was a cult programme, the first of its kind, and had a tremendous influence on how and what to play musically.

Inspired by American rhythm and blues and rock artists, local bands had a heyday with their covers. Amongst the many were strong songs from Little Richard (UK chart-ranking hits from 1956-64), Chuck Berry (UK charts 1957-73) and Bo Diddley (UK charts 1963-65, actually remixing his earlier originals to compete with the local covers).

And so the 1960s were here. The Beatles had their first hit with 'Love Me Do' in October 1962, the Rolling Stones with 'Come On' in July 1963. The times were swinging and Addiscombe's major musical contribution of the times came from Glen Athens & The Trojans. This was a five-piece band that frequently changed personnel, sharing some with the also local 'The Society Five'. The vocalist Glen Athens (who was really Phil Saunders) and Tim Guest (guitar) were in all the line-ups. At various times there was Mike Roberts (guitar), John Gestico (bass), replaced by Dave Coleman, then Matthew Fisher, then Derek (Del) Needham, Ray Cummings and Dave Little (drums), and Ken Howes (rhythm guitar).

The group used to practise in Phil's parents' Morland Road front room. The first Trojans gig was at the 'Ban the Bomb Club' in Enmore Road, Croydon in 1960. Clearly their music was of appeal. Apart from regular gigs at the West Croydon 'Star Hotel', they played the 100 Club and the Marquee in London. As was the thing to do at the time, they toured Germany in an old van with a 'Trojan horse' mounted on the top with surprise light-up eyes! The fact that it was an old rocking horse mounted on springs did not detract from the impact.

The group won in a Surrey Beat Group contest in 1964, which enabled them to record in 1965 a four-track EP (Spot 7E 1018). The record was self entitled, and according to the critics contained the stand-out track 'Let Me Show You How', a slow bluesy number, complete with fuzzy guitar and garage-style vocals. This record is now really very rare and sought after by collectors.

The Trojans (as they were then simply known) called it a day in late 1965. Phil Saunders went on to get a 'proper job' as his mum had always wanted, and is now a solicitor. Mike Roberts continues to write and record songs and in 1997 won an award for 'Sarah Jane' in the Great British Songwriting Competition. Matthew Fisher placed an ad in *Melody Maker*, saying 'Hammond Organist seeks band', and Procol Harum (who had never recorded before) responded. He was not too impressed with them at first: 'I'll give them three months or something, full of big ideas (heard it all before), but at least they write their own songs, something I have been looking for.' Within those three months, in May 1967, 'A Whiter Shade of Pale' hit the No. 1 spot,

remained there for 15 weeks, and became a worldwide mega hit. Over all of this, Matthew reports that he thought it 'would be good to have a pop record that used some of the features of a Bach prelude.' The number is probably better remembered for his sweeping organ playing than the enigmatic lyrics.

Born in Addiscombe, Matthew attended Selhurst Grammar School before moving on to the Guildhall School of Music and divides his time between the band and freelance computer programming. Rock on! Well, he has. At the age of 56, and whilst we were going to press, Matthew has just got married.

Other local pop personalities include Desmond Dekker who lived in Canning Road for many years and in March 1969 had a 14-week No. 1 hit with the 'Israelites'. And just around the corner we still have Mr Otis Grand, the world-famous rock blues guitarist.

The Old Vicarage in Canning Road used to be bedsits before being converted. It was a haven for rock musicians, provided both intimate contact and space to form bands and to make music. We know of at least five bands that are still playing today that went through this excellent schooling. These include Alan Higgins (excellent R&B guitarist and songwriter) and Kevin Gibbons, drummer and vocalist with SKP. Rock on Addiscombe !

For more information do see the excellent *Rockin' and Around Croydon*, Chris Groom, ISBN 0-9531619-0-0.

Alan Higgins playing a charity gig in Croydon for the Parkinson's Disease Society, April 2002. (A.B.)

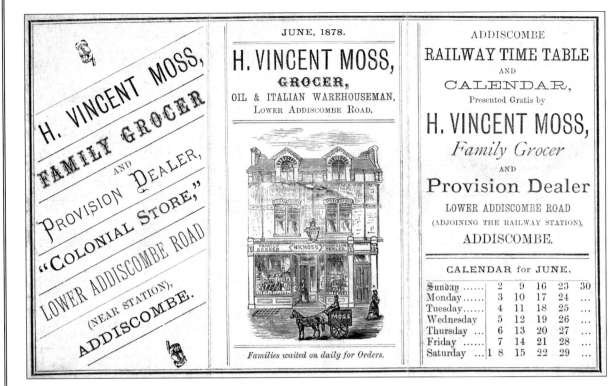

Mr H. Vincent Moss, who had a grocers shop at 127 Lower Addiscombe Road (now part of The Alma), was a Councillor from 1899 until his sudden death in 1918 aged 72. (R.M.)

Albert Jackson, who had a shoe shop in Cherry Orchard Road, was elected the first Councillor of the new Addiscombe Ward in 1921. He did much for people in the area. Mr Jackson is pictured here with his daughter, Ivy, in 1926. (P. & C.L.)

Fifteen

Always a Marginal: Never a Dull Moment

An Electoral History of Addiscombe, by John Cartwright

Addiscombe lies at the geographical heart of Croydon. Neither an inner-city area like Thornton Heath to the north, nor an affluent village like Sanderstead or Purley to the south, it is perhaps a community representative of Croydon as a whole. Its electoral history reflects this central position as well.

When the Borough of Croydon became a political entity in 1883, there were only six large wards, each represented by six Councillors. Addiscombe then was only a part of the East Ward, stretching from East Croydon Station to the edges of South Norwood, Shirley and Croham Road. The first six Councillors elected in June 1883 were Messrs Barrow, Grundy, Gurney, Hobbs, Steele and Thompson. As in the rest of the borough, these Councillors were elected on a non-party basis and would have been local notables rather than the professional politicians of today.

From 1883 to 1920 annual elections were held, with two Councillors being elected each year for a three-year term. Many were unopposed elections (i.e. only two candidates standing). One of the defeated candidates in this period was the intrepid Mr E. Courtenay-Wells, who valiantly stood 16 times in different wards in Croydon from 1899–1920. Despite an all-time record for the lowest number of votes for any candidate in local elections in Croydon, with 13 votes in Upper Norwood in 1900, he managed an impressive 46 votes in East Ward in the same year.

At about the same time local politics were first infiltrated by party organisations. Labour started fielding candidates in a few wards in 1891 and in East Ward from 1902 onwards. Croydon Council was still dominated by independent members and some elected under the label 'Ratepayer' or 'Resident', but the growing involvement of Labour in local elections meant that the 'Ratepayer' label came to be seen by some as a convenient description for crypto-Conservatives. This is not altogether fair; local issues were different from national ones, and the political parties were not controlled by diktats from national headquarters in the same rigid way that is common today. Nevertheless, there would have been a considerable overlap in the membership, social structure and aims of some of the Ratepayers' Associations and local Conservative Association branches in some wards.

In 1919 Cllr W.G. Stapleton was re-elected after 22 years' continuous service, being joined by Mr J.E. Taylor who was elected as the first Labour Councillor in East Ward, defeating the second Ratepayer candidate by some 200 votes in a close four-way contest.

Addiscombe Ward was first made a district ward in 1920, when the large wards were sub-divided into 14 three-member wards. Whereas some in the north of Croydon have undergone substantial demographic change, changing from safe Conservative to marginal or from marginal to safe Labour, Addiscombe is distinct in that, ever since its creation, it has always been a marginal. The very first contest in 1921 set the scene which has continued ever since: A. Jackson (Ratepayers' Association) 1,208; Gilbert A. Foan (Labour) 1,202. Although J.E. Taylor was elected unopposed as a Labour member in 1922, the Ratepayers' Association won again in 1923 and 1924.

In 1925 a wave of discontent swept Croydon as the breakaway Ratepayers' Protection Association was formed in protest against rising rates. The six Ratepayers' Protection Association candidates were all elected, some with substantial majorities, although in Addiscombe Major Rees won another exciting cliffhanger in a three-way contest against the Addiscombe Ward Ratepayers' Association as well as the Labour Party: Major Frank W. Rees (Ratepayers' Protection Association) 1,312; George Nightingale (Labour) 1,291; Mabel Glazier (Ratepayers' Association) 1,216.

The pattern continued, with Ratepayer and Labour Councillors being elected at different times, until the Second World War. This was interrupted by a dramatic sequence of events in the summer of 1936. In May, after 11 years as a Councillor, Major Rees was promoted by fellow members to Alderman, thereby creating a vacancy for the position of Councillor. A brief but vigorously fought campaign ensued in the by-election. The candidate for the Addiscombe Ward Ratepayers' Association was Mr Charles Lewin, estate agent, auctioneer, golf-player and mason. He had been a Councillor from 1932 to 1935, when he was defeated by Labour, and took the chance to win back the seat in the by-election. After a recount, the result was declared at the Town Hall to a cheering crowd on the evening of 19 June: Charles Lewin (Ratepayers' Association) 1,448; Frank Mitchell (Labour) 1,431.

Mr Lewin's career as a Councillor was to be as precarious as his 17-vote majority. After only a week and a half in office, Councillor Lewin was rushed to the Middlesex Hospital suffering from what was described as 'internal trouble' and underwent two emergency operations. He died on 1 July 1936 at the age of only 51, and the voters of Addiscombe were required to turn out again for the second by-election within two months. There was an increased turnout and on 30 July the tables were turned when the Labour candidate, Frank Mitchell, reversed his defeat of six weeks earlier: Frank Mitchell (Labour) 1,684; Harold Watson (Ratepayers' Association) 1,475.

The marginal nature of Addiscombe Ward was again emphasised in November of the same year when Mabel Glazier (who had become Addiscombe's first female Councillor in 1930) was re-elected by a majority of only four over her Labour opponent.

The routine domesticity of municipal politics was enlivened in 1937–38 when the British Union of Fascists put up candidates in Addiscombe, but they received a derisory number of votes (137 and 77 respectively) and the continuing process of alternating Ratepayer and Labour victories continued after the Second World War.

Apart from the intervention of a Communist candidate, a Mrs A. Jarrett in 1947 and 1950, the same two-party contest continued. It was not until 1955 that a Liberal Party candidate contested Addiscombe for the first time, K.H. Simmons, who received 393 votes: H. Lewis (Ratepayers Association) 3,071; Roger Griffith (Labour) 2,237.

Four consecutive years of Labour victories were ended in 1960 when, for the first time, a candidate stood in Addiscombe specifically under the overtly political auspices of the Conservatives. D.A. Nye was Addiscombe's first Conservative Councillor; true to form he too was duly defeated by Labour in 1963.

In 1964 a major reorganisation of local government in London took place. The establishment of the GLC and the expansion of the Borough of Croydon to include Coulsdon and Purley was accompanied by a new electoral system whereby all three Councillors were elected at the same time. Thus the three sitting Labour Councillors – J. Grieve-Smith (elected 1961), R. Taverner (1962) and L. Wood (1963) – all stood (successfully) for re-election in 1964.

By now the fortunes of the political parties locally had already come to reflect more closely the national situation and the mid-term unpopularity of the Wilson government brought about the election of three Conservatives in 1968. Labour won again in the main elections in 1971 and 1974; in October 1973 Mrs Mary Walker was elected in a by-election. The three Labour Councillors were defeated in 1978 and Mrs Walker subsequently became a Councillor in Fieldway (New Addington) and went on to be the first leader of the Labour Council in Croydon in 1994.

By 1986 demographic changes in Croydon meant that a stronger Labour vote was developing in several of the wards further north. In that year Labour gained 21 seats, rising from five to 26 out of 70, and came to within striking distance of being able to win an overall majority. Jerry Fitzpatrick led the field, followed by Martin Walker and Nancy Irwin, who scraped in third place by a margin of 19 votes. And 1986 was also a good year for the Liberal/SDP alliance which was only a few hundred votes behind the Conservatives in Addiscombe.

The 1990 elections were disappointing for Labour. High hopes of victory were dashed when a few Labour gains were offset by a loss of one of the Addiscombe seats: Richard Billington (Conservative) gained a seat from Martin Walker by a majority of 15. In 1994 a tidal wave of national popularity swept Labour to overall power in Croydon for the first time, with 40 seats to the Conservatives' 30. In line with this, Jerry Fitzpatrick was comfortably re-elected and was joined by his colleagues, Sean Fitzsimons and Bernadette Khan. Their majorities were comfortable but not overwhelming; for the second time there was also a sizeable vote, some 500 votes, for the Green Party.

The Labour victory was repeated in 1998 when Ms Khan retired and was replaced by Amanda Campbell. The Liberal Democrats were pushed into fourth place by Local Resident candidate, Steve Collins, with a respectable 533 votes. In 2002 three Labour Councillors were again returned, Mark Watson replacing Jerry Fitzpatrick who retired.

Substantial demographic and political changes have swept through Croydon over the last 20 years. After 100 years of domination by Conservatives (and Ratepayers), Croydon is now on a knife's edge between the two main parties. Although many wards have become safe Labour wards over these last few years, Addiscombe is not one of them. It is still just as marginal as ever and will be high on the target list for potential Conservative gains in future elections in 2006. After 80 years of excitement, there is every prospect for cliffhanger results in Addiscombe to continue. It is a sombre thought, though, that now more than ever, the fate of Councillors and candidates from the two main parties will depend upon the perception and popularity of their respective national leaders, rather than the quality and performance of the candidates themselves.

Sixteen

Rags, Riches & Ruin

A Scandal! by Anne Bridge

The rise in fortunes of James William Hobbs was meteoric. Born in 1843 in Portsmouth, the son of a joiner, Hobbs arrived in South Norwood in 1865 aged 22 as a foreman to a builder. In 1874 he started on his own as a builder and by 1878 was living in his Croydon office at Belmont House, Addiscombe Road with a steam-powered joinery in Morland Road on the site of what is now Burnham Gardens. By 1881 he was employing 800 men and boys. In 1883 Hobbs was elected Councillor for East Ward (which included Addiscombe), Mayor in 1887 and 1888, and - the ultimate accolade - Alderman in 1889. By now he had purchased Norbury Park including the splendid mansion of Norbury Hall in which he and his family lived in the lap of luxury.

As well as having made a fortune, Hobbs was a pillar of society. The *Croydon Review* of November 1887 carried 'An Interview with the New Mayor of Croydon' for which Hobbs welcomed the interviewer into his Norbury mansion, displaying his 'usual heartiness and hospitality'. Hobbs attributed his phenomenal success to very hard work and engaging the loyalty - indeed veneration - of his employees. Hobbs claimed not to have sought the position of Mayor but was accepting it out of duty. This apparent sense of duty extended to active involvement in, and charitable donations to, the West Croydon Congregational Church and included duties as a magistrate in which 'he was voluble in dealing with prisoners, always reminding small boys charged with apple stealing that "these petty thefts lead to bigger ones."'

He should know! James William Hobbs was not quite what he appeared to be. In effect his fortune had been made by stealing money from others through a complex financial scam which was eventually to be exposed.

Let's backtrack slightly. At some point, not long after Hobbs' arrival in Croydon in 1874, he met one Jabez Spencer Balfour, first Mayor of Croydon and possessor of considerable wealth. In 1872 Balfour had created the Liberator Building Society. During the 1860s to '80s building societies had sprung up all over the place. With the rapid development of housing in Addiscombe and South London generally from the 1850s onwards the building societies allowed the less wealthy end of the middle classes to buy property for the first time. Balfour, an active member and benefactor of the Nonconformist Church, exploited the Temperance Movement and Victorian doctrine of self help to encourage Nonconformist chapels and small investors to place their savings in his hands. He deliberately overvalued the assets of his many companies to borrow excessive funds.

By 1879 Hobbs had entered into a quasi partnership with Balfour and a Mr H.G. Wright. It was from this point that Hobbs' financial fortunes appeared to make remarkable progress and in 1884 he purchased Norbury Park and Hall. The following year, unbeknown to the public, Councillor Hobbs was insolvent to the tune of £25,000. This inconvenience was resolved by a ruse which, to cut a long story short, involved turning Hobbs' business into a company limited by guarantee - thus protecting him from its liabilities. This company was ultimately financed by the Liberator Building Society which, as we have learnt, was itself funded by small investors duped by Balfour's exaggerated claims of the asset value of his companies. Hobbs, Balfour, Wright and their business associates managed to escape detection all during the 1870s and '80s thanks to an economic boom which kept funds flowing in freely... and out into their own pockets.

These leading actors of Croydon society were unmasked, however, when the depression of 1890 led eventually to the collapse of all companies in which they were involved in September 1892 with assets totalling £40,000 and debts of £7 million. Jabez Spencer Balfour promptly 'did a runner' to Argentina, leaving his business associates to face the courts.

On 22 and 23 April 1893 James William Hobbs was found guilty in the Criminal Court of forgery, making false entries in the company books and stealing company money. Hobbs had the gall to stand up in court and insist on making a statement in mitigation of his sentence claiming that he had never touched a shilling of commission from these companies! The judge, Mr Justice Hawkins, was unimpressed and proceeded to berate Hobbs for a wicked scheme and a crime of great magnitude. In stealing this money had it ever occurred to Hobbs how many hundreds, aye thousands, he and his associates had rendered desolate by their robberies of the treasured savings they had entrusted to the Liberator Building Society? Hobbs was responsible for leaving 'those innocent people beggars in their old age'. He promptly sentenced Hobbs to 12 years penal servitude and prisoner T180 was duly transported to Wormwood Scrubs.

Having served less than half his sentence, Hobbs secured an early release from prison on 18 January 1898 on the grounds of ill health. Miraculously he managed to recover sufficiently to live a further 16 years in considerable comfort at Norbury Hall. Some of the small investors Hobbs helped to ruin committed suicide rather than face destitution. Hobbs' legacy to our area lives on in houses he built in Cherry Orchard and Cross Roads - and in the red mayoral robes he introduced during his tenure which are still worn in the Council Chamber to this day.

Top: *Hobbs was the Mayor in 1887 and 1888 and is pictured in the red mayoral robes that he introduced.*
Above: *James William Hobbs with his family at Norbury Hall.* (Both C.L.S.L.)

Seventeen

Second World War: The Home Front

Hold Your Fire, A Lady's Diary, A Young Adult's & A Child's View

The Second World War remains vivid in many people's memories. What was life like in the Addiscombe area at the time? We consider this from different viewpoints: the dedicated Home Guard, a lady's diary, a young adult's experience and a child's view.

Hold Your Fire

The Home Guard by Les Ives, Eric Burley, Bill Wood,
Stanley Howey & John M. Haybittle

The Home Guard in Addiscombe and neighbouring Woodside and Shirley played an invaluable role in defending the area and helping those affected by bomb damage. Its members were those who were outside the age range for joining the Army or who were in reserved occupations deemed vital to the war effort. Many of its members were veterans of the First World War who taught the younger men a great deal about being a soldier. The Home Guard members were dedicated individuals who after a full day at work would spend two or three nights a week on Home Guard duties. Les Ives recalls:

The Home Guard did have a serious role to play in the defence of this country. It was not all like Dad's Army. We had all-night guard duties to perform. Remember we all had to go to work next day. There was also night and weekend training. The Home Guard gave help and assistance to the civil defence and police.

There were, however, many funny incidents that occurred. On one night exercise the enemy was another Home Guard unit, their target being the Telephone Exchange in Lower Addiscombe Road. Myself and one other chap were sent out. Making our way up Shirley Road, not a soul in sight, we split up. I had almost reached the top near the shops when I heard hobnail boots coming down at double-quick time. Laying prone under a hedge I watched the boots pass by. Meeting up with my mate we decided to go down to the Exchange and warn them. Now the only way of telling the enemy was that they wore steel helmets and we wore caps. Approaching the Exchange, making sure it had not been taken over by the tin hats, we made ourselves known to the sentry. The Sergeant of the guard promptly took us prisoner in the belief that we were the enemy wearing caps as a disguise.

The Home Guard took their duties very seriously and believed in what they were doing and what they could achieve if asked. For myself I still keep my cap badge with pride.

The 60th Battalion on a route march at Godstone. (E.B. & B.W.)

The Addiscombe and Woodside Home Guard. This picture was taken shortly before they were stood down in December 1944. Numbers are placed under each man's head other than in the back row where numbers are placed above heads. 1. Sergeant Nye, lived in Bingham Road and trained new recruits. 2. Sergeant Yeatman, lived in Capri Road (was bombed out) and worked at Savages, the furnishers in George Street. 3. Sergeant Elfinstone, lived in Morland Road and was an instructor on the Browning M/C gun. 4. Lieutenant Paul, lived in Blackhorse Lane and had a building and plumbing business. 5. Lieutenant Colonel Ward, Battalion commander. 6. A doctor, taught St John's First Aid. 7. Mr Leonard Ellis, lived in Park Hill Road. 8. Mr Arthur James Aveling, lived in Ashburton Road and late in the war moved to Park Hill Road. 9. Mr A.W. Burrows (Bert), competed in local musical festivals and sang in concerts at the Civic Hall in Croydon run by Mrs Salusbury Tardrew (see Chapter Fourteen). He had a great sense of humour and would take part in comedy sketches held in the Cherry Orchard Road Methodist Church Hall. Bert Burrows also had connections with Peter Lockley, working with Peter's paternal grandfather at Surrey Tiles which was owned by Mr H.W. Brimacombe who was also a partner in Hockey & Brimacombe (see Chapter Seven). Mr Burrows played in the Surrey Table Tennis League and took part in a special exhibition match at Kennards. 10. Mr Richard Gilbert, a much respected journalist with the Croydon Advertiser who played an active part in the musical life of Croydon. 11. Mr George Turner, a shoe repairer with premises in Leslie Park Road who lived at 98 Cherry Orchard Road. 12. Mr Spencer, ran a butchers shop in Cherry Orchard Road close to the pub by Cross Road. 13. Mr Stanley Howey, lived in Capri Road and worked on the assembly and tuning of bomb sights. 14. Mr Richard Letts, lived all his life in Norwood. He worked at Handley's brickworks and died in 1993 aged 88. 15. Mr Alf Arthur, worked at Langdon's the butchers in Whitehorse Road. 16. Mr Henry Howey, father of Stanley Howey, lived in Capri Road and worked for W. & T. Avery. 17. Mr Ollie Smith, retired. He lived in Everton Road and was a friend of Henry Howey. 18. Mr J. Strudwick, lived in Grant Road and worked for an engineering firm on war work. 19. Mr Les Ives, an apprentice dental mechanic at Jay's Dental Laboratory, Sydenham Road who lived at 95 Grant Road. 20. Mr Head, ran a cycle shop in St Michael's Road, West Croydon. (P. & C.L.)

Eric Burley was also a member of the Home Guard:

I joined the 60th Surrey 'B' Company at Woodside on 17 March 1941 when I was 19 years old and the officer in charge then was Major Cox. On one occasion on a Sunday morning around 1941 we had a Platoon exercise march starting at Purley and along Godstone Road through Caterham ending up at Tilling Down chalk pits firing range.

Another time we were taken to the Addiscombe small arms (.22) firing range to practise in Radcliffe Road.

The 71st anti-aircraft gun emplacement in which, I think, there were three 3.7" guns, was located at the top end of Mapledale Avenue. We did have some action against the V1 doodlebugs.

We were finally stood down in December 1944.

Below: *The 71st Surrey 'H' anti-aircraft gun encampment at Mapledale Avenue, 1944.* (E.B.)

Right: (E.B.)

Below: *The 71st Surrey 'H' anti-aircraft gun encampment at Mapledale Avenue in 1944.* (E.B.)

165

William (Bill) Wood joined the Home Guard early in the war before joining the Royal Marines in 1941 as one of the first commandos. Bill remembers some of the individuals from the Woodside Home Guard:

The Wood brothers pictured at the back of their father's butchers shop at 304 Lower Addiscombe Road in 1941. Left to right: *Ted, Bill and Jack.* (B.W.)

Harry Roper was well known as the park keeper in Ashburton Park. As a schoolboy we kept him in awe. He had a very wheezy voice; we thought he had been gassed in World War I. No graffiti or litter in 'his' park! Also in his park was Ashburton Library, a place to be admired, almost revered, a real sanctuary.

In his younger days Harry Roper had been something of an athlete. A veteran of both the Boer War and World War I, he joined the Woodside Platoon of the 60th Surrey Battalion of the Home Guard. Sergeant Roper was known for his charm and unfailing courtesy.

Sergeant Bernard Pattenden was a real friend and neighbour, a wonderful, all-round sportsman. His parents owned the grocers and Post Office at 306 Lower Addiscombe Road next to my father's butchers shop. He joined the Local Defence Volunteers just after me. When old enough, Bernard enlisted in the RAF but was tragically killed in an accident. It was a very sad loss.

One of the first men in Croydon to join the Local Defence Volunteers, Lawrence Dunn, was a member of the 60th Surrey Home Guard. Originally from Canada he was a veteran of World War I. He died suddenly while on Home Guard duty on an anti-aircraft gun site.

Stanley Howey joined the Home Guard in 1942 and stayed until January 1945 when he went into the RAF:

Addiscombe Home Guard Company HQ was a big old Victorian house opposite Hastings Road near Addiscombe Station. Parades were at Woodside School two nights a week and occasionally on Sundays at Addiscombe Cricket Ground at Sandilands. There were of course night exercises. My father joined the Home Guard immediately it was formed. He was 60 years old then.

At Company HQ there was a little model of a cannon, about 12" long and 6" high with large wheels each side. On a night exercise against some regular troops Company HQ was about to be captured. The regular Army Sergeant came up the front garden path and shouted 'This HQ is captured!' An elderly, corpulent Home Guard Sergeant placed the little cannon on the top step by the front door and shouted 'Bang!' Everyone dissolved in laughter.

To simulate a rifle being fired, firework crackers were issued. There were about four crackers on a string. One end of the string was tied to the muzzle of the rifle and the other end to the trigger guard. The string was pulled and off went a cracker and another and another, the more you pulled. I and two other warriors were in a strategic position in pitch darkness at midnight crouched behind a low wall in the front garden of Canning Road Church. Suddenly one of my companions whispered, 'There's a head coming along the wall' and indeed there was someone creeping along the other side of the wall. Someone said 'Fire!' so we gave this head a deadly fusillade of bangers. Then our Corporal, Ernie Whitehorn, whose father kept a grocers shop in Dartnell Road, shouted, 'It's me, you bloody fools!' He had come to tell us to go back to Company HQ which we did, giggling like mad. In those worrying days things like this seemed hilarious.

I worked in a factory assembling and tuning bomb sights all through the war. Work started at 7.30a.m. and went on until 7.00p.m. each day, 4.00p.m. on Saturdays and 1 o'clock on Sundays (when not on parade). Getting home, eating a meal and on parade at 8 o'clock two nights a week was a bit wearing. There was also a bit of 'fire watching' to do as well. Still, at 19 or 20 years old, it was not so bad.

Addiscombe Home Guard, with Henry Howey (right) and Ollie Smith (middle). (S.H.)

John M. Haybittle has memories of the 59th Battalion Surrey Queen's Royal Regiment – later after D-Day to become attached to the Royal Artillery when manning the AA (anti-aircraft) guns:

The Company based at Shirley Park Hotel – where Trinity School is now – was under the command of Major Shelton. Second in command was Captain Naylor and third Lieutenant Mills. The Company had three platoons, each under a Sergeant who in turn had Section Corporals and Lance Corporals. Officers and NCOs (non-commissioned officers) were always addressed by rank but curiously the rank and file of volunteers addressed each other as Mister, except the lads who used Christian names.

I belonged to a machine-gun section under Sergeant Williams. Captain Naylor and Sergeant Williams, faced with a motley crew of patriotic civilians, managed to meld them into a reasonably disciplined citizen army. We were equipped with 4.300 Vickers water-cooled machine guns and 600 rounds of ammunition for each. We worked as three-man teams: Lieutenant Corporal Tom Hammond-Smith, Volunteer Ralph Parsons (his brother-in-law) and myself.

Parade was held on Sunday at 10.00 hours and there was one night a week training when we had the use of a large wooden hut belonging (I believe) to Shirley Park Tennis Club located to the rear of the existing Shirley Park Golf Club House. There were a number of fathers and sons in the

company: *Corporal Roddis and son Bobby, Major Shelton and son Michael, Volunteer J.A. Haybittle and myself, his son. The 'boys' were usually 'callers out' because they had bicycles and were separated from their fathers, i.e. in different sections in a platoon.*

We were equipped with Canadian .300 Ross rifles and ten rounds of ammunition. These had ring and blade sights compared with the usual short-nosed Lee-Enfield (Army issue known as the Smelly) which had a V and blade sight and which I could handle. There was of course the problem that these weapons were .003, compared with our own .303, so it was not until the Canadians and Americans came over that we could 'scrounge' any extra ammunition.

We did make one visit to Marlpit Lane Quarry which was a rifle range. We fired a short burst with the Vickers and five-round rifle, a serious drain on our ammunition. To the best of my knowledge there were no casualties either to personnel or targets.

Our duties were to patrol open country in the Shirley Hills, Addington Palace and Shirley Park area. All these areas were dotted with large diameter concrete pipes in order to prevent aircraft landing. We were there to attack any parachutists. My team had a golf course bunker converted into a MG nest and my father had a slit trench just outside Oaks Farmhouse. He was a Lewis gunner. A guard was mounted at Deans Café (now the Chinese Restaurant) on Shirley Hills and at

The 59th Battalion Surrey Queen's Royal Regiment pictured near Lloyd Park and the golf course. (R.G.V.O. & J.Ha.)

John A. Haybittle and John M. Haybittle, father and son, at Selwood Road in 1941. (J.Ha.)

The 59th Battalion. (R.G.V.O. & J.Ha.)

This page: *The 59th Battalion with a 4.5" anti-aircraft gun in 1944.* (R.G.V.O. & J.Ha.)
Opposite bottom: *Lloyds Bank on the corner of Ashling and Lower Addiscombe Road. Taken from the* Advertiser, *15 November 1940.* (C.A.)

Addington Palace. This took place about once a week on a two-hours-on, two-hours-off basis. For this we were paid 1s.6d. a night and 6d. went into the Home Guard funds. A visit to the Davis Cinema in those days cost 1s.9d. For two guard duties and 2s. you could really live it up. As a bank clerk at Westminster Bank in Lower Addiscombe Road I was earning 22s.6d. a week.

We had one or two other Heath Robinson weapons in our 'arsenal'. The Northover Projector was by definition a tank buster. It was a drainpipe on legs which fired surprisingly accurately Molotov cocktails over about 200 yards, bottles containing petrol and a lighted rag fuse. There was a small supply of Mills hand-grenades and we were fortunate that we never had to throw them. The older volunteers tended to suffer from 'screws in the shoulder' and were not the best of throwers.

There was also a large iron pole-like tube called something like a Blacker Bombard. It was about ten inches bore and was filled with any bric-a-brac to hand. This was fired by a Bowden cable from a slit trench in which the operator lay. The thing itself had a spade at its base to stick into the ground. It was unmoveable once in position. I suppose I should also rate Tom Hammond-Smith's motorbike and large hand-built family-sized sidecar as a formidable war machine. He would transport Ralph Parsons and me with the Vickers gun across our area from time to time.

Some of the dedicated men who were personalities of our platoon included:

Captain Naylor, an ex World War I officer and the Manager of Barclays Bank. He lived in Birch Tree Way.

Sergeant Williams worked at the Westminster Bank and lived in Addiscombe Road opposite Shirley Park Golf Course.

Lance Corporal Gunnet, a timber importer who lived, I think, in Mapledale Avenue. His catch phrase was 'Hold your fire!' Every guard night he would produce a bag containing 5s.0d. (25p) of pennies so that all off duty could play pontoon at 1d. or 2d. stakes.

Lance Corporal Tom Hammond-Smith lived off Wickham Road. An auctioneer with Harold Williams, he was the owner of the motorcycle and sidecar secret weapon.

Volunteer Ralph Parsons lived in Craigen Avenue and was the brother-in-law of Tom. A civil servant, he was a cyclist 'caller outer' who joined the Royal Tank Regiment. He ended the war as Sergeant.

Corporal Roddis, ex World War I, lived in Selwood Road and worked at Midland Bank.

Volunteer Bobby Roddis was a cyclist who joined the Army from Midland Bank. He was

accidentally killed by a rifle being discharged while on a daily parade in barracks in Germany with the Army of Occupation.

Corporal Cecil Crabbe was in digs in Selwood Road. He was stationed on the Shirley/Lloyd Park guns. He shared my father's slit trench at Oaks Farm as a Lewis gunner. Ex World War I, he was knighted after the war as head of Friendly Societies.

Volunteer, later Corporal, J.A. Haybittle, lived in Selwood Road. A civil servant, he was on the Unemployment Assistance Board, Dingwall Road. He was the Billeting Officer for evacuees in Godalming before war was declared. Then he went to Whitehall (to the Treasury). He was posted to Algiers as archivist to Harold MacMillan to arrange the American/British landings both there and in Sicily and the Italian Campaign. On returning he rejoined the Home Guard and became Layer for Bearing on the AA guns with the rank of Corporal. He was an ex World War I Signalman in the Royal Navy.

Volunteer J.M. Haybittle came from the Westminster Bank, Addiscombe. I lived in Selwood Road from 29 June 1941 until 26 April '43 and was a cyclist 'caller outer'. I joined the RAF VR on 29 May 1942 as Air Crew and was called up on 26 April 1943. I undertook Canada flying training on 13 November 1943 and worked as a meteorologist from 9 January 1945 until 26 June 1947. I was the 'last of the lot' not the 'first of the few'. Officially I flew Tiger Moths, Cornells and Harvards. Unofficially I flew Ansons, Oxfords, DH Dragons and PBY Catalinas for which there will be no record as I was 'scrounging the trips'.

Sergeant Jepp, Platoon Sergeant, lived in Craigen Avenue.

Sergeant Morris was Platoon Sergeant.

Volunteer Peter Booth lived in Northampton Road and was training to be a solicitor. He joined the Fleet Air Arm and was commissioned. He flew twin-engined aircraft, training navigators and other air crew. After the war he became a very successful solicitor with his own partnership.

Major Shelton's son, Michael, joined the RAF from the Home Guard and was later shot down and killed.

Lieutenant Mills must have been in his late seventies and had been a regular Army Colonel.

A night to remember: *It must have been early on Sunday morning about 2.00a.m. It was thought that the Germans were on their way at the start of Operation Sea Lion, the invasion of Britain. Captain Naylor called with the order 'Home Guard turn out!' 'Stupid Boy' Haybittle and other cyclists had to jump on their bikes and call out about ten other Home Guards on their pre-rehearsed list. It was of course raining.*

You can well imagine the responses I got from various bedroom windows. Of course everybody knew it couldn't happen here. It was certainly a very resigned but calm response. A particular individual in Lower Addiscombe Road was known for his lack of enthusiasm:

Myself: *'Home Guard turn out! Report to HQ. Immediately.'*
Wife: *'Bert, Bert, there's a bloke from the Home Guard says you've got to turn out.'*
Bert: *'But it's only 2 o'clock. We don't parade till 10.'*
Wife: *'He says you've got to go now. It's raining, Bert. It won't do your shoulder any good, will it?'*

I returned to Shirley Park HQ. I collected the gun, the ammo and six Mills bombs, toted them to the MG nest and was operational by about 4.30a.m. My father meantime had set up his Lewis gun in his hole at Oaks Farm. During the next few hours the platoon began to gather and manned their posts. At about 9.45a.m. someone, who I will not name, arrived in his Lanchester car, drove up to our carefully camouflaged MG nest, parked beside the sand-bagged enclosure and informed us that he had stopped for a bath, had his breakfast and looked in at the newsagents to bring us all the Sunday papers to read. It's a bloody good job it turned out to be a false alarm!

A truly defensive operation: *There were of course incidents of a much more serious nature. Parade and patrol duties on Sunday mornings often ended with the platoon or section adjacent to the Sandrock Pub. This was most unpopular as at that time the Sandrock only had a six-day licence. There was also an occasion when there was a serious shortage of beer in the area. The White Bear at Fickleshole was known to have a supply and the Addington Home Guard made it a priority to mount guard there to prevent any other units taking advantage of the situation - a truly defensive operation. Giles the cartoonist made a cartoon about it and for some years this hung in the bar.*

Fire Watching at the Bank: *Fire watching at the bank took place every Wednesday night. On one occasion some time in the winter of 1942/3 a stick of incendiary bombs fell upon the houses and gardens on Lower Addiscombe Road between the old railway bridge and Baring Road. I tackled a number of these. Later a high-explosive bomb landed on the corner of Ashling Road opposite J. Page's china shop. The corner house was then a sub-branch of Lloyds Bank manned by a clerk for limited hours and containing a strong safe about the size of a modern washing machine. Remarkably the door blew off and a fair amount of copper and silver coins were strewn around the crater. In no time at all, although it must have been around 2.00a.m., a crowd gathered. For the following week it was surprising how many 'honest citizens' came into the bank and paid in several £5 bags of rather muddy and bent silver coins. I seem to remember that St Mildred's Church collection contained some in the offerings.*

At home: *My family slept under a large mahogany dining table in the front room of the house. We had a long-case grandfather clock which chimed the quarters and struck the hours. As the raids went on, we became exhausted and sleep became fitful. The German aircraft had unsynchronised engines giving a particularly nasty beat. A sort of WROOM, WROOM, WROOM. The reaction was 'Here they come again!' The grandfather clock would strike twelve with the gongs reverberating WROOM, WROOM, WROOM and we would fall into a fitful doze, probably waking at 3.00a.m. The claim would then be that the so and so clock had just struck fifteen. I never understood why we didn't have the sense to stop it.*

The first bombs to fall near us were in Ashburton Avenue near the junction with Craigen Avenue. We were all in bed. I heard them whooshing down, rushed into Mum and Dad's room and shouted, 'Get downstairs quick!' My dear mother, bless her heart, insisted on 'putting the bed tidy' before going downstairs. That's house proud for you - didn't want to be caught with an unmade bed if the roof blew off.

And finally: *The people of Argentina presented a Ford shooting brake to the Surrey Home Guard. It was Army green with 'Presented by Argentina' painted along the roof in red. It was presented at a big parade on Fair Field with lots of VIPs present. We never saw it again.*

At that time the Davis Cinema used to present a local news reel which they screened after the Gaumont British or Pathe News. I have not met anybody who can remember this. The reels could have been lost when a bomb fell into the auditorium, killing, I believe, nine, but fortunately it didn't explode.

A Lady's Diary

Recollections by Mrs Elsie Gilbert based on diaries kept at the time

Mrs Elsie Gilbert with David in 1940.
(D.G.)

Mrs Gilbert's husband, Richard, was for 25 years a journalist with the *Croydon Advertiser*. Born in 1894 in Eastbourne, he developed an early love of music and nature. His other interests included local history and archaeology. Richard Gilbert came to Croydon in 1935 to join the *Advertiser* as senior music critic, although during the war he had to cover other functions with the newspaper. Mr Gilbert was known for his quiet, scholarly and gentle manner. He was also a respected conductor and composer. Richard Gilbert was a veteran of the First World War and appears in the Home Guard photograph taken at Woodside School. When leaving for Home Guard duties, he was not allowed to tell his family where he was going so it was something of a revelation for his sons, David and Richard, to spot him in the photograph. The family lived at 48 Chisholm Road.

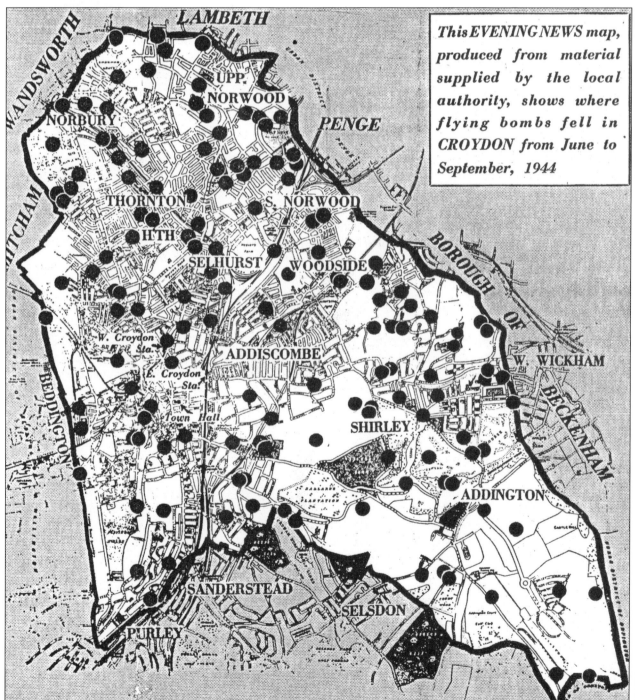

This EVENING NEWS map, produced from material supplied by the local authority, shows where flying bombs fell in CROYDON from June to September, 1944

(D.D.)

1939

With not unexpected foresight Richard saw the need for an air-raid shelter in Croydon, with the threat of impending war, and he made arrangements for a dugout to be made at the end of our garden. It was about eight feet deep (we could stand up in it). There was room for a wide plank lengthways to take a mattress and another shelf on the same level, with walking space between, to hold an electric kettle, flasks, lamp, etc. Richard made a cradle of chicken-wire and a wooden frame fitted to the wall in which baby David slept, suspended over our feet.

The floor was of wood and the sides of corrugated iron. The entrance was a square extension of this which contained the ladder by which we descended, closing the lid over us, which eliminated all sound. A heavy cable connected the dugout with the house electricity.

1940

4 AUGUST 1940: Richard had joined the Home Guard on 8 June 1940 and was on regular night duty. Air-raid warnings sounded at all times in those days, and one was sounding in the afternoon of 24 August when Ellen, Richard's sister, arrived at the station. I ran all the way home with David in his pram and took to the shelter, but Ellen, watching later at night the searchlights and anti-aircraft guns firing at the planes on the way to bombing London, said, 'Isn't it MARVELLOUS!' We could see the fires in London from our bedroom window.

8 SEPTEMBER: There was an alert at 8.00p.m. Richard was on duty at 8.30p.m. so had to go out.

9 SEPTEMBER: He saw three planes brought down. Battle of Britain day was 15 September.

27 SEPTEMBER: We watched the rout of Nazi planes by anti-aircraft guns at 3.30p.m. Richard was on night duty on the following night guarding evacuated areas.

Richard received his Home Guard uniform on 1 October.

Warnings continued to sound at all times. A raider hovering in low cloud from 12.00p.m. to 5.30 was rather unnerving. Sometimes we had day protection from a Lysander. On 10 October David and I spent 12 hours in the shelter. There were heavy night raids in the next few days and Croydon gasometer was hit and there were incendiaries in Cedar Road. Richard had night duties, gave a lecture to the Home Guard, and went to Bisley rifle

range. We may wonder how he continued to do his work at the Advertiser.

1 NOVEMBER: Bombs fell in Radcliffe Road at 1.00p.m. and there was a fire in Havelock Road 8.30p.m.

3 NOVEMBER: We risked an evening by our own fire, and there was no night raid; but on 5 November an alert lasted fourteen hours – 6.15p.m. until 8.15a.m. We found shrapnel on the lid of the dugout.

A few evenings indoors and Richard slept in the house, but by 24 November there were bombs on the Town Hall and Scarbrook Road. Richard was on night duty. 6 December was Richard's 'free day'. He had a temperature.

16 DECEMBER: Mr Thomas (Editor) went to hospital. Richard was Sub-Editor, and on 23rd was Editor.

Richard was made a Corporal in the Home Guard. Fires in the City of London.

1941

Richard, then a Sergeant, was given ammunition on 26 January, and had to have 24 hours' food. Fire watching 12.00–2.00a.m and on 1 March he had to fire a Lewis gun.

We became accustomed to the routine of raids, nights in the shelter and Home Guard night duties. We took walks around Croydon country places when 'All Clear' and would pick blackberries for jam or bottling, and we even tried stinging nettles (a substitute for spinach, we were told).

We had to go to the Food Office, which I think was at the Public Hall, about our ration cards, and David's cod-liver oil and orange juice were issued

Orange ration coupons. (M.R.)

Tunstall Road, April 1941. (C.T.)

there. Our grocers shop in Lower Addiscombe Road was bombed in April.

Also in May there was a blitz, 11.00p.m. to 5.45a.m. We slept well in the shelter but bombs had fallen in Canning Road and Park Hill Rise, we discovered the next day.

On 22 May Richard was fire watching, 11.00p.m to 2.00a.m.

There are few entries in the diary for 1942.

1943

Home Guard weekend course, 19 June. I bottled 27lbs of cherries.

14 AUGUST: Home Guard night operation. Richard very sleepy next day (Sunday).

In October Richard had a threatening duodenal ulcer. On 24 October he was 'called out' at 5.00a.m.

5 NOVEMBER: A large bomb was dropped in Clyde Road at 9.15p.m. Richard had just returned from Home Guard duty. On 9th he developed laryngitis and was unable to lecture to the Home Guard.

1944

23 FEBRUARY: Alert, late evening. Shower of explosive incendiaries in Chisholm Road. Roof on fire next door (No. 50). Windows were broken, and an anti-aircraft shell fell into the garden of No. 52. Neighbours fought the flames with buckets of water.

24 FEBRUARY: School 9.30a.m. Alert 9.45p.m. Took David to the shelter.

19 APRIL: Richard was back on Home Guard duty 8.30–12p.m.

10 JUNE: Richard has holiday from the Home Guard. There were two alerts, 4.00 to 5.00a.m.... There are rumours of radio-controlled planes.

Four arrived. On 15 June, 200 were sent (V1s). On 16th sirens sounded at 12.15a.m. Pilotless planes came over till 3.00p.m. There were alerts all day. Shelter was in great demand.

On 19 June guns were removed from London to the North Downs with the balloon barrage but many penetrated this.

The part which women played in the war effort, as it was called, should not be overlooked. They worked in munition factories and on the land as Land Girls.

On 16 July four or five bombs fell in the night after five quiet nights. Richard had to help with the bomb damage. Next day our guns were moved to the coast. Clothing coupons were being issued.

7 JULY: The Advertiser protested against censorship by printing front-page lead story about flying bombs, leaving blanks wherever censored.

21 JULY: Bad day. Dozens of flying bombs. 20,000 women and children evacuated. School breaks up. On 23rd Richard was again helping with bomb damage. Elmer's End bus garage was hit.

28 JULY: Doodlebugs came over in packets on that day and it was a noisy night which shook the dugout. There was trouble near the Parish Church.

30 JULY: Electricity supply was cut off 6.00–7.30p.m. by a flying bomb.

9 AUGUST: At 6.00a.m. a bomb fell in Ranmore Avenue.

12 AUGUST: Richard was working on bomb damage with the Home Guard.

15 SEPTEMBER: It was reported that eight weeks of flying bombs in Croydon killed 211 and injured 1,991 people, destroyed 1,400 houses and damaged 54,000.

26 NOVEMBER: There was Home Guard parade and shortly after the Home Guard was 'stood down'.

1945

28 MARCH: The last siren sounded at 7.30a.m.

22 APRIL: Our blackout restrictions were lifted.

8 MAY: VE Day. All-night street dancing and bonfires.

A Young Adult's View

Naturally a person's perspective of a situation is influenced by their age. Ivy Binstead, Bill Angell and Elsie Pamphilon were young adults during the Second World War. Ivy (born 1915) recounts:

War was declared over the radio at 11.00a.m. on 3 September 1939 and almost immediately the sirens wailed out. We rushed around. Should we close the windows or leave them open? But about ten minutes later the 'all clear' sounded. Over the next six years we often thought our end had come. We always had to carry our gas mask and be prepared to run for shelter. There were of course some long periods without raid alerts, and children were brought back from evacuation, but did have to return later.

Sometimes going and coming home from work the siren would go and you had to dive to shelter, sometimes in one of the big shops in Croydon, or under a hedge if I was cycling to work. Once we were dive-bombed while on the bus, bullets were flying and we were hustled off and into a café. We shared their cellar with rats and mice.

One night we had a direct hit on a house two or three doors from us. The whole family was killed. We were doing a jigsaw puzzle. The bomb blew all our windows and doors out, and most of the roof. Mother decided she wanted to go upstairs and get her best coat, but as there was no roof, we dared not show a light. We had to boil kettles over an open fire and collect water from a stand pipe at the top of the road. A large piece of red-hot shrapnel landed on our doorstep. Several families moved out but we decided to stay. We slept under the kitchen table and Dad in the cupboard under the stairs and later in the war in the Morrison shelter taking up most of the kitchen. In spite of all the troubles, everyone was friendly; you helped one another. You could walk safely in the blackout unless there was a raid, no fear from muggers.

Once or twice I was out in the summer evening and unexpectedly a plane would dive-bomb, bullets flying. At the top of our road was the railway line and a mobile gun used to run up and down and make a lot of noise.

Everything seemed to be rationed; clothes, furniture and worst of all food. I suppose it was all very fair but most things that were on ration seemed to be a few ounces a week; sugar, butter, fat, meat, bacon, sweets, etc.

We were fortunate as we had relations in Canada who sent us food parcels from time to time. My Aunt used to give our address to any of her friends, some of whom came over so we had a

succession of Canadian soldiers paying us a visit. They used to spend days with us and brought food and much extra rations, but sometimes they were a nuisance.

I can remember buying clothes coupons from people who did not need them, and when someone was able to get parachute silk it made wonderful underclothes and, if big enough pieces, a blouse. You could sometimes buy coarse white cotton flour bags off ration. We made all sorts of queer and useful things from these – pillow cases and cushion linings, sheets and I can remember making a skirt and dying it.

From time to time we would get a whisper that the chemist had certain cosmetics, lipstick, powder, perfume, etc., also combs, so we would rush round and get in a queue and were lucky if we got them.

Stockings (no tights) were a problem; they were not fully fashioned and had to have a seam up the back. So legs were painted and you had to get someone to draw a black line up your leg. There were many, many ways we had to make do and mend.

There were always socks, scarves, helmets, etc. to knit for the troops and, when I was in the Guides, we adopted a mine-sweeper and sent them books, magazines, cakes, etc.

I would have liked to go in the Land Army or maybe Air Force, but I was exempt from call-up as I was in a firm who supplied building materials which was considered a reserved occupation.

Mother and I went to London several times during the war to see the ruins in the City and elsewhere. The devastation around St Paul's was dreadful.

At the end of the war, Mother and I joined with thousands of people in London, seeing Winston Churchill driving along Whitehall and later at Buckingham Palace standing on the Victoria Memorial to see the Royal Family on the balcony and some weeks later going with Vin and his sisters at 6.00a.m. to London for the VE parade – a grand march-past of regiments of troops; English, Canadian, Australian, Polish, American, ARP, Land Army, Home Guard, etc.

It was good to have street lights again, to take down the blackout curtains, and no longer hear the Street Wardens cry 'PUT THAT LIGHT OUT'.

Rationing was continued well after war was over until about 1953. At one point I can remember a shipload of bananas arrived and many children did not know what they were. I made cakes with liquid paraffin and dried egg powder and mashed potatoes with banana essence to make a spread. Rationing was still on when we got married in 1948, but everyone helped out with

Left: *Kathleen Huntley in front of the air-raid shelter at 87A Cherry Orchard Road, with St John's Terrace in the background, 1941.* (K.S.)

Right: *A clothing ration book.* (M.R.)

Elsie Pamphilon recalls:

15 February 1941 was my wedding day. Captain McKinney was giving me away; the Revd Wright was marrying us. My husband-to-be was in the Navy taking his first leave from Chatham Barracks. Unfortunately he did not leave Chatham when expected, missed the only train, found a taxi and arrived nearly two hours late!! The church was packed with people, the vicar had a Church Council Meeting in the Crypt scheduled for after the wedding. However, he went on with his meeting, popping up now and then murmuring 'Usually it is the bride we wait for; this time it is the bridegroom.'

The organist gave a recital and eventually the wedding service was performed with the bridegroom in his sailor's uniform and the bride thinking she was marrying the wrong man. She hadn't seen him for three months and he looked very strange in uniform!! Of course the small reception was practically nil. Wartime people had to reach home before dark.

extras; even the Co-op Manager secretly gave us ingredients for our wedding cake. We had to have dockets to sparsely furnish our house.

Bill Angell (born 1923) was 16 when war broke out. His parents had an elderly lodger by the name of Mrs or Miss Johnson. During the war a bomb dropped over the junction of Tunstall and Addiscombe Court Roads. This was in the same raid that badly damaged Turners Garage. The blast came through a gap between the houses across the road, blasting in the windows and blowing Bill off the couch. Mrs Johnson, being deaf, didn't realise the severity of the raid and was standing by the upstairs window which came in on top of her. Miraculously she wasn't hurt but there was dust everywhere. To this day, the bomb site has not been rebuilt. Bill was 17 at the time and the event made him resolve to join up as soon as he was 18.

Bill volunteered for the Navy and ended up in the Royal Marines. He was a founding member of the present-day 40 Commandos, called 44 during the war. During the conflict Bill's future wife, Joan, was in the ATS and, having seen a photo of Bill, was dared by a friend to write to him, which she did. They married in 1943. Just 27 days after this, Bill sailed to India and did not return for two years.

A wartime wedding in 1942. Pictured are Harold and Evelyn Adams. (E.A.)

A Child's View

Ann Butler's father, Richard Letts, was a member of the Home Guard. Ann remembers seeing him cleaning his boots and leather gaiters. During the war the family lived off Portland Road. Ann remembers seeing her father on manoeuvres with his platoon. They were crouching behind a wall in Seymour Place and she waved to say hello. Her father put his arm out sideways and Ann rushed all the way home in tears because she thought her father had indicated to go away. When Richard Letts returned home, he explained that he had in fact been waving to her but, because he wasn't able to put his hand above the wall, he had waved sideways. Richard Letts lived all his life in Norwood. He worked at Handley's brickworks and died in 1993 aged 88.

Arthur Burns (born 1925) recalls:

I remember the infamous sneak raid on Croydon Airport by German planes one summer evening in 1940. I had just finished my evening meal when I heard the noise of aeroplane engines that sounded somewhat different from usual. ... I wandered into the back garden (126 Lebanon Road) and looked up over the next door roof to see a number of planes high up in the direction of the airport. As I watched, still idly wondering why the engine note was different, I was just able to see tiny little objects drop from the planes to quickly disappear from my line of vision over next door's roof and, after a short pause, the distance-diminished sound of their landing. We were caught on the hop! In fact all those planes succeeded in getting away, though it was announced they'd all been shot down.

The British Restaurant, I think it was called, was located at the corner of Lower Addiscombe and Morland Roads, which produced cheap lunchtime meals. I'm afraid they were not only cheap, but nasty! – at least on the one visit I made there. That was rather typical of cafés, etc. generally during the war...

We spent months at a time in the Anderson shelter in the back garden during the raids. Until bunk beds came along we all had to sleep on the floor which my mother had made really comfortable with broken-up orange boxes to a depth of about eight inches, on top of which was laid a feather mattress. She and our father, younger sister and myself all lay on that, and a tight squeeze it was too, definitely a case of one turn, all turn together. The 'ordinary' raids tailed off eventually so that we were able to return to the house to sleep, only for a hasty return to the garden when flying bombs came along in 1944. As you will know, Croydon was the worst-hit area with those

and for me the frightening part was the silence when the burbling noise they made as they approached cut out before reaching us, so that you knew it was on the way down. ... on hearing it explode elsewhere brought two reactions: relief and sorrow for those whom it hit.

Otherwise land-mines were the most destructive bombs, descending relatively slowly by parachutes so that their destructive power on ground contact was spread over a wider area than bombs which caused deep craters. One such landed in Park Hill, 50 to 100 yards inside the main entrance on the right of the path. Years later the area was clearly visible by virtue of rough grass that had grown on it, compared with proper grass.

Cliff Marlow was just ten when the war began. A week before it started all children were given gas masks and evacuation was initially seen as an adventure, although it did not necessarily remain so. Neither children nor parents knew where the children would end up. Ten-year-old Cliff, his friend, Geoff, and Geoff's sister each had a letter asking if all three of them could be kept together. This made them more difficult to place. They and many other children were taken to Brighton Station and then to a hall where they were each given a bag of corned beef, biscuits and chocolate. From there they were put in buses that drove around with teachers getting out, knocking on doors and asking if the occupants would take in evacuee children. Cliff, Geoff and Geoff's sister were the last three remaining on the bus. By now they were tired and afraid. Eventually a lady in Queen's Gardens took them in to her tiny cottage but was not kind to them. Her husband in contrast was lovely. He was the Stage Door Manager at The Hippodrome. This was no longer an adventure for Cliff and he missed his mother; he cried his eyes out once in bed. The three stayed in the cottage a while and then moved on back to Addiscombe.

In early 1940 Cliff's family moved to St James Lodge on Lower Addiscombe Road. This was because a chap living further up Lebanon Road had caught a burglar one night and chased him with a shovel. Cliff's father did some night work and his mother was nervous of being in the house after the burglary. There were 25 flats in St James Lodge in a block built about 1923 behind the front building. The rent was 26 shillings rent a week (£1.30). Cliff's father told the family 'These are nice flats but we're not snobs.'

On one occasion during the war 23 of the 25 flats were alight at the same time because of an incendiary bomb. Turners Garage also suffered extensive damage during the conflict. At the time Turners comprised two very large Victorian houses with big staircases and pumps outside. Turners' lorries carried a sign across the back 'There goes Turners of Addiscombe.'

Cliff used to stand on the roof of St James Lodge and watch the East End being bombed. There was an air-raid shelter at the front right-hand side of St James Lodge. Cliff and his family were in there in 1941 when the bomb that destroyed the shops on the corner of Warren and Lower Addiscombe Roads fell. Charlie Whybrow's family were trapped under rubble for some time before eventually being rescued.

There were some old flats on the corner of Lower Addiscombe and Grant Roads which had been condemned before the war. A lot of Canadian troops were billeted there.

Peter Lockley (born 1931) recalls:

I was evacuated at the beginning of the war, as was my sister. I returned home in 1942, a little after my sister. By this time we had moved to 186A Lower Addiscombe Road, which had an Anderson shelter in the garden and a Morrison shelter in the front room, put in for the use of an elderly lady and her three grown daughters who had been billeted on my parents after being bombed out.

My mother was a chiropodist and had the shop as her surgery. Our front room was used as a waiting room, the plate-glass window had been painted for privacy and some curtains hung up. During an air raid a bomb fell a short way away and the blast bent the glass and sucked the curtains round the side, the glass went back into place leaving the curtains hanging outside and they had to be cut off.

I joined the St John's Ambulance cadets and I used to act as patient to help with the first-aid training of ARP Wardens, etc. On Guy Fawkes night 1943 I was doing my bit in Fair Field when the siren went off and the doctor taking the training session had to return home and decided to run me home on his way. I remember it was a lovely night. As we turned in to Park Lane, we were stopped for a moment by the traffic lights at George Street, then turned right and past the East Croydon Station, along Addiscombe Road. Just as we passed the top of Addiscombe Court, there was an almighty explosion. The houses and nursing home at the top of Clyde Road were hit. That was one time I was grateful to be stopped by the lights. As I was only 12, the doctor would not let me stay and help and sent me home. I can still remember the cries from those trapped in the buildings - no panic, just calling to show where they were, and seeing the plane trees lying in the road. I had to come up to Croydon just after the storm of 1987 and seeing trees down brought it all back to me.

In 1944 I was cycling along Lower Addiscombe Road on my way to school when a

German fighter came flying down the road with all guns blazing. It was then I found that a bike will go up curbs as I went into a hedge. As far as I can remember, no one was hit.

Another time I was cycling to school with my friend, Ray Tarry. We arrived on top of Gloucester Road Bridge when we noticed a plane making a strange noise and looking as though it was on fire. We suddenly realised it must be one of the new secret weapons we had heard about that morning on the news! We rode like hell to school.

John Wellfare also spent most of his childhood years in wartime Addiscombe:

My earliest recollection of the war was standing in the garden in Dalmally Road and watching a doodlebug being chased by a Spitfire. I was nine years old. I also remember being sent home early from Woodside School as an air raid was imminent. My most vivid memory was the day that a doodlebug came down in Dalmally and Capri Roads. We had a Morrison shelter in our front room, and we lay awake listening to them going over, the engine cutting out and the explosion somewhere.

It was 1945, a Saturday morning around 9.00a.m. Mum had gone to the shops. I remember my sister, Pat, and I were in the front room. Pat was in the shelter and I was playing on the floor outside the shelter. We had heard the drone of the doodlebug and suddenly she pulled me into the shelter and within no time at all the windows all blew in. If I had still been on the floor, I would have been cut to pieces. My sister had really saved my life. I can remember the front door was at the top of the stairs. The emergency services, as I remember, were on the scene almost immediately as if they were following these things around.

When repairs on the houses began, slate tiles were stacked outside houses that needed roof repairs. I ran into our house one day and sliced my leg against the edge of the slates which meant being rushed to Mayday Hospital to have it stitched. That is still vivid in my mind.

After the war we had the street party... The bomb site became the playground for us and we had... great times playing there, especially 5 November when we used to have a big bonfire. It seemed a shame at the time that the houses had to be rebuilt.

Clyde Road Nursing Home, November 1943. (B.W.)

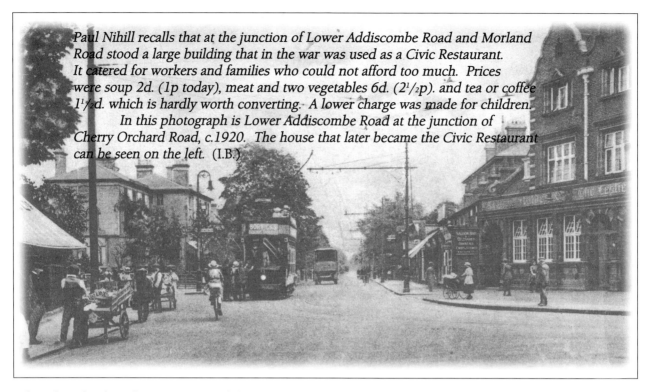

Paul Nihill recalls that at the junction of Lower Addiscombe Road and Morland Road stood a large building that in the war was used as a Civic Restaurant. It catered for workers and families who could not afford too much. Prices were soup 2d. (1p today), meat and two vegetables 6d. (2½p). and tea or coffee 1½d. which is hardly worth converting. A lower charge was made for children. In this photograph is Lower Addiscombe Road at the junction of Cherry Orchard Road, c.1920. The house that later became the Civic Restaurant can be seen on the left. (I.B.)

John Blunsden has clear memories of the war:

The word 'Addiscombe' first entered my consciousness when I was at least 120 miles away. It was in 1941, when as an 11-year-old lad I was living with my mother and younger sister in Bristol, my birthplace. It was a lovely city, or at least it had been until the centre was systematically destroyed by one blitz after another; by 1941 it had become an extremely dangerous and uncomfortable place in which to live. By that time, of course, in the South East of England the Battle of Britain was long over, and Croydon had been enjoying several months of relative tranquillity. So it was with the best of intentions that my maternal grandmother suggested that we should leave Bristol and join the rest of the family, at least for a while. It would be a squeeze, but it could be managed.

So one afternoon early in March we duly arrived at 237 Addiscombe Road, saying that we were looking forward to the rare treat of an uninterrupted night's sleep. No chance! Our arrival preceded the first of a new series of visits by the Luftwaffe by just a few hours.

Some six decades on, my memories of Addiscombe during those war years probably echo those of hundreds of other youngsters who lived here at the time, although inevitably, some have remained far more vividly than others. I recall, for example, the many times we had meticulously to check the blackout curtains to ensure that not the slightest chink of light penetrated the darkness outside (though bearing in mind the enemy were flying at the very least some 5,000 feet above us,

and were probably surrounded by exploding anti-aircraft fire, it is difficult to imagine how on earth they could have reacted to the output of a 60-watt bulb!).

Then there was the eagerness with which we tuned into the BBC Home Service to hear the latest news, good or bad, from the various war zones. If nothing else, the Second World War taught we youngsters a great deal about geography and the location of many places in distant lands which otherwise would have escaped our attention - places like Mersa Matruh, Sidi Barrani, Tobruk, Benghazi, Tripoli - we could pinpoint them all along the North-African coast as confidently as the stations between East Croydon and Victoria (perhaps even more so because, of course, the station names had disappeared from the platforms in the hope of confusing any spy who happened to have been parachuted into our midst!). We studied the war maps avidly in the thin newspapers, and we stuck pins in our wall maps to indicate the latest movements in the various battles...

Like everyone else, of course, we were encouraged to 'dig for victory', and we took over one of the allotments which filled the then undeveloped stretch of land at the top of Radcliffe Road, beyond the turning into Harland Avenue, where we spent many a weekend and, in the summer months, part of the evenings as well. The first picking of the new season's potatoes was always an occasion to celebrate - for some reason, their taste has never been bettered!

We slept in the semi-basement of No. 237, conscious that if we received a direct hit we would probably end up with a lot of bricks and plaster on top of us, but comforted by the knowledge that we had a fair chance of surviving. Fortunately, the theory was never put to the test, and then, in October 1943, we had a lucky break when 37 Ashburton Road became vacant and was available for us to rent.

Kenley Lodge, as it was called, no longer exists, having been replaced by a block of apartments, but for us it provid-ed a comfortable home by the standards of the time (though visitors usually reckoned it was freezing cold inside – we must have been a hardy lot in those days!). Built in the Edwardian era, it had an in-and-out drive with a central entrance up a short flight of steps, and that ele-vated front doorway was to come in quite useful during 1944, for more than one reason.

John Blunsden with his mother and sister by one of the concrete pipes, which were laid to prevent aircraft landing on the golf course at Shirley, c.1943. (J.B.)

At that time there were tennis courts... opposite us, on the other side of the road, backed by the railway line, which used to run between Bingham Road and Coombe Road stations. The open space of the courts gave us an excellent view of the line, and during the weeks leading up to D-Day we saw an almost non-stop flow of trains, many pulled by those giant locomotives brought over from America, ferrying troops and equipment down to the coast in preparation for the invasion of Normandy.

It was clear to see that the Second Front, as it was referred to, was fairly imminent, but by a freak accident and a curious set of circumstances I was to get more than an inkling as to precisely when the big day was likely to be. I was out on my bike, riding on the main road through Catford and keeping well to the left of the tram track, when the driver of a Canadian Army truck suddenly swerved left towards me as he passed, hoping to get clear of a tram ahead that was slowing to pick up passen-gers. One of the grab handles on the side of the truck caught my handlebar and threw me off the bike. I fell backwards onto the edge of the kerb outside a private house, the lady occupant of which, who was in the front garden, picked me up, dust-ed me down and took me inside for a cup of tea.

There I met her husband, who was working for the Port of London Authority, and inevitably the conversation came around to the question everyone in England was asking at the time: 'I wonder when it will be – the Second Front?' All he would say was: 'Some people already know; they know because they need to, because of their job. But you tell me, lad, when do you think it will be? What's

your guess?' I thought for a while (this must have been around 20 May), and eventually I said: 'If I had to bet on it, I think I would go for, let's say, June 5.' He simply said, 'Would you now?' and left it at that. But a few minutes later, when his wife had finished patching me up and I was about to get on my way again, he simply said: 'In future, try to avoid those Army trucks... and remember that date.'

I took this to mean he knew something he was not allowed to tell me and I had soon convinced myself that June 5 really was to be the big day. As D-Day approached, the traffic on that railway line grew heavier by the day until at times the trains were running nose-to-tail, just like buses in a traffic jam. It was all very exciting, so you can imagine my disappoint-ment when June 5 came and went and still there was no inva-sion. In fact, of course, that really had been the intended day, but the bad weather in the Channel had caused a 24-hour postponement, which is why D-Day became June 6.

A couple of weeks later that view from our front doorstep was put to a very different use when we found ourselves in the middle of a new bombardment by 'doodlebugs'. Their noise travelled a tremendous distance, and after a while people became so used to the deep drone that they went about their normal chores, hoping that if they had to they would still have time to take cover at the last moment.

So when I was around I offered to become the family's lookout; I would stand by the open front door, checking the path of the V1s as they (hope-fully) flew past before their fuel ran out. With only a small, low clubhouse opposite there was a useful field of vision, and I remember on one occasion seeing no less than three of them in the sky on more or less parallel paths.

Like so many people, our sleeping quarters became a group of Morrison shelters, which we had erected in the basement of the house, and we were there the night that the first pair of V1s came our way. Of course, at the time we knew nothing about flying bombs, and the unfamiliar noise from the first one made us believe that it was an aircraft in severe engine trouble; when the noise stopped and a few seconds later there was a huge explosion we were convinced that the plane had been shot down. But when a short while later the same thing happened again, it began to seem too good to be true, which of course it was.

The reality became all too apparent the next day, and everyone had rapidly to adjust to the new threat, including the Army. The crew of the anti-aircraft battery in Lloyd Park were kept very busy banging away at those early V1s until it was recognised on high that trying to bring them down in such a highly populated area was not a very sensible idea, whereupon the guns were hastily redeployed on the South Coast, though not before one of them had showered a load of shrapnel around me one afternoon as I walked home from school past Elgin Court! Shrapnel, of course, was high on the list of 'collectables' in those days, and most of us had some prize possessions tucked away in a tin box or two. We came to terms with living with V1s quite quickly, just as we had with the blitzes earlier in the war, but the tension was always there in the background, and of course the V2s, which came later, were the worst of all. At least with conventional planes or V1s you could hear them coming, but the shock factor of a V2 exploding without any prior warning was difficult to deal with. I still have a vivid memory of the afternoon when we switched on the radio and heard: 'This is the BBC Home Service, here is the 6 o'clock news and this is Alvar Liddell reading it', then in the middle of the few seconds' pause which always followed the introduction came an almighty crash as a V2 hit another target. We reckoned that had been the biggest bang of our war!

But once again we had survived, and a few months later we were able to celebrate VE Day, then VJ Day, in the knowledge that the entire family had come through the six years intact, which was more than so many others could say. On the positive side, the war had brought people so much closer together – the climate of mutual help that was so quickly generated throughout society has never been equalled since, more's the pity – and as we went about our lives at least we were free of the sort of on-the-ground dangers which seem to engulf us today. On a personal note, it was of course the Second World War which brought me to Addiscombe in the first place... and you know, I think my wife and I might hang around here for quite a while longer!

The Dalmally Road street party held to celebrate the end of the war. John Wellfare is dressed as a red indian (right, far left), with his sister, Pat (front, 2nd from right), as Victory Flower Girl. (P.S.)

Eighteen

A Meander Around Old Addiscombe

With Woodside

Enjoy this meander around old Addiscombe, some of which is long gone, some of which remains.

Lower Addiscombe Road. The Methodist church was destroyed in an arson attack in 1948. (J.G.)

Addiscombe Station can be seen on the left, with Canning Road on the right, c.1930. (J.G.)

Ashburton Cottage on the corner of Lower Addiscombe Road and Ashling Road, c.1924. (J.G.)

181

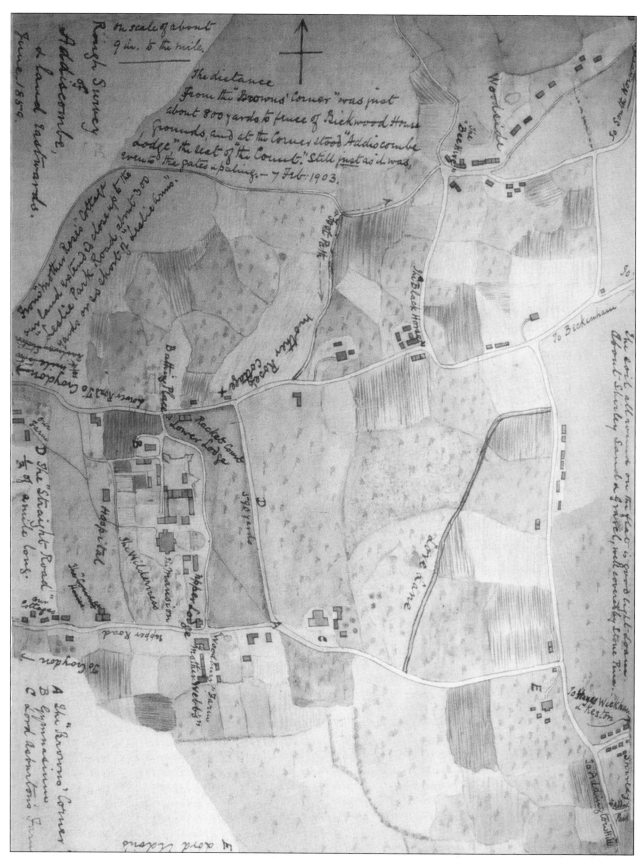

A map drawn by an East India cadet, Sydenham Renaud, in June 1859. The cadets were trained principally as engineers with cartography playing an important role. The Upper Road is today's Addiscombe Road; the Lower Road is today's Lower Addiscombe Road. The road marked 'D' is Ashburton Road. Love Lane was a country walk linking the Addiscombe Road with Shirley Road; it ran from today's Fryston Avenue, ending at Ashburton Avenue. The Bathing Place was also known as Canal Mead or the Coldstream and is the site of the grounds of today's Havelock House. (C.L.S.L.)

The Beehive at Woodside was one of the cadets' favourite pubs. (J.T.)

∾ Woodside Green ∾

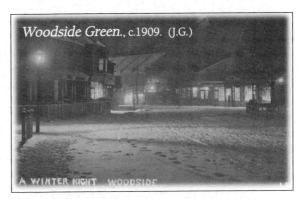

Woodside Green., c.1909. (J.G.)

The Parade at Woodside. (J.G.)

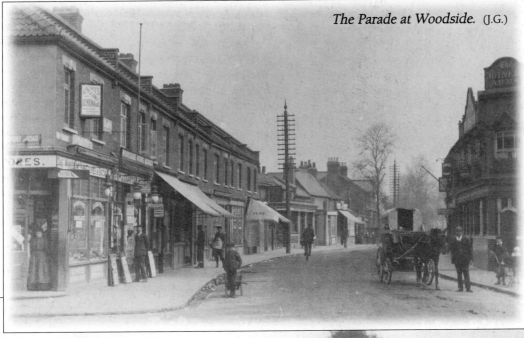

The Beehive and Woodside Green, c.1906. (J.G.)

183

Chestnut Avenue lined the drive to the North Lodge of the East India Company. The North Lodge was demolished when the estate was sold for building development. The site of North Lodge was opposite where a house called the Chestnuts was built at 15 Havelock Road. (S.R.)

Right: *Woodside Carnival, 1914.*
(J.F)

Left: *Addiscombe House, 1920s, formerly the residence of the Steward of the East India Company, stood on what is now Mulberry Lane. It was said that cadets would conduct mortar practice a short distance from this spot and the shot would land about where St Mary Magdalene Church now stands. There was an underground tunnel linking this house to the big house which stood on what is now Outram Road.* (S.R.)

Above: *Ashburton Road divided the Addiscombe and Ashburton estates. It was said that cadets carved their initials on beech trees along this road, which is pictured here in around 1910.* (J.G.)

Left: Lower Addiscombe Road at the junction with Sherwood Road, c.1910. (J.G.)

Brickwood House, 1907. (C.L.S.L.)

Left: *Woodbury Farm, Addiscombe Road. Sydenham Renaud describes Woodbury Farm as the home of the much-loved Mother Webb, the college matron. 'Here we bought for the season gooseberry and currant bushes in advance, early in spring, for one shilling each, and took our chance of the crop when ripe. It was a farmhouse where we had milk and eggs also.'* (C.L.S.L.)

Addiscombe Road by Park Hill Road. (J.G.)

Left: *The front of Brickwood House, an early view. A map of 1847 shows that the Brickwood estate ran along Addiscombe Road from Cherry Orchard Road to what is now Lebanon Road, and at its northern edge alongside what is now Cedar Road. After the estate was sold, the land was built upon in stages. Marian Gilliam (b.1913) lived in Lebanon Road and remembers playing in the fields between the Cedar and Addiscombe Roads before the area was fully developed.* (C.L.S.L.)

Park Hill Road, c.1909. (J.G.)

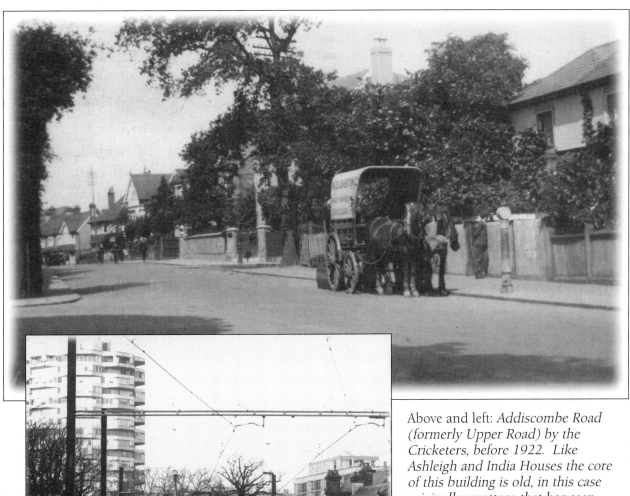

Above and left: *Addiscombe Road (formerly Upper Road) by the Cricketers, before 1922. Like Ashleigh and India Houses the core of this building is old, in this case originally a cottage that has seen additions over the years. The delivery cart is of Page and Overton, a Shirley brewery; a similar view in 2001.*
(J.G. & A.B.)

∾ Memories of Dick Boetius ∾

Going back to history beyond my deeds I gather that Ashleigh and India House were actually named by the East India Company in the 1840s. Prior to that it was a single house which in fact was smaller than the Ashleigh half. Part of Ashleigh and most of India House were incorporated in a house that I don't know the name of, but in 1796 the Honorable Felinda Tollymarsh of the brewers (not that she was a brewer) lived in the house until the East India Company bought it. One of the families in Croydon were the Pulfords who lived in the large house with the cedar trees in the Addiscombe Road bordering Elgin Road. This family had been established for some considerable time and it was in fact Mr

Pulford who told me about the Tollymarshes. In the 1840s the East India Company built on what would be the wing to Ashleigh, and the

Addiscombe Road, 1920s. Ashleigh (Dick's home, left) and India Houses still stand. They were at one time inhabited by professors of the East India College. (S.R.)

stable complex, and put the French professor in Ashleigh because the officers at Addiscombe College had to learn French. It wasn't long before the East India Company didn't have to produce its own army so the two houses were sold off separately.

Ashleigh was bought by Tom Easton. The Eastons had the house from roughly 1850 through to about 1930. Miss Easton was born in the house and in fact died [there]. She was clearly quite a character in Croydon; she had five servants in the late 1920s and '30s, including the coachman who lived in the stables. A plumber came to the house and continued to work for my father often mending one burst and making two more. The plumber recalled several times Miss Easton leaving the house in a coach and pair. [She] was well known for walking down to Croydon frequently with a fox fur stole and a parasol either furled or spread out.

One of the aspects that often interests people is the way Addiscombe was affected by the war. I was obviously young at the time but [Ashleigh] had five bombs affecting it. The first was one of the small incendiaries which only destroyed the asparagus bed. I can remember being stood in the back-room window and all I could see was the whole of the outline of the Crystal Palace hill lit up by the glow at night of London on fire. The next bomb was the one that took out the half house, No. 16 Clyde Road, and blew a street tree straight across what were the tennis courts of 139 and through the ash tree into the garden. Somewhat later another bomb took out half the house at No. 5 Canning Road and this blew across the orchard which was at the bottom of 137 and 135. In fact the orchard was basically plum and apple but there was a magnificent mulberry tree which must have dated back certainly to the time of the East India Company. Then I suppose the biggest bomb was the one that hit the nursing home on the corner of Clyde and Addiscombe Roads. This was, ironically, 5 November 1943. It was one of the limpet bombs that was lowered by parachute and the detonators hit the chimney-stack which did damage to 139 and 137. The surgeon from Radcliffe came down and they pulled everybody out, mothers with newborn babies from the first floor and elderly people from the ground floor. That was then pulled down and for a long time... we had the old

prefabs coming up Clyde Road and into the Addiscombe Road. Some time after the war the prefabs were removed, the Pulfords' house pulled down and Beverley Hyrst was built. During the war we started off by going down in the cellar but there was a better chance of catching pneumonia so we went under the stairs; eventually we thought, well, this is getting silly, so we'll go back upstairs. I got blown out of bed but it was alright. [Ashleigh was hit again but by then Dick and his mother had left.]

Towards the end of the war there was one of the first radar stations based in what was subsequently the Guides' grounds, three-quarters of the way up Radcliffe Road on the left-hand side. This news was relayed to me, only a youngster, by one of the doctors and the old gardener who knew most of the people round here. He was an old stalwart of the First World War who was gassed but was able to do stirling work during the Second World War.

Another character, who lived in the Elizabethan cottage at the corner of Sandilands and Addiscombe Road, was old Col Henry who was a Colonel from the First World War, an established Croydon person.

Another feature of the Addiscombe Road was Winton House. A lot of people weren't sure why it was called Winton House. This is because Mr and Mrs Childs, elderly people, came up from Winchester where they had a school. They established it here in Croydon and their daughter also taught there.

Before the war this particular area of the Addiscombe Road was really quite a medical zone if you like. At 135 Addiscombe Road you had a physician, at 139 a surgeon, on the corner of the Addiscombe Road and Park Hill Rise a physician and at the bottom on the eastern side of the Radcliffe Road another surgeon with my father, the dental surgeon, sandwiched in the middle between the whole group at 137. Opposite 137, where the Guiness Trust now stands, was yet another physician.

NOTE: In the 1930s Dr Thompson lived at 135 Addiscombe Road on the corner of Canning Road. The house was called Glendalough. Dr Thompson originally lived at 1 Morland Road which itself had been called Glendalough (Chapter Four). Glendalough in Addiscombe Road no longer exists, Ashleigh House is still at 137 and India House at 139.

Nineteen
≈≈⊖≈≈
And Finally...

How to Trace Your Family History by Brian Roote

Brian Roote and Cliff Marlow.
(S.C.)

New to family history research? For the benefit of people who are just starting, or intending to trace their family tree, I hope these brief notes may be of help. I have been through most of the stages of discovery and frustration which beset many researchers during the five or so years of my addiction!

Start by listing your known family and draw a rough family tree, together with as many dates as you can. Collect together any photographs, documents etc. Then start talking. Contact as many family members are you are able and write down reminiscences, anecdotes and known facts. One of the most familiar cries of the genealogist is 'I wish I'd asked before it was too late.'

It is probably best to work on one family at a time, at least to begin with. Later, with more experience, you can expand research parameters. Keep your notes in a loose-leaf ringbinder and never discard anything – it inevitably becomes useful at some time!

A beginner can find a way around the basics by reading some of the many books now available. Many well-known booksellers stock genealogy books and there are specialist stockists too.

The biggest change in recent years has been the way in which computers have become a major information source. The internet has put information at people's fingertips but do not assume that what is available is infallible; believe me, it's not! A slight lapse in transcription of documents or indexes can lead to many people barking up the wrong family tree!

When you have made a start as outlined, then you can progress to the Civil Registration of Births, Marriages and Deaths which commenced in England and Wales on 1 July 1837. These records are kept in quarterly ledgers at the Family Record Centre in Islington. Some of the records can also be found on microfilm/fiche in some large libraries and county records offices. The records are each referenced and from these references, copies of the certificates can be ordered. At the time of writing copy certificates cost £6.50. Information on the certificate type varies. For instance, on birth certificates, the mother's maiden name is recorded; on marriage certificates both father's and mother's occupations are shown. In all cases, however, the information should be viewed circumspectly as economies with the truth are not infrequent. Much information can be obtained from Census records. You can consult the Census records 1841 to 1891 and before the end of 2002, we hope, the 1901 record. Copies can be seen at the Family Record Centre and other sources, including CD-ROM.

Registers of baptisms, marriages and burials have been kept in parish churches since the sixteenth century and the majority are now in county record offices. Many have been indexed and are available on microfilm, CD-ROM and the internet.

Military records can be found at the Public Record Office at Kew. Many regiments also have their own museums and some keep individual details. Take heed, however, that without a person's service number it will be almost impossible to research.

Family History Societies are a very helpful source, so don't hesitate to join the one nearest your research area. The cost is nominal but the help you'll get is phenomenal.

For anyone starting on this quest may I say that I hope you get as much pleasure and surprise as I have!

NOTE FROM THE COMPILERS: We have met many interesting and lovely people in the course of preparing this book and we are indebted to all for their generous help. One of the greatest thrills has been realising one afternoon that Cliff Marlow sitting on the living-room sofa was the long-lost cousin of Brian Roote due to come round that very same evening. Their reunion made it all worthwhile!

Subscribers

Evelyn Adams, Addiscombe, Surrey
Mr and Mrs Albert Adegbite
    Addiscombe, Surrey
Valerie Allen, New South Wales, Australia
Dawn Patricia Allum, Addiscombe, Surrey
Jennifer Andreas, Addiscombe, Surrey
George and Eileen Argent, Woodside
    Green, London
Pat and Arthur Ashby, Shirley, Croydon,
    Surrey
Mary (Joy) Atkins, Richmond,
    North Yorkshire
Ivy Ayling, Addiscombe, Surrey
J.H. Bainbridge
David Bair, East Croydon, Surrey
Tony Ball, Lower Addiscombe,
    Croydon, Surrey
Alan and Jean Barber, Shirley, Croydon,
    Surrey
Phil Barber, Croydon, Surrey
John E. Barker, Woodside, London
Peter and Tom Barry and Trisha
    Holmes, Addiscombe, Surrey
The Barthaud family, Whitgift Estate
Roy Bartlett, Cornwall (formerly
    Addiscombe)
Jacqueline and Keith Bartley,
    Addiscombe, Surrey
The Basic Skills Centre, Elmers End
David G. Bate, Keyworth, Nottingham
Pat and Alan Bates, Addiscombe, Surrey
Heather and Christopher Bates,
    Addiscombe, Croydon, Surrey
Marion and George Battley,
    Addiscombe, Surrey
Rick Biddle, Wallington, Surrey
Ivy Binstead, Croydon, Surrey
Michael Bowler, Addiscombe, Surrey
Alma Boxall
The Brashier family, East Croydon, Surrey
Gwen Braund (née Smith), Isle of Wight
Mrs C.M. Brennan, Addiscombe, Surrey
Ann Broad, Addiscombe, Surrey
David E. Brookes, Wareham, Dorset
Barbara Broughton, Addiscombe, Surrey
John W. Brown, Local History Publications
Gloria E. Browne, Addiscombe, Surrey
Mrs Doreen F. Buckley, Addiscombe, Surrey
Emma C. Budgen, Addiscombe, Surrey
Bertha Bull (née Henbest), Peacehaven,
    Sussex
Eric H. Burley, Addiscombe, Surrey
Jean Burrows, Addiscombe, Surrey
Gordon R. Button, Addiscombe, Surrey
Rosemary Button, Addiscombe, Surrey
Deborah Campbell-Cooke, Chisholm
    Road, Croydon, Surrey
Anthony John Cane, Shirley, Croydon,
    Surrey
Margaret K. Card, Capri Road,
    Addiscombe, Surrey
Mrs Veronica M.C. Card,
    South Croydon, Surrey
Lisa and Roy Carey-Bailey
Michael J. Carpenter, Selsdon, Croydon,
    Surrey

John Cartwright, Park Hill, Croydon
Margaret Chapman, Woodside Green
Mr Colin Chatten, Croydon, Surrey
Dick Clarke, Ashurch Road,
    Addiscombe, Surrey
Phyllis D. and David J. Clarke
Robin and Susan Clarke, Croydon, Surrey
Adrienne and Graham Cluer
    Addiscombe, Surrey
Clive and June Coles, Capri Road,
    Addiscombe, Surrey
Nigel Collins, Canning Road, Croydon,
    Surrey
Maureen and Stephen Collins,
    Addiscombe, Surrey
Patrick Connelly, Shirley, Croydon, Surrey
Trevor R. Constable, Oxted, Surrey
Mrs Lesley Elizabeth Cook
Terry Cooper, Sheffield
William G. Cooper, Croydon, Surrey
Ron and Geoff Couchman,
    Addiscombe, Surrey
Mrs Dorothy Joan Cowland
Jane Cox and Jill Lucas, Shirley, Surrey
Mrs Julia Cross, formerly of
    Addiscombe 1985–93
Miss Margaret Crouch, Addiscombe,
    Surrey
Lucinda Currie and Stef Giza, Stamford
    Brook
Rosie and Alwyn D'Costa
Melanie De Villiers, Addiscombe, Surrey
Mrs Olive F. Dear (née Cane),
    Addiscombe, Surrey
Mr P.R. Dennison, Kenley, Surrey
John and Jan Dixon, St Ouen, Jersey
Mr Paul Dixon, Addiscombe, Surrey
Denis S. Driscoll, Addiscombe, Surrey
Hazel Dummer, Devonshire Way,
    Croydon, Surrey
Mr N. Dunmore, Grant Road, Croydon,
    Surrey
Edward Jobson Court, Canning Road
Barbara Edwards, Addiscombe, Surrey
Lyn Egan (née Garland), Croydon, Surrey
Robert C. Eichert, Addiscombe, Surrey
Mrs Sheila Falconer, formerly of Lower
    Addiscombe Road
S.J. Farage, Croydon, Surrey
Graham Feakins, Herne Hill, London
Mr and Mrs D. Fearn, Addiscombe,
    Surrey
David and Ann Fenner, Addington,
    Surrey
Ronald and Irene Fielder, South
    Australia 5114
Ian A. Francis, Woodside Green,
    London SE25
Full Steam Ahead Ltd, Addiscombe,
    Surrey
John Gallard, Addiscombe,
    South Croydon
John Gent, Croydon
Barbara M. George, Addiscombe, Surrey
R.C. Godden, Addiscombe, Surrey
Mr W.A.G. and Mrs J.F. Goddin, Hastings
Anthony Gomesz, Addiscombe, Surrey
Hermione G.E. Graham (née Hockey)

John Greasley, Croydon, Surrey
Christopher James Green, Addiscombe,
    Surrey
David A.W. Green, Addiscombe, Surrey
Mark John Green, Addiscombe, Surrey
Greenwood UK
Henry and Joy Griffiths, Bexhill-on-Sea
Patricia Hadland, Barrington, Somerset
John R. Hailey, Addiscombe, Surrey
Susan M. Hall, Addiscombe, Surrey
Paul and Derry-Anne Hammond,
    Canning Road, Croydon, Surrey
Ken Harman, Sanderstead,
    South Croydon, Surrey
David Harmes, Addiscombe, Surrey
Phillip Harris, Southampton, Hants
Harris and Bailey Ltd
Jeremy G. Harrison, Addiscombe,
    Surrey
David A. Harwood, Addiscombe, Surrey
Matthew L. Haughton, Addiscombe,
    Surrey
Mr Henry G. Hawkins, Addiscombe,
    Surrey
Edward John Hayler
Ivy Haynes, Addiscombe, Surrey
John Head, Truro, Cornwall
Geraldine L.M. Healy, Addiscombe,
    Surrey
Peter Heyman, Chulmleigh, Devon
J. Hibbert, East Croydon, Surrey
S.J. Hicks (Nobby), Woodside
Anne High, Addiscombe, Croydon,
    Surrey
Christopher Hitchen, Addiscombe, Surrey
Mary Hogarth, Tenterden, Kent
Stella and Brenda Hogg, Addiscombe,
    Surrey
Neville Hortas, Addiscombe, Surrey
William A. Hoskins, Woodside, London
Barry F. Houghton, Addiscombe, Surrey
Janet M. Houghton, Addiscombe, Surrey
Eileen Howell (née Beare), formerly of
    Addiscombe
Master Taylor Hughes, Brendon Road,
    Addiscombe, Surrey
Mr Ken Hughes, Addiscombe, Surrey
Mary and Steve Hughes, Addiscombe,
    Surrey
Gill Hulme, Shirley, Surrey
Roger Hurrion
Betty M. Huston, Addiscombe, Surrey
Jackie and John Hutchings,
    Addiscombe, Surrey
Ian Isham, Park Hill, Croydon, Surrey
Zena A. Ivens, Addiscombe, Surrey
Lisa Jackson and Graham Williams,
    Addiscombe, Surrey
Andrew R. Janes, Taunton, Somerset
R.F. Jewell, Long Lane, Croydon, Surrey
Mr K.N. Johnceline, Wenhaston, Suffolk
Mrs Carole Johnstone, Cazals, France
Sharon L. Jones, Shirley, Croydon, Surrey
Sara Jones and Daniel Whitmarsh,
    Exeter Road, Addiscombe, Surrey
Anne R. Keeley, Addiscombe, Croydon,
    Surrey
William Kehoe, Addiscombe, Surrey

SUBSCRIBERS

Dennis and Marjorie King, Hailsham
Vera King, Addiscombe, Surrey
Howard F. King, Croydon, Surrey
Pamela King (née Rippingale),
    Addiscombe, Surrey
Patrick, Mary and Clare Kingman
James Kingswell, Wallington, Surrey
Mr and Mrs P. Knott, Addiscombe, Surrey
Robert M. Krarup, Addiscombe, Surrey
Paul Derrick Lane, Burgess Hill,
    West Sussex
David P. and Sonja Lane, Oslo,
    Norway/Addiscombe, Surrey
Patrick Charles Lane, Addiscombe, Surrey
Peter J. Langsdale, Addiscombe, Surrey
Gaynor Lawrence, Addiscombe, Surrey
Margaret and Michael Lewis,
    Addiscombe, Surrey
Nora G. Lewis (née Nash), Uttoxeter
Chris Liddle, Croydon, Surrey
R.J. Long, Addiscombe, Surrey
Pauline Macbroom, Addiscombe, Surrey
Sharon E. Marshall, Addiscombe, Surrey
Peter D. Maryan, Addiscombe, Surrey
Mr and Mrs Masters, Birchanger Road,
    South Norwood
Jean C. Mayo, Woodside, London
Michael R. Mead, Beckenham, Kent
Graham R. Medcalf
Roy and Shelley Mercer, Addiscombe,
    Surrey
Peter Miles, for Maureen and Geoff
Miles, Addiscombe, Surrey
Shirley Mills, Outram Road, Croydon,
    Surrey
Lynn Mills (née Beadle), Woodside,
    London
Barbara Mitchell, Camberley, Surrey
C. Morley-Smith, Addiscombe, Surrey
Miss Sasha Emilia Morris, Ashburton
Road, Addiscombe, Surrey
Martin, Paula and Harry Murray,
Addiscombe, Surrey
Geoffrey Myers and Lester Thorpe
Jeanette Nathan
Patricia and Frances Newman,
    Addiscombe, Surrey
Tony and Sue Newman, Addiscombe,
    Surrey
David Nicholls, Addiscombe, Surrey
Nichola Nicholls, Addiscombe, Surrey
Ken and Ann Nicholson, Addiscombe,
    Surrey
Paul Nihill MBE, formerly of Addiscombe
John Nobes, Addiscombe, Surrey
Graham Norcutt, Toronto, Canada
Peter O'Kill, Alexandra Road, 1947-67
Mr and Mrs Overton
Lisa A. Page, Woodside, London
Mrs Elsie Pamphilon, Shirley, Croydon,
    Surrey
Alan and Francesca Parsons,
    Addiscombe, Surrey
John Pauling, Hunmanby, North Yorks
Catherine Peck, Canning Road,
    Addiscombe, Surrey
Mrs J.M. Pentecost and Miss J.M.
    Pentecost, Addiscombe, Surrey

Miss Rachel Perrins, Addiscombe,
    Croydon, Surrey
Mr Michael Perrins and Mrs Gillian
    Perrins (née Pamphilon), Addiscombe
Marie Pickering, Whyteleafe, Surrey
Jim Pickett, Addiscombe, Surrey
Denis Piggott, Croydon, Surrey
Doris Piggott, Shirley, Surrey
Patricia Anne Power, Addiscombe, Surrey
Barry Press, Addiscombe, Surrey
Mrs Julie Ann Pretlove
Mr and Mrs B.E. Price, Bridge Row,
    Croydon, Surrey
Alan and Debbie Purchasen,
    Addiscombe, Surrey
Mrs Susan Putnam, Farnham, Surrey
Madeleine Quiney
Elaine and Adrian Ralph, Addiscombe,
    Surrey
Chris Reeves, Woodside, London
C.X.F. Rich, East Croydon, Surrey
 Richard and Judy, Shirley, Surrey
Ron Richens, Addiscombe, Surrey
Mary Riches, Addiscombe, Surrey
Michael F. Ridden, Addiscombe, Surrey
Gilly Ridout, Addiscombe, Surrey
Tony and Kathy Rigby, Addiscombe,
    Surrey
Jonathan and Kathryn Roberts,
    Melbourne, Derby
Margaret Robson, Shirley, Croydon,
    Surrey
Mick and Frances Ross, Addiscombe,
    Surrey
Dennis and Margaret Rowe, Paignton,
    Devon
Joyce Russell (née Stredwick), Earley,
    Berkshire
Chris and Jenny Rutter, Shirley,
    Croydon, Surrey
Mrs M.C. Scherr
Miss J. Scherr
Michael J. Semeta
Alan Shillabeer, Addiscombe, Surrey
Mr and Mrs Shillingford, Addiscombe,
    Surrey
Monica Shuttleworth, Outram Road
    1959-1975
Jill and Tony Simpkin, Addiscombe, Surrey
Deryck A.P. Sinclair, East Croydon, Surrey
Tony Skrzypczyk, Addiscombe,
    Croydon, Surrey
Bob Sleeman, Addiscombe, Surrey
Brenda Smart (née Yearley)
Jodie Smith, Addiscombe, Surrey
Peter Jervis Smith, Croydon, Surrey
Mr Cyril C. Smith, Basingstoke, Hants
Joyce Smith (née Wawman),
    Addiscombe, Surrey
John Snashfold, Addiscombe, Surrey
Richard Snashfold, Addiscombe, Surrey
K.E. Snow
R. Soles, Addiscombe, Croydon, Surrey
Paul W. Sowan, South Croydon, Surrey
Diane Spicer, Addiscombe, Surrey
Les Steadman, formerly of Addiscombe,
    Surrey
Betty and Ivor Steer, Colyton, Devon

Martin J. Sterling, Addiscombe, Surrey
Robert A. Streeter, Addiscombe, Surrey
John and Sheila Stretton
Andy and Jenny Strevens, Addiscombe,
    Surrey
Beryl Suckling (née Pauling),
    Deddington, Oxon
Patricia Vanda Sullivan (née Bylett),
    Kingston, Ontario, Canada
Sid and Joyce Swain, Addiscombe,
    Surrey
Mark J. Swain, Addiscombe, Surrey
Dawn Symes, Croydon, Surrey
Frank and Audrey (née Hasdell) Taylor,
    Addiscombe, Surrey
Loraine and Sean Taylor, Addiscombe,
    Surrey
Mrs D. Tedder, Addiscombe, Surrey
Mr Barry F. Thatcher, Addiscombe,
    Surrey
Mr and Mrs I.D.M. Thewless,
    Woodside, London
Gordon Thompson, Addiscombe, Surrey
Tighearnan and Sorcha, Shirley, Surrey
Margaret Todman (née Saunders),
    Addiscombe, Surrey
Anne Tompsett, Croydon, Surrey
Fred Turner, Hooley, Surrey
Sylvia B. Turner, Addiscombe, Surrey
Steven Turner, Shirley Park, Croydon,
    Surrey
Ron Turner, Copthorne, Sussex
Simon P. Vaughan, Addiscombe, Surrey
Peter Walker, Croydon, Surrey
John F.W. Walling, Newton Abbot, Devon
Jane Ward, Addiscombe, Surrey
Mrs D. Ward, Addiscombe, Surrey
Douglas Waters, New Addington, Surrey
Jeanne E. Watts, Addiscombe, Surrey
Eileen and Gordon Weaver, Coulsdon,
    Surrey
Don and Pam Webb, Addiscombe, Surrey
Stephen and Natasha Weller, Croydon,
    Surrey
Beverley and Bob Wheatley, Shirley,
    Surrey
Dave and Vanessa Wheeler,
    Addiscombe, Surrey
Terry and Greer White, Shirley Park,
    Surrey
Mr Raymond and Mrs Eileen White,
    formerly of Addiscombe, Surrey
Mary Whitfield, Thakeham, Sussex
Peter A. Whybrow
Frank and Jo Williams, Owslebury,
    Hants
Mrs Leonora M. Williams,
Kate Wilson, Addiscombe, Surrey
Nicky and Colin Wilson, Addiscombe,
    Surrey
Michael Winch, Addiscombe, Surrey
Doreen and Ian Wood, Addiscombe,
    Croydon, Surrey
John Wood, Seaford, East Sussex
William J. Wood, Shirley and
    Addiscombe, Surrey
Jennifer and Norman Young,
    Addiscombe, Surrey

Titles from the Series

Forthcoming

For details of any of the above titles or if you are interested in writing your own history, please contact: Commissioning Editor Community Histories, Halsgrove House, Lower Moor Way, Tiverton Business Park, Tiverton, Devon EX16 6SS, England; email: naomic@halsgrove.com

In order to include as many historic photographs as possible in this volume, a printed index is not included. However, the Community History Series is indexed by Genuki. For further information and indexes to volumes in the series, please visit: http://www.cs.ncl.uk/genuki/DEV/indexingproject.html